History of the 12th West Virginia Volunteer Infantry

BY WILLIAM HEWITT

and
The Story of Andersonville and Florence

BY JAMES N. MILLER

© Copyright 2011 by 35th Star Publishing.
All Rights Reserved.
Printed in the United States of America

35th Star Publishing
Charleston, West Virginia
www.35thstar.com

No part of this book may be reproduced in any form or in any means, electronic or mechanical, including photocopying, recording, or by any information storage and retrieval system, without permission in writing from the publisher.

ISBN-10: 0-9664534-1-7
ISBN-13: 978-0-9664534-1-6
Library of Congress Control Number: 2005903843

On the cover:
Private Joshua Fortney, Betty L. Alley Collection
U.S. Army Military History Institute

Private Joseph McCauslin, Dr. Kathleen Dietrich Collection
U.S. Army Military History Institute

Book cover & interior design: Studio 6 Sense • studio6sense.com

History of the Twelfth West Virginia Volunteer Infantry

The Part It Took in the War of the Rebellion 1861 – 1865

BY

WILLIAM HEWITT

Published by the Twelfth West Virginia
Infantry Association, 1892
35th Star Publishing, 2011

*To the Surviving Comrades and the
Families of the Fallen of the
Old Twelfth this work
Is Respectfully
Dedicated*

Preface

COMRADES:

You conferred upon me at our reunion, held at New Cumberland, in 1889, the honor of selecting me to compile a history of the Twelfth. The matter was taken into consideration afterward by me, and owing in part to the magnitude, burden, and difficulty of the proposed task, my inexperience in this kind of undertaking, and because I believed that there were other survivors of the regiment much better qualified to write the history, it was concluded to forego the undertaking. But at our next reunion, because Col. Curtis was disappointed that nothing had been done in the matter of the history, and was anxious that it be written, and for the reason that the comrades present again expressed a desire that I should undertake the work, I promised to attempt it and do the best I could. Laboring under the unavoidable difficulties that it has been thirty years since the old Twelfth was making its history in the field, the almost total lack of official records pertaining exclusively to the regiment, and the uncertainty of memory at this late day, I have tried within reasonable fidelity to fulfill my promise. In reason more should not be expected.

If you, the survivors of the Twelfth, be pleased with the history, this fact will be a sufficient reward for my labors; but, on the other hand, if it shall not come up to your expectations, you should be charitable to its faults and short comings, remembering that however great its imperfections you, yourselves, are largely responsible, for the task was not one of my own seeking, but was rather thrust upon me. The plan aimed at in writing the history is to not go outside of our own organization in what is related, except to give a brief account of the operations of the various armies to which we belonged, and to intersperse the work with incidents, anecdotes, and matters mainly personal to the members of the regiment.

Whatever possible merit may be found in the history is largely due to the assistance of comrades in furnishing valuable data. Some of them were quite liberal in their contributions. And where there is failure to make mention of incidents worthy of record, or of daring deeds of individuals or detachments, it is because they were not or are not known or remembered by the compiler. Reasonable effort was made to get all such details. A card was inserted in various newspapers, and letters were written to different comrades asking that they be furnished. If comrades shall fail to find, as no doubt they shall, a record herein of certain incidents worthy of mention, they will be forbearing toward the historian when they consider there is a number of such matters herein given that they did not know of or have forgotten. The comrades will all feel like thanking Mrs. McCaffrey, formerly Mrs. Bengough, wife of the late Lieut. Bengough of the Twelfth, for the vivid and stirring story of the capture, detention and final release of herself and sister-in-law as prisoners by the Rebels, kindly furnished for this history.

Surviving Comrades, this attempted record of the history of the old Twelfth is now submitted to your charitable consideration, and may your days be long, peaceful, and prosperous.

WILLIAM HEWITT.

June 20th, 1892.

Preface

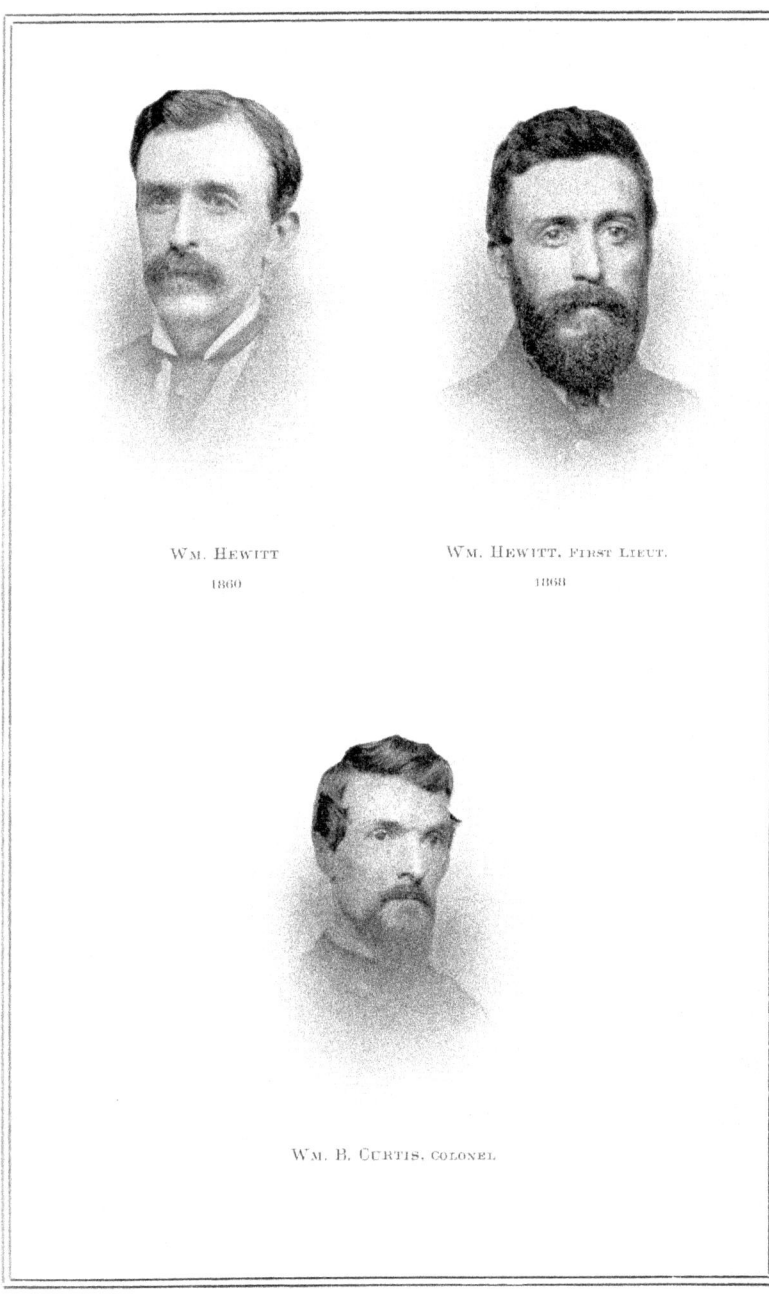

Wm. Hewitt
1860

Wm. Hewitt, First Lieut.
1863

Wm. B. Curtis, Colonel

Contents

CHAPTER ONE 1
The Circumstances Under Which the Twelfth Was Organized - The Character of the Men Composing it - The Organization.

CHAPTER TWO 9
March to Clarksburg - Marches and Operations in West Virginia in the Fall of '62 – Incidents.

CHAPTER THREE 19
The Movement into the Shenandoah Valley - Stationed at Winchester Under Gen. Milroy - Moved to Berryville - The Capture of Capt. Lapole - Joke on Sergt. Porter - From Berryville to Clarksburg - The March Through Charlestown.

CHAPTER FOUR 31
The Battle of Winchester - The Retreat - The North Mountain Girl - Halted at Bloody Run, Pa. - Marched to Bedford - Left Bedford for Loudon - Milroy's Men Capture One of Lee's Trains and Many Prisoners - Marched to Hagerstown – Anecdotes - Marched to Sharpsburg - Thence to Martinsburg.

CHAPTER FIVE 43
Col. Klunk's Resignation Accepted - Troops Pass from the Army of the Potomac to Grant - An Incident about Van and Tom - Capt. Bristor's Capture of Spy - Capt. Moffatt's Capture of Gilmore's Men - Lieut. Blaney's Observation - An Incident Concerning Adjt. Caldwell - Mrs. Bengough a Prisoner - Her Story.

CHAPTER SIX 63
An Attack Expected - March to Maryland Heights – Incidents - Brigaded with the Thirty-fourth Mass. - A Move up the Valley - Incidents - The Return - Incidents - Followed by Early - Threatened Attack at Harper's Ferry - Moved to Cumberland, Md. - Comrade Haney's Story - Gens. Kelly and Crook Captured.

CHAPTER SEVEN 75

Under Gen. Sigel - March to Beverly, via Webster - March back to Webster - The Story of the Camp on the Rebel Farm - The March up the Valley - Two of Company C Captured - The Battle of New Market - Gen. Sigel's Letter - Corpl. De Bee's Scout - An Incident - Comrades Miller and W. C. Mahan as Prisoners - Their Stories.

CHAPTER EIGHT 95

Sigel Relieved - Hunter in Command - The Lynchburg Campaign - The Battle of Piedmont - List of Killed and Wounded - Marched to Lynchburg – Anecdote - The Battle - The Retreat to the Kanawha - Hunter's Loss of Artillery on Way - The Men Hard Pressed for Food.

CHAPTER NINE 115

Back in the Valley - Threatening Early on His Retreat from Washington - Battle of Snicker's Ferry - Marched to Winchester - Battle of Kearnstown - Our Retreat via. Martinsburg and Sharpsburg to Halltown - An Incident - R. W. Mahan's Prison Trials - A Large Army Concentrates at Halltown - The Wild-goose Chase Into Maryland.

CHAPTER TEN 127

Sheridan in Command - The Move up the Valley - The Twelfth Charges Rebel Skirmishers - Sheridan Retreats to Halltown - Early Demonstrates Against Him - Early Withdraws - Sheridan Moves to Charlestown - The Fight at Berryville - Grant's Visit to Sheridan - The Battle of Opequon - Anecdote of Sheridan - Battle of Fisher's Hill - Pursuit of the Enemy up the Valley - Destruction by Sheridan - He Falls Back to Strasburg - Battle of Tom's Brook - Our Brigade Starts for Martinsburg - Mosby Attacks an Ambulance Guard - The Twelfth Starts for the Front - Early Shells Thoburn's Camp - The Battle of Cedar Creek - The Twelfth on the Way to the Front - Sheridan on His Ride - Col. Thoburn Killed - Capt. Phil Bier Killed - The Twelfth Marches to Cedar Creek - Thence to Newtown.

CHAPTER ELEVEN 141
  The Army Moves Back to Kearnstown - Early Follows Far as
  Middletown - Sheridan's Cavalry Drives the Rebel Cavalry -
  Early Returns to New Market – Anecdotes - The Twelfth Moves
  to Stephenson's Depot - Salutes for Gen. Thomas's Victories -
  The Twelfth Sent to the Army of the James - Put into the Twenty-
  fourth Corps - The Opposing Pickets - Lieut. Col. Northcott's
  Resignation - The Sinking of Rebel Gun Boats - Rebel Deserters -
  The Peace Commission - Grant Reviews Our Corps - Gen. Turner
  Commands the Division - It Moves to Aid Sheridan - Asst. Surg.
  Neil's Lecture.

CHAPTER TWELVE 151
  Part of Our Army Crosses the James - The Second Division
  at Hatcher's Run - The Capture of Fort Gregg - The Enemy
  Evacuates Richmond and Petersburg - The Pursuit - The March
  to Cut off Lee's Retreat - An Incident - The Second Division and
  One Other Were the Infantry Forces Cutting off the Retreat - The
  Surrender - Both Armies Cheer - Lieut. McCord - The Col. and
  Citizen McLean Talk - An Incident - Marched to Lynchburg and
  Back - Thence to Richmond - Some of the Boys Presented with
  Medals - Mustered Out - Sent Home – Memorial – Conclusion.

CONCLUSION 167

THE STORY OF ANDERSONVILLE AND FLORENCE 171
  by James N. Miller, Company A, 12th West Virginia Infantry
  Originally published in 1900.

CONGRESSIONAL MEDAL OF HONOR RECIPIENTS,
12TH WEST VIRGINIA INFANTRY 235

ROSTER 237

INDEX 261

Chapter One

The great War of the Rebellion had gone on for a year, and had assumed proportions of a grand scale, dwarfing any other ever fought on this continent, so far as there is any history; in fact, making all other wars on this side of the ocean appear, by comparison, to be Lilliputian in character; and so far as the magnitude of its theater or geographical extent was concerned, the greatest war in the history of the world.

Previous to our great war it had been supposed that modern times had only one man surely - possibly others - capable of efficiently handling a hundred thousand men - Napoleon Bonaparte. But this mighty conflict was developing more than one man fully able to command that number of men in action; and at least one man capable of having a general supervision over fully a million of men in the field. We were exhibiting to the world new methods of warfare both on land and sea, and showing it that we had the most effective and intelligent soldiers in the world.

Several hundred thousand men had been called into the field, armed and equipped. Men and money had been lavishly expended. There was a willingness on the part of the loyal people to spend the last dollar and furnish the last man, if they could see any evidence of progress on the part of our arms, or have any assurance of final success in the suppression of the Rebellion.

The war on the part of the Government, however, had been begun with an entirely inadequate idea of the magnitude of the undertaking.

It is well known that one [Secretary Seward] high in the councils of the nation had predicted before hostilities actually began that there would be peace in sixty days, and even the good President seemed to think that all the threatening aspect of affairs would pass away if a little time were allowed for the passions of the people to cool. There seemed to be a want of comprehension on the part of the loyal people generally, and not less so on the part of those holding the reins of government, of the terrible earnestness and deadly determination of those who had taken up arms to disrupt the Government.

Hence the first call for troops to cope with what was to prove to be the most determined and formidable rebellion recorded in history, was for only seventy-five thousand men, and what was worse, for only the short term of three months, as though the suppression of the Rebellion was comparatively a trivial affair.

There was some reason, however, aside from the supposed sufficiency of the first call for troops, for not calling out a greater force, namely, the lack of arms and other munitions of war; but this excuse could not be offered for the deplorable blunder, which all now can see, of making the term of the first enlistment only three months, many regiments' time expiring when they were sorely needed.

In the outset of hostilities and actual conflict of arms, there was a remarkable lack of earnestness and the customary severity, which is generally supposed to characterize grim-visaged war, shown by some of our generals in the field. In some instances the first prisoners were merely sworn to not take up arms again against the Government and then let go - "a process," says Greeley in his *American Conflict,* "about as imposing and significant, in their view, as the taking of a glass of cider." This treatment of prisoners soon became a by-word and jeering jest among the soldiers. It is related that during the Three Months' service, when a comrade had captured a snake and was holding it up by the tail, a fellow soldier called out to him to swear him and let him go.

There was great tenderness, too, in the beginning of the war, shown by professed friends of the Union, for the people of those States which assumed to be out of the Union; and for the people of the States which were nominally within the Union, yet whose loyalty was of an exceedingly questionable kind, as was manifested by their objecting to the soldiers of our country marching under our common flag, setting foot upon their soil. It was alleged by these professed friends that, by treating the Rebels with severity, the people of the seceded States, would be so exasperated thereby that all hope of restoring the Union would be forever destroyed. Just as though they were not already inflamed to the highest pitch, and enraged to the last degree, when a timid, halting policy of being afraid of hurting them, was only bringing the Government into disrespect, encouraging the enemy, and making more Rebels every day, and when a decided, vigorous course toward the traitors was needed to sharply draw the line between the enemies and friends of the Government.

There was also a halting, half-hearted policy shown in the disposition and handling of the eastern army - a dissipation of its strength which resulted in bringing only little more, if any force, on the Union side, than about one-half of the available strength in the first Battle of Bull Run, fought July 21st, 1861, and resulting in a humiliating defeat, which defeat had the effect of stimulating and vitalizing the Rebellion into tremendous vigor, and giving it high hope and great energy.

This defeat at the time was universally regarded as a great calamity, though it is now seen, in view of the fact that it necessitated the prolonging of the war, thereby compelling more extreme and radical measures for the suppression of the Rebellion, and consequently making a more substantial and durable peace, that that reverse to our arms was a blessing in disguise.

It was followed by the calling out of five hundred thousand more troops, and the next spring, by General McClellan's dilatory, sluggish and worse than abortive attempt to take Richmond with the Grand Army of the Potomac. And this failure of this magnificent army to still further encourage the Rebellion. At the end of that campaign the Rebels were as full of the spirit of determination and as sanguine as ever. And although some substantial progress had been made by our arms in the Southwest, yet the results of the war so far were not satisfactory, nor at all equal to the great expenditure of men and money.

Under this condition of affairs, and in this exigency, "Father Abraham" called on July 1st, 1862, not for "three hundred thousand more," but for six hundred thousand additional soldiers. And it was in response to this call for more defenders of the Union that the Twelfth West Virginia enlisted and was mustered into service along with the other reinforcements, to do what it might to keep the Old Flag aloft, and "that government of the people, by the people, and for the people might not perish from earth."

The Twelfth was made up of exceptionally good material. The men were mainly American born and native Virginians. They were a hardy, robust, vigorous, self-reliant class of men, mainly from the farming districts, of more than average size, many of them mountaineers. They enlisted under trying and embarrassing circumstances, and in great measure from patriotic impulses, their surroundings and circumstances in many cases tending to lead them to join their fortunes with the Rebel cause. It was a common thing for a West Virginia Union soldier to have friends and relatives in the Rebel army, and in some cases for brother to fight against brother.

One of our faithful and efficient surgeons, of the Twelfth, F. H. Patton, now having the important and responsible position of being in charge of the Soldiers' Home at Dayton, Ohio, at a reunion at Wheeling in 1886 paid the boys of the Twelfth the compliment of relating that he was sometimes asked why it was that there were so few West Virginia soldiers found in the Soldiers' Home at Dayton, and said that he replied to that question, that the boys of West Virginia were a self-reliant class of men, used to and feeling themselves fully capable of looking after and taking care of themselves during the war, and that he thought the same trait, characterizing them yet, of looking out for themselves, accounted for so few West Virginia soldiers being found in soldiers' homes.

Another incident will further illustrate the character of the men of this regiment. During the winter of 1864-5, the Tenth, Eleventh, Twelfth and Fifteenth West Virginia regiments, along with some other regiments, were sent from the Valley of Virginia to the Army of the James, and organized into a small division, General T. M. Harris, commander. This division was afterward known as the Independent Division. It so happened that members of some of the regiments of the corps to which our division was assigned were so inclined to desert to the enemy when on the picket line, that it was not considered safe to put those regiments on picket. Shortly after arrival, General Harris was asked by his commanding officer if he would be responsible for his men's deserting from the picket line. Harris replied that he would guarantee that not a man of his would desert. His confidence was not misplaced. The men were put on picket and not a man of the Twelfth deserted. The same is true, it is believed, of the other regiments of Harris' command. Of course the Twelfth, like other regiments, had its deserters; but that class was long since weeded out, and those left, the men in general, were determined to stand by the old flag to the end of their enlistment. They would rather die than desert.

The Regiment was made up from the counties named below, as follows: Cos. A, B and C, in Marshall; Co. D, in Ohio County; Cos. E and G, in Harrison; Co. F, in Marion; Co. H, in Taylor; Co. I, in Hancock; and Co. K, in Brooke County.

The Twelfth West Virginia Volunteer Infantry was mustered into the United States Service August 30th, 1862, at Camp Willey on Wheeling Island, and the organization completed as follows:

FIELD AND STAFF.

(Mustered in August 30th.)
Colonel - JOHN B. KLUNK, Grafton
Lieut. Colonel - R. S. NORTHCOTT, Clarksburg
Major - F. P. PIERPONT, Harrisville
Adjutant - GEO. B. CALDWELL, Wheeling
Quartermaster - N. U. THURBER, Moundsville
Surgeon - JOHN FRIZZELL. Wheeling
Asst. Surgeons - DWIGHT RUGGLES, Moundsville
   S. P. BRYAN, Limestone
Chaplain - THOMAS H. TRAINER, Moundsville

NON - COMMISSIONED STAFF.

Sergeant Major - JAS. W. DUNNINGTON, Fairmont
Q. M. Sergeant - DAVID B. FLEMING, Independence
Com. Sergeant - WM. A. SCOTT, Fairview
Hospital Steward - CHARLES H. ODBERT, Wheeling
Principal Musician - GEORGE HAMMOND, Grafton

COMPANY A.

(Mustered in August 16th.)
Captain - HAGAR TOMLINSON, Moundsville
First Lieut. - T. S. MAGRUDER, Moundsville
Second Lieut. - WILLIAM BURLEY, Moundsville
Five Sergeants, eight Corporals.

COMPANY B.

(Mustered in August 20th.)
Captain - MARTIN P. BONAR, Rosby's Rock
First Lieut. - NATHAN S. FISH, Rosby's Rock
Second Lieut. - JOHN C. ROBERTS, Moundsville
Five Sergeants, eight Corporals.

COMPANY C.

(Mustered in August 23rd.)
Captain - ERASTUS G. BARTLETT, Rosby's Rock
First Lieut. - WM. L. ROBERTS, Moundsville
Second Lieut. - JOHN B. LYDICK, Rosby's Rock
Five Sergeants, eight Corporals.

COMPANY D.

(Mustered in August 25th.)
Captain - W. B. CURTIS, West Liberty
First Lieut. - WM. A. SMILEY, West Liberty
Second Lieut. - DAVID M. BLANEY, West Alexander, Pa.
Five Sergeants, eight Corporals.

COMPANY E.

(Mustered in August 26th.) .
Captain - CORNELIUS MERCER, Clarksburg
First Lieut. - OSCAR H. TATE, Clarksburg
Second Lieut. - JAS. R. DURHAM, Clarksburg
Five Sergeants, eight Corporals.

COMPANY F.

(Mustered in August 26th.)
Captain - AMOS A. PRICHARD, Mannington
First Lieut. - THOS. A. FLEMING, Fairmont
Second Lieut. - THOS. H. HAYMOND, Fairmont
Five Sergeants, eight Corporals.

COMPANY G.

(Mustered in August 27th.)
Captain - JAMES W. MOFFATT, Shinnston
First Lieut. - VAN B. HALL, Shinnston
Second Lieut. - ELAM F. PIGOTT, Shinnston
Five Sergeants, eight Corporals.

COMPANY H.

(Mustered in August 27th.)
Captain - J. H. BRISTOR, Grafton
First Lieut. - DAVID POWELL, Flemington
Second Lieut. - THOMAS H. MEANS, Grafton
Five Sergeants, eight Corporals.

COMPANY I.

Captain - R. H. BROWN, Fairview
First Lieut.. - JOHN H. MELVIN, Fairview

Second Lieut. - THOS. W. BRADLEY, New Cumberland
Five Sergeants, eight Corporals.

COMPANY K.

(Mustered in August 30th.)
Captain - THOMAS WHITE, Wellsburg
First Lieut. - JOHN B. JESTER, Wellsburg
Second Lieut. - J. R. BRENNEMAN, Wellsburg
Five Sergeants, eight Corporals.

Chapter Two

The Regiment did not remain long in Camp Willey. On the day after its completed organization it was ordered to Clarksburg, W. Va., which place was then threatened by a force under the Rebel General, Jenkins, who was then on a raid through West Virginia. Clarksburg is an old town, the county seat of Harrison County, situated on the Baltimore & Ohio Railroad, by rail 122 miles from Wheeling. Clarksburg will be remembered by the great abundance, in its vicinity, of blackberries during the early fall of that year. They were so plentiful that there seemed to be enough for the Twelfth and the citizens of the town, too.

The regiment arrived by rail at Clarksburg Sept. 2nd, and on that day a detachment of four companies under command of Lieut. Col. R. S. Northcott was ordered to Beverly, the county seat of Randolph County, lying in a southeast direction, and distant from Clarksburg 60 miles. The detachment arrived at Beverly September 6th. This place is a small town situated on the Tygarts Valley branch of the Monongahela River, at the western base of Cheat Mountain.

The remaining six companies under command of Col. John B. Klunk were ordered September 4th to Buckhannon, W.Va., the county seat of Upshur County, distant 28 miles. Buckhannon is pleasantly situated in apparently a good country.

The detachment under command of Col. Northcott marched from Beverly September 13th for Webster, Taylor County, distant 42 miles, arriving at the latter place the 15th. On this march the detachment was followed by slaves, some half dozen, who were striking for freedom, saying that they had run away because their master had threatened to sell them. They seemed to attach themselves to Capt. Brown's Company (I), and appeared inclined to remain with it during the stay at Webster. One or two of these slaves were nearly white, and some of the boys inclining to talk to and hang around them, Capt. Brown concluded to get rid of them; so in a few days two of the boys going to Grafton, a few miles distant, he sent them with the boys.

When the boys got to Grafton, a train of Ohio soldiers was about to start for Wheeling. One of the boys informed the colonel of the presence of the slaves and their story, and asked him if he would take them aboard of the train. He refused peremptorily. It looked blue for getting them off in that way. However, the Twelfth boys, in passing to rear of the train - a long freight - caught sight of, as it appeared, some of the non-commissioned staff in the rear car. They were told what was wanted. One of them having an eye to the main chance, wanted to know how much money would be given to take the "darks" on board. In a few moments some money was paid, the Twelfth boys contributing in part, and quickly and slyly the fugitives were hustled aboard; and a little later the train was off. They were never heard of afterward. It is to be hoped, however, that the sweets of freedom were not a disappointment to them.

The detachment left Webster on the 22nd and marched to Clarksburg, distant 18 miles, arriving there the same day. It remained at this place until October 1st, when it marched to Buckhannon, rejoining the other companies there. There was considerable rejoicing when the boys all got together again. In fact, the detachment met on its arrival with quite an ovation, the band coming out to greet it with stirring martial airs.

The regiment remained at Buckhannon, doing guard and picket duty, and drilling until the 19th. It was at this place that a drill-master appeared, and he put the regiment through quite a course of drilling, having it out every day practicing, while he stayed. Among the other exercises, he practiced the regiment considerably on forming a correct equipment. He would place the Sergeants, two from each company, in a line, say ten steps in advance of the regiment; the Colonel or the Major would then march the men forward to the line of the Sergeants; and when a particularly good alignment was made in this way, the drill-master was in the habit of remarking, to the amusement of the boys, "I say, Colonel," or "I say, Major, that is a capital line."

It is remembered that more than half of the companies, while having company drill at this time and place, would, on moving by different flanks on the march, in marching to the rear, have the order of the men reversed, so that No. 1 was on the place of No. 2, and vice versa. But it was never observed that this circumstance in any way interfered with the efficiency with which the boys afterward moved upon the enemy, or in case of an emergency, with the celerity with which they could "limber to the rear," as one boy expressed it. A little story, as "Father Abraham" would have said, relating to a later period of the war, will perhaps be not impertinent in this place.

We were in the Valley under Gen. Sheridan. The Twelfth and Fourth West Virginia Infantry, under command of Lieut. Col. Northcott, had been to Martinsburg, and was returning to the camp at Cedar Creek, on a four-days' round trip. The Battle of Cedar Creek was fought while we were on the return. It is a matter of history that the Army of West Virginia, or the Eighth Corps, was surprised in that battle. It was attacked before daylight, its works carried, and it put to rout almost before it knew it. The men not captured "fled to the rear, as the only thing they could do." In order to the better appreciation of the story, it may be well to say that Gen. Sheridan had employed this corps, doubtless on account of its celerity of movement, to flank the enemy at both the Battle of Opequon and the Battle of Fisher's Hill. The Twelfth and Fourth reached the camp at Cedar Creek with a supply train on the forenoon after the battle. It should have been said that these two regiments belonged to the Eighth Corps. Just as they were getting into camp, while passing some of the Sixth Corps, one of the latter yelled out, seemingly in allusion to the former's flanking movements, and its rout at Cedar Creek, "There goes some of that d---d Eighth Corps. They are always running one way or the other!"

On the 19th six companies under command of Col. Klunk marched to Beverly, and November 1st they were rejoined there by the other four companies. At this period of our service we had Sibley tents, which were circular in form, having a center pole, and a hole at the top of the center of the tent. They were capable of holding about sixteen men. We had tin-plates, tin-cups, knives and forks, one of each for each soldier, and a camp-kettle for, say each mess of ten or fifteen men. We had also a mess-box, in which to pack the plates, etc., for transportation. When in camp during pleasant weather the boys would eat in the open air on tables erected for that purpose. In fact, there was considerable style put on in the outset of the regiment's service. It took time to pack mess-boxes, strike tents and get ready to march. It took six wagons to carry the camp equipage. A large army having a proportionate number of wagons would have had enough to seriously embarrass it, and it might be, to whip it, in an engagement. Later in the war, the last year or more, the camp equipage for the men was reduced to a piece of shelter-tent and a tin-cup. This was a deprivation, but it had its advantages, for the men did not have to wait on the wagons, as they had to do sometimes when the camp equipage was hauled; but they could pitch their tents and make their coffee whenever and wherever they stopped, for they carried their tents and tin-cups in which to make their coffee.

At the time of this second march to Beverly, the regiment was pretty nearly full, not having been reduced by sickness or otherwise, there being not far from 800 men present for duty, and it made rather a formidable showing on the route. The impression that it made at that time upon a private soldier, as to its formidableness, may be here spoken of. "I used to think," said he later in the war, when he had had more experience, "that when I would take a survey of our regiment on the march from some point on the route, we were not likely to meet any enemy that could withstand us." This shows that he, like thousands of others, who were under a mistake in a less degree as to the magnitude of the Rebellion, had a ridiculously inadequate idea of the numerical strength of the enemy, or of the vastness of the force necessary to overcome it, there being, if not just then, not long afterward, the equal of more than a thousand such regiments required to achieve that purpose.

On our way to Beverly we passed over the battlefield of Rich Mountain, the first view we had of the sad havoc of war. Quite a number of Union and Rebel dead were buried here at the side of the road. It was said that when our forces drove the enemy from this position they found a trench dug at the side of the road over which this inscription was placed: "TO HOLD DEAD YANKEES." But the trench was utilized by filling it with dead Johnnys, about sixty of whom were buried here. A few of our men belonging to Ohio and Indiana regiments were buried in the corner of a garden nearby. The surrounding trees gave evidence of the struggle at this place.

The regiment as a whole remained at Beverly only a few days. The stay at this place of the six companies first there was over two weeks. The Eighty-seventh Pennsylvania Infantry and the Ninth West Virginia Infantry were there with us at the same time. The Eighty-seventh and the Twelfth were camped near together, a short distance north of the town on the bank of the Tygart's Valley River. Col. Hay of the Eighty-seventh was a very pleasant man, and a good tactician; and while we were here used to drill the Twelfth; and a friendship sprang up between his boys and ours that was strengthened and never lost by after association in the same brigade or division.

While we were at this town an unfortunate occurrence took place. A detail of the Ninth West Virginia was on guard in the town with orders to not allow any soldiers enter it without a pass. Some of the Eighty-seventh boys undertook to force past the guards, when one of the former was shot, it is not remembered whether fatally or not. When the news of the shooting came to camp there was a great commotion, like that of a disturbed hive of bees, in the camp of the Eighty-seventh. The boys went rushing to their tents, many of them from the river where they were washing clothes, to get their guns to avenge the shooting of their comrade. The aspect of things looked quite threatening for awhile. Finally, however, the officers of the regiment managed to quiet the men down, and further trouble was prevented.

Sergeant Thomas J. Orr of Company D thus relates a couple of incidents of our stay at Beverly:

Provisions being a little short, our larders were sometimes replenished from surrounding flocks and herds. An effort in this direction came near being attended with serious consequences. Jake McCormick of Company K concluded that bull-beef was a great deal better than no beef; so he and a chosen comrade or two walked deliberately down to the river, where a herd of cattle was quietly grazing, and selecting the patriarch of the herd, proceeded to extreme measures by shooting him to death, after which they dispossessed him of his hide, quartered and divided him among their hungry chums. Shortly an order was issued for Jake's arrest, but as the whole regiment was *particeps criminis*, the authorities concluded that it was too big a contract, and Jake escaped punishment, and went his way rejoicing.

On another occasion a fine flock of sheep was reported a mile or two down the river. A squad from Company D concluded to sample the mutton of that part of the country. Selecting a fine moonlight night, and led on by Tegard and King, who located the flock, they soon arrived at the objective point. But here a difficulty arose that they had not anticipated. How would they get the sheep captured? For they were wild as deer. After thinking the matter over and discarding many proposed plans, King, who stuttered, said: "B-b-b-boys, I have it. Tegard and I will go down to the lower end of the field, make a gap in the fence, and the rest of you drive the sheep through. Tegard and I will lie down just inside the gap and catch our sheep as they go through." This being a feasible plan, the boys proceeded to carry it into execution. Tegard and King laid down the fence and laid themselves down just inside, to await coming events, or rather the coming of the sheep. They had not long to wait; the sheep, frightened by the other boys, made a drive for the gap in the fence, the largest and strongest, of course in the van. Now here was where the fun commenced. King was greedy and concluded that one would not be quite enough for him; so he grabbed two of the first that came through by the legs. Being large and strong, they dragged him a short distance from the fence, where the rest of the flock would light on him as they jumped through the gap. King held on to the mutton, but he was a sorry looking King when he got straightened up. And an inventory being taken of him, it stood something like this:

G. W. King + two sheep.
G. W. King + two black eyes.
G. W. King + countenance demoralized generally.
G. W. King - cap, coat and half his pants.

After dressing three sheep the boys returned to camp in safety. But it was fun to hear King tell the boys the next day in his stuttering way how he got his black eyes.

If there was anything a soldier would stake his all on, it was on something good to eat; and this further remark is ventured while on this subject: that there were members of the regiment who contented themselves with Government rations, but if any article of food was placed before them not found in "Uncle Sam's" bill of fare, they ate what was put before them, asking no questions for conscience's sake.

The circumstance of the killing of the bull is well remembered, and it is not forgotten that the officers of the Twelfth, accompanied by the owner of the bull, went through the camp pretending to search the tents for that bull-beef, all the while trying to assume a serious face; but at the same time betraying in their countenances a manifest consciousness that the whole proceeding was a glaring farce. They did not want very much to find any part of the remains of the defunct bull. In fact, the whole performance gave the impression that it was a vigorous attempt at "how not to do it" and that the undertaking was succeeding admirably.

Our stay at Beverly now came to a close. On November 5th three companies, F, D and I, with a detachment of the Ringgold Cavalry, a battalion of Pennsylvania troops under command of Major Pierpoint of the Twelfth, were ordered on a scout through Pocahontas and Bath Counties, by way of Elkwater and Huntersville, to Monterey, the county seat of Highland County, Va., where they joined the other companies of the regiment, they, the latter, having started from Beverly one day late, and marched a different route, through Pocahontas and Pendleton Counties, under command of Col. Klunk, arriving at Monterey on the 9th.

As there is no data at hand regarding events or incidents in connection with the seven companies on this expedition to Monterey, the account given will relate exclusively to the three companies under command of Major Pierpoint.

On this scout the detachments of the three companies and the small cavalry force, traversed a section of country where Yankees had not been seen before. The opportunities for foraging here were good, and the boys improved them. One day an incident occurred that gave an intimation of the licentiousness and hardships of war. A citizen was met in the road. He wore a fur overcoat made of coonskin, and one of the cavalry men made him take it off and surrender it to him. The citizen passed on minus his overcoat, and in a predicament that should have enabled him to realize, in some measure, the beauties of secession.

Camp was made one night at a place called Mingo Flats. While here a laughable affair occurred, for the relating of which as follows Sergeant Orr is drawn upon once more:

There was not house room for all the command so Company F and part of each of the other two companies, D and I, went into a meadow where there was a bunch of hay stacks. The men took the fence from around the stacks, and built square pens four or five rails high, leaving the side next to the fire open. Then filling the pen up with hay they placed rails over the top, and covered all with hay, making excellent quarters for ten or a dozen boys.

Capt. Prichard of Company F, and Lieut. Melvin of Company I, were both with this squad. The former was very much opposed to foraging, while the latter didn't care whether school kept or not, so they didn't bother him too much, and he got enough to eat. There was also in this squad a character of Company I we called "Nosey." Now it happened that there was a drove of calves in the meadow. And after we had our quarters prepared and fires built, some of the boys were peering to see if there was anything in view appropriable. Among the number was "Nosey," who spied the drove of calves. Visions of fresh veal at once began to dance through his brain. With "Nosey" to think was to act. He made at once for the calves, selected his veal, grabbed the tail, and then the circus began. The calf was large and strong, but "Nosey" had a splendid hold. The calf broke for the fires at a 2:40 gait, "Nosey" keeping on as best he could. Capt. Prichard, hearing the racket, drew his "cheese-knife," and ran out to intercept the culprit, whoever he might be. The first thing he saw was "Nosey" and his calf coming at full speed, whom he greeted with "Hold on there! Hold on there!" "Nosey" replied: "I will, by ____." Just then a member of Company D, catching on, snatched an ax and relieved the breathless "Nosey" by tapping the calf gently on the head. We had veal for supper.

On the second day out we passed over the Elkwater battlefield where the Rebel Col. John A. Washington, was killed. At Huntersville we surprised a number of Johnnys, who were sleeping off heavy potations of apple-jack, and took them along as prisoners, passing, on our way, up Knap's Creek Valley in Pocahontas County, a section of country of rich farm land, abounding in fine cattle and horses. It was a fine and amusing sight to see Acting Quarter Master Lieut. Bradley of Company I sailing over the broad meadows on horseback, endeavoring to capture the splendid horses grazing on the luxuriant pastures there. Some of the horses were too fleet to be captured, and maintained their freedom.

The boys fared well on this raid, getting milk, honey, apples, etc., in abundance. The apples were buried in holes, as is frequently done with potatoes. And it was a laughable sight to see the boys fairly tumbling over each other and almost standing on their heads, as they dived into the apple holes, trying to not get left in their attempts at getting a fair share of the apples.

Sergeant Orr has the floor once more for the narration of an incident said to have occurred here, for the truth of which, however, he does not vouch. He tells it thus:

"Two men of the expedition went into a house to get something to eat. It happened that the male folks were all away from home, as was generally the case in that section when the Yanks were about, leaving only two single ladies of age in charge of the premises. When our two Yanks made their appearance the two ladies became frantic with terror; and holding up their hands exclaimed, 'Take our money, take everything we have, but do not harm us personally!' 'You personally be damned,' said the Yanks, 'have you any corn-bread?' That soothed them."

On this raid of the three companies we captured 60 head of horses and mules, 300 head of cattle, 41 prisoners and a wagon load of fine butter on its way to Staunton, Va. The owner of the butter was sent to Camp Chase. Where the bulk of the butter went is not known, but the boys made use of some of it.

We arrived at Monterey on the night of the 9th, rejoining here the other seven companies, as before stated, which had accompanied an expedition under command of Gen. R. H. Milroy, to this point. The regiment remained here but one day, when we started on our return, by way of Crab Bottom, resting one day there in the old Rebel winter quarters. We resumed our march on the morning of the 13th, by way of Franklin, the county seat of Pendleton County, thence by way of Circleville and Hunting Ground Mountain, back to Tygart's Valley River, five miles below Beverly, our starting point.

A sad accident occurred while crossing the mountain. A member of the Eighty-seventh Pennsylvania, who was along with the expedition, was accidentally shot by a comrade. His comrades attempted to carry him, but they could not do so, and they were compelled to bury him on the lonely mountain, using their bayonets to dig his grave.

Leaving our camp below Beverly, we marched to Webster, on the Parkersburg branch of the Baltimore Railroad, where we arrived on the 18th, marching 238 miles in fourteen days during the most inclement season of the year, fording mountain streams, swollen by melting snow and rain, many of the men bare-footed, and the roads half knee-deep with mud. It is not to be wondered at that many of the men succumbed to this ordeal, and were candidates for the hospital on our arrival at Webster.

One more incident of this raid will perhaps bear relating. Some of the boys took the measles on the route. On the return to Beverly a sergeant was sent in charge of an ambulance containing four sick boys, something in advance of the regiment, and over a different route, it is believed, from that taken by it. One evening, second out, perhaps, after ascending and descending Cheat Mountain, the driver halted the ambulance just at the base on the west side, where there was a hotel.

Now it happened that Gen. Milroy and his Adjutant General, Capt. McDonald, if his name is not mistaken, were going to put up at that hotel. The boys being quite sick, the Sergeant spoke to the landlord to procure beds for them. He seemed reluctant to comply with the request, and perhaps, to baffle the Sergeant, he told him to see Capt. McDonald about the matter, saying it would be just as the Captain said.

It often is the case that a man holding an inferior rank or position assumes an air of more importance, and of "the insolence of office," than do his superiors. This Captain was no exception to this rule. In fact, he was a specimen of the type of fellows represented by the fellow who was "a bigger [sic] man than old Grant." So when the Sergeant spoke to him regarding the getting of the beds, he put on a forbidding and repellent air and sarcastically that "he was not quarter-master." The Sergeant replied with somewhat of offended dignity that he would not have come to him at all, only that the land-lord had referred him, the Sergeant, to him, the Captain.

Here Gen. Milroy spoke up in a courteous and considerate manner, quite in contrast with that of the Captain, saying "We do not assume to have the disposition of the landlord's beds; they are entirely at his own disposal. As for myself, I can sleep on the floor." The Sergeant, being thus left to his own resources, secured beds for the sick boys.

The regiment left Webster on the 19th, going the Baltimore & Ohio Railroad to New Creek, in Hampshire County, West Virginia, distance 89 miles, arriving there the same day. There were other troops besides the Twelfth. One of the regiments of these was the Twenty-third Illinois Infantry, Col. Mulligan's regiment. This command was made up almost if not entirely of men of Irish birth, Mulligan himself being of that nationality. He was a fine, tall, erect man, with a military air, and a general mien and bearing that would attract attention anywhere. For this reason, and because of his national reputation, no doubt, and, it may be, the circumstance that he wore a green shirt, he attracted considerable attention from our boys.

As the weather was now pretty cold, and severe winter was approaching, and as we had established a camp here with regularly-laid-out streets, it looked as though we might winter here. But we stayed here only three weeks. On the 11th of December our regiment marched by way of Burlington and Petersburg to Moorefield, the county seat of Hardy County.

On the march to this place Lieut. Col. Northcott, stopping at a house on the way between Petersburg and Moorefield and getting thus behind the command, was taken prisoner by a Rebel scout. One of our scouts, however, followed the Rebel and his prisoner, and recaptured the Colonel, after, it was said, a severe hand-to-hand fight, in which each scout surrendered alternately, the Union scout coming out final victor.

Chapter Three

At Moorefield the Twelfth was assigned to Gen. Cluseret's brigade of Milroy's division, and on the 17th Gen. Cluseret started on an expedition to Strasburg, Va., the Twelfth being part of his command. We marched 26 miles the first day, camping on Lost River, four miles from Wordensville. That night was cold and stormy. The wind blew so that it made the soldiers' blankets flap as they lay under them trying to get a little sleep, and it was so cold that in some cases they had to get up in the night to go to the large fires they had made to get warm. That night it froze so hard that the creek was frozen so as to bear up a horse, but not quite the artillery. There was some difficulty in getting it over the creek. It was to this bleak and inhospitable place that the eccentric genius, "Barney" Wiles of Company D, alluded when he spoke of "the place where fire froze and turkeys chewed tobacco."

The second day the command marched through Wordensville to Capon Springs, 18 miles, encamping there for the night in the Mountain House, a magnificent building of 410 well-finished rooms, situated right in the midst of rather a dense forest. Owing to the torturous mountain roads we were close to this building before observing it. Making a sharp turn in the road, its grand proportions flashed upon us suddenly, as if by magic. The water in these springs is quite warm, and much steam was arising from it that cold weather.

We had good quarters that night, having nice mattresses on which to sleep. But we had to get up very early in the morning to resume our march to Strasburg. Surgeon Bryan of the Twelfth, in a half-jocular and half-earnest way, protested against getting up so early, saying "It's not the ideal thing, and I don't believe in it - this thing of getting up at midnight to stuff victuals and start out on a Rebel hunt."

After "stuffing victuals" we pushed out for Strasburg, a distance of 18 miles, where the Rebel Gen. Jones was, with a small force, which retired before the advance of Cluseret's brigade, leaving only his rear-guard to skirmish with the advance, as it entered the town.

Gen. Cluseret was a spirited, dashing Frenchman, who afterward figured prominently in belligerent affairs in Paris, after its evacuation by the Prussians, in the late Franco-Prussian War. And it was a picturesque sight to see him in his corduroy pantaloons, on nearing the town, dashing ahead of the infantry with a very small body-guard, while some skirmishing was going on with the cavalry. Some prisoners were taken here.

On nearing we got our first sight of the far-famed Shenandoah Valley, which had already been the scene, so far in the war, of some bloody battles, and was destined to be the scene of some far more bloody. And at the same time we got our first view of the no less famed Blue Ridge.

We camped at Strasburg that night. This was a small town of quite ancient appearance, situated on the north bank of the North Branch of the Shenandoah River, and at the base of the Massanutten Mountain, lying to the south. The next day the command marched six miles to Middletown. We remained here until the 24th.

Our movement from Moorefield had been a rapid one, and all subsistence and camp equipage had been left behind, except what the men could carry. So we had, in part, while at Middletown, to live off the country, regular foraging details being sent out for the purpose of getting subsistence, which were fairly successful. And we had to extemporize such quarters as best we could, while staying at Middletown. We built up rail-pens, filling them in and covering them over with straw for quarters. They answered very well for that purpose, as the weather then was quite fine for that season of the year.

On the 24th the command marched to Winchester. For a little while, until our tents arrived, we occupied the abandoned Rebel winter quarters at that place made of cedar brush. It appeared that when the Johnnys vacated their quarters they were not entirely abandoned - we found other occupants of them. It was here that we made our first acquaintance with "grey-backs." We found them companions whose acquaintance was hard to cut. They seemed to be no respecters of persons. It was not an uncommon sight to see a Colonel with his shirt off looking industriously for the little enemy, just the same as though the said Colonel were a fellow of low degree. As Artemas Ward would perhaps have said, he, the "grey-back," was a "little cuss," who seemed to love war against the human species for its own sake, not caring a continental whether he attacked a Union soldier or a Reb.

When the regiment started on the raid by way of Strasburg, a part of it was left behind at Moorefield. This detail of about 75 men, and about the same number of the Tenth West Virginia Infantry, the latter under command of Capt. Darnell of the latter regiment, and the whole under command of Capt. J. W. Moffatt of Company G of the Twelfth, struck tents and started for Winchester with a wagon train of supplies for Cluseret's command, leaving Moorefield the 28th. At Wordensville, four miles out, they were attacked by Rebel cavalry. The Wheeling Intelligencer of June --, 1865, in a sketch of the history of the Twelfth, said of this affair: "They were attacked by about 300 of Imboden's cavalry, and, notwithstanding the largely superior force of the enemy, Capt. Moffatt repulsed them handsomely, driving them several miles, and conducted the train safely to Gen. Cluseret at Winchester."

The Intelligencer's statement regarding this affair is not strictly correct, for the Rebels captured 52 from the train. No blame attaches to Capt. Moffatt, however, as he was a brave and faithful officer.

After this attack and repulse Capt. Moffatt and his train-guard had no further trouble. On the route they crossed the south branch of the Potomac, passed through Romney, crossed Lost River, passed through Blue Gap, crossed Capon River, and on the fifth day out, January 1st, 1863, arrived at Winchester, the train-guards of the Twelfth rejoining here their regiment. This was the day on which the President's Emancipation Proclamation was to take effect, but strange to say the colored people of Winchester seemed utterly ignorant of the fact that there was such a thing as any proclamation of freedom.

One was struck with the number of colored people in this town with white blood in them. They were of all shades of color, from, say half white to nearly white. An incident in this connection is perhaps deserving of a place. After we had been in Winchester for some time, and had begun to get a little acquainted, Surgeon Bryan of the Twelfth one day got into a conversation with a lady of the city, and, pertinent to the subject of the conversation, remarked that he could scarcely distinguish the negroes from the whites.

"How is that," inquired the lady, "are the white people so dark?"

"Oh, no," he replied, "it is not that the whites are so dark, but that the blacks are so white."

To go back a little, some skillful maneuvers by Gen. Cluseret, shortly after his arrival at Winchester from Strasburg, should be mentioned. One day there seemed to be some signs of an attack by Gen. Sam Jones. And it appeared as though our General wished to avoid, at that time, an attack from the enemy; so he moved the bulk of his brigade, consisting in all of about 2,500 men, over a ridge to the north, a half mile distant, out of sight; then he brought them in view again, on the ridge several hundred yards to the right, marched them along the southern slope of the ridge, and passed over it out of sight, at the same place as before. Thus making it appear that two had crossed the ridge instead of one.

This maneuver was calculated to deceive the enemy if he viewed it from a distance, for some of our own men, looking on from a distance, thought we were getting reinforcements. Some of the citizens of the town remarked afterward, it was said, that they thought that Cluseret's strategic handling of his brigade on that occasion was well done.

Winchester at the time of our occupancy of it was a rather pretty old town pleasantly situated, and of about 6,000 inhabitants. It was a place of historic associations, among which may be named the fact that it was the burial spot of Gen. Daniel E. Morgan of Revolutionary fame, and it was destined to have still further historic associations.

The citizens were almost universally disloyal; and the women especially took particular pains, on our coming among them, to show their hostility toward, and aversion for, the Yankees, by pulling their veils over their faces on passing the men on the street, and other like demonstrations. But time and association have their influence, and after awhile these manifestations of dislike and enmity almost entirely ceased. In fact, on entering their houses the women would treat you courteously and, in some instances, it is remembered, that they used, in a half pleasant, half tantalizing way, to sing for and at us their Rebel songs, such as "The Bonny Blue Flag," etc., and then apologetically ask us to not be offended at their doing so.

The women here were notably handsome and fine looking, so much so as to be the subject of remark among our soldiers to that effect. A little incident may be here pertinently given. There was an old colored woman in the town who used to work for the boys. On one occasion there was an allusion by some of them, in her presence, to the fact that there was a general concurrence of opinion among both officers and men that the women of Winchester were quite handsome. The colored woman did not quite relish this compliment to the white women, and said that if they were handsome in appearance they were not pretty in disposition, adding, "Indeed, honey, they could just cut your hearts out." Perhaps it was not without reason that this negress entertained this opinion.

There were more than 1,000 Rebel dead buried here, many of whom had been wounded at the Battle of Antietam and died of their wounds at this place.

This post was destined to be our winter quarters for the remainder of the winter. We spent the time here in guard, picket and fatigue duty, the latter duty being in work on the fortifications; and in drilling, target practice, and an occasional scout, filling in the interims growling, playing cards, corresponding, reading the papers, and occasionally talking on politics and disputing about the Emancipation Proclamation. Something about this last matter will be mentioned further along.

The arrival of the mail was always looked forward to with especial anxiety and interest by the boys. So eager were they to hear the news from home, some of the men in some of the companies, who could not write, inducing others to help them in their efforts, so applied themselves to learning to write that they were enabled to do their own corresponding before the war was over. The army was, in this particular, as well as in some others, a good school for some of the boys.

Citizens used to come into camp at this place to sell pies, cakes, etc., to the soldiers, and the boys would sometimes cheat them shamefully. In one instance at least, a soldier passed a label taken from a bottle of Perry Davis's Pain-killer for money. Where a peddler of pies could not read and the boys paid in scrip they, in making change, would very likely take more money than they gave. It is not to be wondered at, in view of the simplicity and lack of intelligence on the part of many of the South, that they manifested the ignorance they did, implied in the question, "What are you alls coming down here to fight we alls for?"

Even the citizens of apparently general intelligence seemed to have very hazy ideas of the real nature of the war. On one occasion a lady of Winchester, who did not seem to be of the ignorant class, asked the question, "How long do you intend to carry on the war against us?" and when told that the war would be prosecuted until the people of the South submitted to the authority of the United States, she seemed to regard the idea with horror and repugnance, and as a thought not to be entertained for a moment, throwing up her hands and exclaiming, "Oh! Oh!"

Possibly this lady's conception of the war, and that of thousands of others in the South, was that it was a fight to satisfy a spite or grudge, and after a sufficient revenge should be taken the war would stop. They seemed to have very little idea of the deep devotion to the old flag, on the part of the Union soldiers, and the loyal citizens generally, that made them willing to stand by it at any sacrifice; and perhaps no understanding of the demands of the future welfare of the nation, requiring the maintenance of the Union, and appealing to all Unionists to fight the war to a successful issue, if it was among human possibilities.

Our present occupancy of Winchester continued for three months. During that time little of important interest took place. The cavalry here had some brushes with the Rebel cavalry. On one or two occasions some Pennsylvania cavalry (either the Twelfth or Thirteenth) was sent down the valley from the direction of Strasburg, pell-mell into Winchester by the Rebel cavalry, some of the former, in one instance at least, losing their hats in their hasty retreat.

A reference to a diary kept by one of the boys, under date of February 27th, says that on that day our cavalry had an engagement with the Rebel cavalry ten miles out on the Strasburg road, in which our force was rather worsted, losing about 200 men.

During March we received some reinforcements, three regiments and a twelve-gun battery of Regulars. On March the 17th the voters of the West Virginia troops marched to the nearest point of that proposed State, to vote on the question of the adoption of the constitution.

On the 27th we struck tents and marched to Berryville, about ten miles distant. This was a small town, on the road to Harper's Ferry, and near the Shenandoah River. Two days later two regiments, the Sixth Maryland and the Sixty-seventh Pennsylvania Infantry, reinforced us at this place.

There were guerrillas, whose retreat was just across the Shenandoah River in the Blue Ridge, that were very bold and annoying at this place, frequently firing on the outposts. On the night of April 8th they captured two cavalry pickets and five horses of our command. On the night of the 21st a detail of 40 men under command of Lieut. David Powell of Company H, all of the Twelfth, crossed the river into London County, Virginia, and captured the desperate and dangerous Capt. Lapole and seven of his men of these daring guerrillas, bringing them in safe to camp as prisoners, receiving therefore the hearty thanks and commendation of the commander of the post at Berryville.

A comrade tells the story of the capture as follows:

While the Twelfth West Virginia Regiment lay at Berryville, Va., during the months of March and April, 1863, the pickets, outposts and reconnoitering parties were constantly annoyed and harassed by frequent attacks from guerrilla bands, under command of Capt. Lapole, a noted desperado belonging to Mosby's command. Quite a number of men had been killed by this Captain and his party. To capture them was no trifling undertaking.

Lieut. David Powell of Company H had been provost marshal of the command. In this position he had an opportunity to quiz and learn from all parties who came to his office the whereabouts of Capt.

Lapole and his men. At length a negro man, name forgotten, came and wished a permit to buy some sugar and coffee of the post Sutler.

On inquiry Lieut. Powell learned that he was from the east side of the Shenandoah River, where Capt. Lapole and his men always made their escape after making their attacks. At once the Lieut. suspected that the negro man had been sent to obtain the articles he desired, and took him into a back room to question him. The negro stoutly denied that he had been sent by Lapole or any of his men, but admitted that he knew Lapole and quite a number of his men, and after close questioning said that Capt. Lapole and seven of his men were at his master's home and would remain there for the night.

At this Lieut. Powell told him if he would give such information as would lead to Capt. Lapole's capture he would give him $50. This was increased to $80 by Gen. Milroy. The negro at once acceded to the proposition, and agreed to join in the work of his capture, and admitted that Capt. Lapole and his men had sent him for the coffee and sugar. He was allowed to purchase his articles and return to his home, with the understanding that if Capt. Lapole and his men remained at his master's he would come to the eastern bank of the river and light three matches in succession. Then someone would cross the river and learn all the facts respecting Lapole and his men. At the appointed time the lights flashed across the river and Lieut. Wycoff of the First New York Cavalry crossed the river, and learned that Lapole and his men were there at his master's and would remain all night.

Lieut. Powell accompanied by Lieut. Thos. H. Means of Company H, came to the river, and while there signals were displayed from an upper window of a farm house, which display Lieut. Powell with a part of his command went to the house to put a stop to. On going to the house he found quite a number of the fair sex collected and a bounteous supper prepared for the boys on the other side of the river.

Lieut. Powell allowed his men to eat at the first and then after giving strict orders that no lights be exhibited from the house that night, he took from the house a negro guide and made for the river again. But on his return, Lieut. Means and his men could not be found, and no one dared to make a noise to call him.

Presently he came across Lieut. Wycoff, who had secured a leaky old boat and was waiting for Lieut. Powell and his men. As soon as Lieut. Powell came he, Wycoff, told him what the negro had done and said. At once Lieut. Powell entered the boat with three other men - Samuel McDaniel and Harvey Haddox (the latter was afterward killed in the assault on battery Gregg, in front of Petersburg, Va.) as rowers of the boat. The other soldier was Elijah McIntosh, all of Company H, (McIntosh died at Winchester, October, 1864, from an overdose of morphine given him by a drunken doctor of the regiment.) Then the oarsmen returned and brought two others over until there were twenty-eight men in all on the east side of the river. With these twenty-eight men Lieut. Powell pushed on to where Lapole and his men were lodging for the night.

McDaniel and Haddox took charge of the boat and started down the river, which was fearfully high and rapid, and the night was so dark that no one could see an object ten feet away. Thus three miles had to be traveled down the river, before coming to the house where the men sought, were to be found.

Before reaching the house the chickens were crowing for day and already the dawn of light was beginning to show above the mountain height. (Blue Mountain)

The negro guide made a mistake and led to the wrong house, not more than four hundred yards away. The noise here in bursting open the door was loud, but fortunately not loud enough to waken the sentinel, who, not more than twenty minutes before had been permitted by his Captain to lie down and sleep, for he had announced the dawn of day and all quiet.

Lieut. Powell had divided his men into two sections - the first, was to move on to the house, and then open order and quickly move around the house, so as to enclose it. The other section was to rush with all their force against the door, and if possible mash it in upon the men who were sleeping on the floor. The first crash, the door flew from its hinges and fell within upon the now frightened foe.

Without firing a shot, the whole crew cried for quarter. A light was struck and just as the light flared up, one of the men fled up a stair way. When pursued, he was found close in by the side of a fat chubby girl who had been sleeping alone upstairs. When requested to come forth, he quickly obeyed and begged for quarter. The girl was heartily scared. Some of the men were for capturing her, but on closer view they decided that she was a woman and ought to be left to finish her morning nap.

All the prisoners, Capt. Lapole and seven men were properly searched, their arms secured, and a rapid fall back upon the river was made, where the two men with their boat was in waiting. Lieut. Wycoff had also secured another boat.

Lieut. Means and his men were on the other side; also, two pieces of artillery were planted to secure a safe crossing of the river, against an attack from Mosby and his men, who were only a mile or so distant.

Lieut. Powell saw all his men and his prisoners safely across, then he the last of all, came across, having with his brave men, accompanied one of the most daring feats of the war. The crossing of the river alone, was one of the most perilous adventures one could undertake.

After crossing the river, and forming his men, Lieut. Powell marched with his prisoners to Berryville, where he securely placed them in the county jail, under a vigilant guard. He and his men received the complimentary notice of Col. McReynolds, commanding post; of Gen. R. H. Milroy, commanding at Winchester, Va., and of Gen. Robert Schenck, who commanded the northern part of Virginia and of Maryland.

Lapole, the morning after his capture, proposed that if he could be allowed fifty yards, and then a chance for escape, he would allow six or eight men to shoot at him. But when told there were that many men in the command who could kill a deer 100 yards running, he gave up the matter as a dangerous undertaking.

He was afterward tried by a military court at Fort McHenry at Baltimore, and was sentenced to be hung, which sentence was executed on the 8th of May, 1864, one year and one month after his capture.

The negro who informed, was literally shot to pieces afterward, by Lapole's comrades in their guerrilla warfare.

The men who crossed the river and captured Lapole, did their duty nobly. Not one of them failing in a single duty assigned them.

It was a mortification to Lieut. Means, that he did not get to cross the river and to share the danger with others.

The men who participated in the capture of Lapole and his men, were largely volunteers from the several companies of the regiment. There was never any need of a detail when it was known that Lieut. Powell was to command.

A company of the Twelfth, on the night of the twenty-ninth went out from camp a few miles to a house to capture some "bush-whackers" supposed to be there; but they failed to get any.

In this connection may be told a little joke on Sergeant James Porter, who was of the detachment. There was a beautiful girl at the house whom the sergeant got to see, and with whose beauty he was, it seemed, much impressed. It appeared that the matter rested upon his mind; and the next day, though a quiet man, he referred to her beauty in evident admiration, saying, "Boys that was a mighty pretty girl that we saw last night, and I have a notion to go back there."

Our stay at Berryville, now May ninth, came to a close. The regiment at this date received orders to proceed to Clarksburg, W. Va., to protect that place, which was threatened with an attack by a rebel force under Gen. Jones, who was raiding the country about there generally.

We started on our march to Clarksburg in the afternoon, to go by way of Harper's Ferry to take the cars there, to the former place. We marched through that old town of Charlestown, W. Va., near Harper's Ferry, which old town is destined to be historic, and a noted place for long years to come, because of its association with the name of John Brown of Osawatomie, whose memory is world-wide. As showing the extent of the name and fame of John Brown, an incident is here given in substance, as related some years ago by the late Thomas Hughes, "Tom Brown of Rugby," then ex-member of parliament.

It was after our late Civil War that he, Thomas Hughes, was one day walking along in London, not far from London bridge, when he heard a sound of voices that arrested his attention. He listened and soon discovered that the sound proceeded from a regiment of British soldiers crossing the bridge singing, "John Brown's body lies mouldering in the tomb," etc. In writing about this occurrence he indulged in this reflection. That when such men as he should be forgotten, the name of John Brown would still be remembered.

It was perhaps between nine and ten o' clock at night - that night in May - when we passed through the old town. The lights were out, the streets deserted, the citizens apparently had retired for the night; and the town seemed wrapped in slumber. There was nothing to disturb the quiet of the night, and the solemn stillness of all about, but the monotonous tramp, tramp of the soldiers as they marched; when suddenly the quiet was broken; Company A, at the head of the regiment struck up the song of "John Brown," and other companies taking it up, soon all were singing.

Pretty soon windows were hoisted, shutters were thrown open and lights flashed out on the streets. It seemed as if the citizens of the old town were startled! Possibly they thought the spirit of John Brown had come back from the spirit world to haunt them.

A few years before the soldiers of Virginia were here to see that John Brown should be hanged, that human servitude in the land might be made more secure. Then the moral atmosphere of our land was murky with greed, selfishness and prejudice. Men's understandings were perverted; they called wrong right, and preached it as a holy thing. It was almost true, that he had no friend, that dared proclaim the fact, and that none were so poor as to do him reverence. Then, too, there were distant rumblings of a coming storm, but the cloud on the horizon was no larger than a man's hand.

Today the storm of war had burst upon the land with threatening fury. The whole country was turned into a field of war. There were other soldiers on duty now. They were fighting to maintain the Union of their fathers, "shouting the battle cry of freedom," and every step they took was leading to the doom of slavery.

The thunder and lightning of war was clearing the moral atmosphere. Men saw things differently now; and while the men of the old Twelfth, like many others, gave a sort of superficial disapproval of the conduct of John Brown, deep down in their hearts, in these perilous times which were anew trying men's souls, they felt an admiration for the old hero who died bravely, in an insane attempt to free from bondage a despised race; and hence, they sang with gusto the John Brown war song, as they marched through that town in the Valley which will suggest his name for generations to come.

Considering the wonderful contrast between the spectacle of this regiment's then singing the battle hymn whose refrain is, "But His Soul Goes Marching On," and that which was to be seen there only a few years before, the incident was a most extraordinary and impressive one.

On the eleventh, we arrived to within five miles of Clarksburg, where the enemy had destroyed a railroad bridge. We got off the cars here, got our dinner, and marched the same day to Clarksburg. The Rebel Gen. Jones made no attack on the place. During this stay at this place, Mr. Nathaniel Wells, of Brooke county, brought tickets out from Hancock county, for the soldiers of the latter to vote.

We remained at this place doing picket duty and drilling nearly every day, with nothing particular occurring until June second, when we had orders to march, taking a freight train for Grafton on the Baltimore and Ohio railroad, where we were paid on that day two months pay. The next morning we took the cars at this place for Martinsburg, arriving there the following night; and in the morning following, we started on the march up the Valley Pike for Winchester, more than "Twenty miles away" arriving on the fifth at that place. We camped on the southwest of the town. Here at this time we drew shelter tents. This appeared like getting down to business - looked like stripping for a fight.

Chapter Four

The time for the taking place of important events was approaching. The near future was pregnant with events for the Twelfth; the time for the battle of Winchester under Gen. Milroy was not far off. And an important crisis for the entire nation in the progress of the war was almost at hand, involving the welfare of the country and the better interests of mankind generally; for the battle of Gettysburg, the greatest battle of the war, and the greatest battle ever fought on American soil - a battle which is now regarded as the turning point of the war, was about to be fought.

We had now been in the service for nearly ten months and the regiment, as a whole, had never been in an engagement. We sometimes wondered whether we should ever get into a battle. It is safe to say that most of the boys were anxious to see at least one fight; and some of them were want to say somewhat boastfully, that they were "spoiling for a fight." Any doubts, however, as to whether we were to see a battle were soon to be dispelled; and the desire to see one, or to be engaged in it, was destined to be more than satisfied, at a later period.

"Coming events cast their shadows before." There are frequently harbingers of future occurrences; but the difficulty is to measure their significance, and to know what is best to do in view of them. There began to be signs of a coming conflict in this field of operations. The next day after our return to this place we had orders to lie on our arms the succeeding night; and the next night, Sunday, the seventh, at 10 o'clock, three companies, D, E, and I, were sent out on the Strasburg road to reinforce the picket there. The three companies stayed out till morning, when they returned to camp. Two days later the situation was becoming more threatening. Companies F, I, C, and H, under command of Col. Northcott were ordered out to support, at night, a section of artillery, which at the time was placed in position every night to be ready in case of an attack.

In the morning, no enemy having appeared, the four companies returned to camp. This day, the eleventh, Major Pierpont gave us a farewell address, he having resigned as major, to accept the office of adjutant general of West Virginia. He left much to the regret of the Twelfth, being a general favorite.

The bloody ordeal of a general battle for the whole command was just now at hand. The next day the Eighty-seventh Pennsylvania with some cavalry and artillery went out the Strasburg road five miles, and ambushing a force of Rebel cavalry, they killed and wounded some fifty of them, and captured about forty prisoners without the loss of a man of the Eighty-seventh. The boys of that regiment came back in good spirits saying that they had "skunked them."

That night four companies of the Twelfth were again ordered to support a battery. They returned from doing that duty at 7 o'clock next morning, but before they got their breakfast, the whole regiment was ordered into line. After standing in line for awhile, we got orders to fill our canteens with water and get one day's rations in our haversacks; and about 11 o' clock we marched out on the Strasburg road. At the same time, cannonading commenced on our left, which told us the battle was on.

We changed our position several times until we got into a piece of woods. Here we were ordered to take off and pile up our knapsacks, which we did. The Rebels were advancing a heavy skirmish line in front; and soon were heard those peculiar sounds, the whistling of the minnie-balls, to which the men afterward became quite accustomed. So unaccustomed were they to the whistling sounds, that they began to question among themselves as to what they were, some saying that they were the sounds of flying bullets; others that they were not. An officer hearing the talk said: "Boys those are bullets as sure as you live." This assurance together with the increasing frequency of the sounds, settled the matter in their minds; and they never afterward had any doubts as to what it was, when they heard the whistle of bullets.

We opened on the advancing enemy, and for about an hour we kept up a heavy fire. We held the Rebels in check in our front. After a while Adjt. Caldwell reporting that the enemy was flanking us on our right, Company A, under command of Lieut. Burley was ordered to form a skirmish line, and move to that flank to protect it. The force there, however, moving against us was too heavy to be kept back by one company of skirmishers; so the Colonel ordered us to fall back behind a small creek which position we held till dark.

When we retired from the woods to the creek, the Colonel marched us to the rear by file, instead of in line of battle, which latter order under the circumstances, military tactics, it is taken, would demand. We filed off the field by the left flank, and in doing so the right had to march the length of the regiment before gaining a step to the rear. It was while thus marching to the point of filing left to the rear, Lieut. Bradley, of Company I, was shot dead. We left our knap-sacks in the woods, where we had unslung them. They, of course, fell into the hands of the Johnnys, who, no doubt, examined them with a good deal of interest. This, our first engagement, was the only one in which we met with anything like a general loss of equipments.

Col. Curtis, then Captain of Company D, used to tell this anecdote concerning this day's fighting. There was an Irishman in his company whose name was Tommy Burke, who, like his nationality in general, was quick-witted and humorous. During the fighting in the woods the hammer was shot off his gun, and about the same time he missed his haversack. Tommy believed - no doubt correctly - that it had been shot away too. Being thus completely knocked out as it were, he turned to the Captain saying, with reference principally, it is presumed to the loss of his haversack, "Captain, Captain, the bloody Rebels have cut ahff my supplies."

After dark we fell back from the creek to a stone wall at the outskirts of town, when it began pouring down rain in torrents. At 2 o'clock in the morning, Sunday the 14th, we marched up into the fortifications, remaining there till 7 o'clock. At this time while in the fortifications, Lieut. Melvin of Company I, arrived from home, showing that the rear was still open till near that Sunday morning, at least.

Our regiment was the first to go out of the fortifications that morning. We took a position behind a stone wall between the Strasburg and Romney roads, and about a mile from the main fort, which we held till ordered back. A little later two companies as skirmishers took position behind the stone wall we had just left. The left wing was held in reserve, while the right supported a battery placed at about 900 yards from the Rebel lines.

In front of this battery off to the southwest the Johnnys were behind a stone wall. Our artillery did some very accurate shooting, knocking several holes in the wall behind which the Johnnys were, causing them, when the wall was struck, to scatter in a lively manner, and thus affording for the time being, at least, great sport for our boys, though they were quite worn out from want of sleep, having had little or none the night before. Occasional shots from the enemy reached this battery. It was one of these that struck and killed Lieut. Beugough of Company F, who was lying sleeping at the time, being overcome by want of sleep.

About 5 o'clock P.M. the whole regiment advanced to the stone wall. A half hour later the Rebels opened a tremendous fire with their artillery which heretofore, during the day had been quiet, on our fortifications. The whole force then fell back to the forts, the Rebels having shortly before this captured battery L, of the Regulars. Thus practically ended this day's fighting. However, our siege guns replied to the Rebel guns about night, the roar of our heavy guns being deafening.

The Rebel artillery fire came from a ridge southwest of our forts, and was directed seemingly to the flag staff of the main fort; and when Gen. Milroy climbed the flag staff, as he did, in order to get a view of the Rebel batteries, it may be, or to note the effect of our fire, the boys cheered him lustily.

Greeley in the American Conflict says in regard to this capture of Winchester by the Rebels, that our men took a prisoner Saturday night the 13th, "who rather astonished Milroy by the information that he belonged to Ewell's corps; and that Longstreet's also was just at hand - the two numbering about 50,000 men."

In regard to the operations of the next day, Sunday, 14th, he says that at 4 P.M. they (the Rebels) made a charge up the Front Royal road to the edge of town, but were repulsed. A little later they opened fire from two eight-gun batteries on the northwest, hardly a mile from town; and forthwith Ewell's infantry swept up to and over our breastworks, disregarding the fire of our guns, driving out the 110th Ohio with heavy loss, and planting their colors on our defenses. Meantime, the city had been substantially invested on every side, and was now virtually lost; though an attempt to storm the main fort from the position first gained was repulsed."

Referring to the foregoing alleged attempt to storm the main fort, if there was any made, it was after dark. It is remembered that there was heavy firing from the fort, on the northwest side, as though the enemy was making an attack, but it never seemed quite clear that he was, as it was so dark at the time that an object could be seen but a short distance.

At 1 o'clock A.M. Monday, 15th, Milroy held a council of war which decided to evacuate our force of all arms being only 10,000, and not all of it effective, against a corps of 25,000 and more if necessary. The artillery was spiked, the harness cut up, the axles and wheels sawed to pieces, and at 2 o'clock, the whole command began moving out to evacuate the fort, the soldiers hastily breaking some boxes of crackers (conveniently placed for the purpose) with the butts of their muskets, and putting some of the crackers in their haversacks, as they marched out.

We started on the road leading to Martinsburg. A mile or two from the fort, Gen. Milroy rode along the road past the men telling them to push along, that he wanted to get as far out the road as possible before daylight. The Twelfth was somewhere about the middle of the line. Four miles from Winchester our advance was attacked by a division of Rebels holding the road in our front. It was at this time just breaking day. There was very heavy firing for about a half hour - heavier than at any time during the two proceeding days.

We were halted when fighting began in our front; and stood in line seemingly waiting on orders, but none coming we filed to the left of the pike, and started in the direction of North Mountain. It was just here where we left the pike, that Lieut. Col. Northcott, getting separated from the regiment, was captured. We encountered no enemy until we got to the base of the mountain several miles distant. Here we were fired upon by some Rebel cavalry, from a road running along the base of the mountain. Company A, being at the head of the regiment opened fire in return upon the Johnnys, pouring it in briskly, and they soon got out of the way. We had now got outside of the Rebel ring. None of our men were hit at this place.

The One Hundred and Sixteenth Ohio, the First New York cavalry and the Twelfth West Virginia, were the only regiments that came out of the fight retaining their organizations. We lost no men as prisoners except those who had in some way got separated from the regiment; though our loss in prisoners was considerable, about 200. Among these were, Lieut. Col. Northcott, Asst. Surgeon F. H. Patton, and Lieut. Henry F. Anshutz. Among the killed were, Lieut. Thomas W. Bradley of Company I, and Lieut. John T. Bengough of Company F, and among the wounded was Lieut. James R. Durham of Company E.

This fight at Winchester was a disastrous one for the Union cause. Milroy lost between 3,000 and 4,000 men, all his artillery and some 400 wagons, the troops coming out of it, retaining their organizations, had only their small arms.

It was an opinion entertained by many of Milroy's men, that this disaster to our arms was largely compensated for, by the alleged fact that his stubborn resistance at Winchester had so detained Lee in his invasion of Pennsylvania, that Hooker and Meade were the better enabled to concentrate their forces to protect Washington and meet him in battle. There is seemingly not much in this view; for it was only a part of Lee's army that was detained; the bulk of it kept moving on, not being detained, in the least, by Milroy. Days after his rout the enemy was still on the road south of Winchester, marching down the Valley, as will appear further along.

It was more than two weeks after Milroy's defeat that the battle of Gettysburg was fought. He could have got out his entire command if he had started one day sooner. Considering the length of time after the defeat, before the battle of Gettysburg took place, this detention of the advance of Lee's army for only one day longer than was consistent with his escape, was of not very great importance. Greeley says, "Milroy's great mistake was holding on just one day too long - his communications with Schenck and Halleck having already been severed." This will doubtless be the verdict of history. It was for this blunder and its consequences, that he was relieved from command of his army.

Going back a little, Col. Curtis tells this story about Lieut. Phil Bier of Company A, in reference to our being fired upon by the Rebels at the foot of North Mountain. When our men began returning the fire, some one shouted, "You are shooting the cattle." Lieut. Bier replied, "D---n it! whoever heard of cattle shooting - give it to them boys."

In this connection it is proper to speak of the conduct of Sergt. Henry Spear, of Company D, at this time. When we were fired upon, some of the boys, not knowing, of course, the strength of the enemy, and being taken by surprise, began shying off to one side of the road into the woods. Sergt. Spear, however, walked toward the Johnnys, so as to get a good view, and spying a fellow behind a fence, took deliberate aim at him and fired. He got from behind the fence quickly. Spear had unknowingly exchanged guns with a comrade at night in the fortifications. He insisted that if he had had his own gun, he would have shot the Johnny.

In closing any reference to the fighting of our regiment at this battle of Winchester, it is but simple justice to say that the manner in which Company B acquitted itself on the first day's engagement, as skirmishers, called forth deserved praise.

Here is an incident of our retreat copied almost verbatim from an old letter written at the time, well worthy of a place. After we had driven off the cavalry at the foot of the mountain, and were ascending it along a road, through a sort of defile, near the top, a girl of some fourteen or fifteen years, barefooted, bareheaded, her hair hanging loosely down over her shoulders, came out from a humble, unpretentious dwelling near by, and with a coolness and confidence calculated, under the circumstances, to excite admiration, inquired for the Colonel telling him that she thought it best to not take the road he was on; that she had heard that the Rebels held it at the point where it intersected the Baltimore and Ohio railroad, about 35 miles distant; and when inquiry was made of her as to whether she could show us another route that was open, she said that she thought she could.

When the Colonel told her that we would burn their house if she deceived us intentionally, and got us to take a road on which we would be intercepted by the Rebels, she showed no alarm, and was not in the least disconcerted. She went with us about four miles along a path on the mountain crest, where we had to walk in single file. Striking another road here, she left us. Before she left, however, each of several officers gave her some money.

This young heroine talked very rapidly - was not bold, but had a simple confidence - and was not a bit afraid of the soldiers. Her hair was blonde, her forehead high, she was intellectual in appearance, and had native beauty of person. This mountain maid needed only a little polish to make her highly attractive. It is to be hoped that she never had to suffer at the hands of the Rebels for giving aid and comfort to the enemy. The soldiers of the Twelfth who met her that morning on the mountain will long remember her.

We continued our retreat in a somewhat northerly direction, camping at night in the mountain. At about midnight we renewed our march and in the forenoon of the next day, crossed the Potomac into Maryland, at a place called Millstone point, wading the stream. Passing on up the river five miles farther we reached Hancock on the Baltimore and Ohio railroad about noon. The men, of course, by this time, were much exhausted from two or three days' fighting, little sleep since the fight began three days before, little to eat for the last day or two, and hard marching. It is believed that the men generally, got something to eat here.

The One Hundred and Sixteenth Ohio, which arriving on another road, and portions of the First New York, and Twelfth Pennsylvania cavalry, with some stragglers from various commands; joined us at this place. Scouts reporting that some Rebel cavalry coming from the direction of Martinsburg were going to receive them; but no attack was made however. We stayed here till 10 o'clock at night, when we marched to Little New Orleans, eighteen miles distant, arriving there sometime the next day. We expected to take the cars here for Cumberland, Md., but no cars came.

We waited here till dark, when Col. Washburn of the One Hundred and Sixteenth Ohio, receiving a dispatch from the colonel of the First New York, that the enemy held Cumberland, we went a little back on a hill and camped for the night in some woods. Having got some coffee, meat and flour at Little New Orleans we managed to make out of these articles a slim breakfast in the morning, and began our march for Bloody Run, Pa., about thirty-five miles distant, arriving there the 19th.

When we got into Pennsylvania we struck a new atmosphere. If hitherto, when we were in the so-called Confederacy there was always a feeling present, that we were out of our country, we now felt that we were once more in the land of the "stars and stripes," the United States of America. The people all along the road gave us a hearty welcome, and freely gave us food. There was no danger of being bush-whacked here, if you should chance to become separated from your command.

When we arrived at Bloody Run, we met Gen. Milroy there. This meeting was the first knowledge we had, that he had escaped from Winchester. He proceeded to reorganize his command, but was soon relieved because of his disastrous defeat. The members of the Twelfth generally, regretted very much to part with their brave old commander, who was familiarly known in his command as the "Old Grey Eagle," as he was a general favorite with them. They felt that he had been harshly dealt with, considering that the last order he had received from Gen. Schenck at Baltimore, commander of the department, communication being soon thereafter cut off was to "hold the place until further orders." They thought that his fault, if it was such, was in too literally obeying orders.

Col. Pierce of the Twelfth Pennsylvania cavalry being the senior of the officers present, took command of the remnant of Milroy's demoralized force after Milroy was relieved of his command; and Col. Klunk of the Twelfth West Virginia, was put in command of the infantry. We remained at Bloody Run till the 30th, when we marched to Bedford, Pa., starting in the morning and passing up the Juniata river we arrived here about 1 o'clock P.M. of that day. Here we drew blankets and clothing the first after leaving Winchester.

We stayed at Bedford till July 3rd, when we had orders to march starting in the direction of Gettysburg, but too late to participate in the battle that was then going on there. We passed through Bloody Run and Connellsburg, arriving at London, Franklin county, the 5th, making a distance of about forty-five miles. Somewhere on the road, perhaps on the 4th, we got a daily paper of the date of July 3rd, which gave a vague, indefinite, unsatisfactory mention of the battle, taking place at Gettysburg which, of course, made us exceedingly anxious for more news.

Most of the infantry went on six miles farther to Mercersburg to meet 200 or 300 of our cavalry who had captured a Rebel train of wagons, with the guards, hauling wounded and plunder to the crossing of the Potomac at Williamsport, Md. There were 110 wagons and ambulances, and about 600 prisoners, half of whom were wounded in this capture. The wagons were loaded up with quartermaster's stores, and all kinds of plunder of which they had robbed the people on their invasion. There were several thousand dollars worth of fine cloths, cassimeres, silks, and etc., in whole bolts in this plunder.

Hospitals were established at Mercersburg, and the Rebel wounded were cared for. They were in a horrible condition, having been there from three to five days without having had their wounds dressed. The next day the infantry returned to London bringing back the unwounded prisoners, about 300 in number, and the wagons and etc. The wagons, ambulances and stolen goods were turned over to the quartermaster's department.

We remained at London until the 13th, when we were ordered at 3 o'clock A.M., to prepare one day's rations and get ready to march. We started at 6 o'clock A.M., marching through Mercersburg and Greencastle, we reached Hagerstown, Md., the next day. Passing through the town, we camped about two miles south of it in the middle of the afternoon, having marched thirty-two miles.

The battle of Gettysburg had been fought, the Rebels had met "a bitter crushing defeat," and "the Army of the Potomac had won a clean, honest, acknowledged victory." Lee's army had retreated as far as the Potomac but when it reached there it found its pontoons gone, they having been destroyed by some of our forces, sent up from Harper's Ferry for that purpose and the river was so high from recent rains that it could not be forded. Lee was compelled to halt until he could restore his means of crossing. In the meantime the Army of the Potomac had come up and was again facing its old enemy. Gen. Meade, however, was hesitating to make an attack, when he received orders from Washington to do so, and accordingly he would have attacked the Rebels the day, the 14th, we of the remnant of Milroy's army passed through Hagerstown in the vicinity of which place the two armies confronted each other; but on the previous night, Lee got his army across the river; not however, without considerable loss, Kilpatrick having, after a sharp engagement, captured 1,500 of the Rebel rear-guard. If there had been a battle there, as Meade expected, it is more than probable that the Twelfth would have been on the ground in time to have engaged in it.

Here is an anecdote of Lee's invasion of Pennsylvania, heard at the time of his retreat, that should not be lost. A Rebel officer, as Lee was marching north through the state stopped at a private house for some purpose. The woman of the house with some curiosity asked him where they were going, which presumably, he did not know, and would not have told if he had known. But he replied, "We are going to

Boston." The woman said to him, "You'll get 'Boston' before you get back."

When Lee's army was retreating the same officer stopped at the same house and reminded the woman that he had stopped there before, saying to her, "Madam, I have just called to say that we got 'Boston.'"

The next day after Lee crossed the Potomac, the First Corps of the Army of the Potomac passed our camp en route to Harper's Ferry. They had been on the go marching and fighting for about a month, with no time to do any washing or to get new clothes; and, of course, they were covered with dust and dirt, and were hard looking generally. A large part of Milroy's men had new uniforms and were pretty bright and clean looking, and the First Corps boys tantalizingly called us Sunday soldiers.

The Sixteenth, we of Milroy's late command, marched to Sharpsburg, Md., ten miles distant. Some time during the latter part of July, while we were at Sharpsburg, Capt. W. B. Curtis of Company D, received his commission as major of the regiment, to rank as such from June 17th, 1863.

This vicinity is Maj. Curtis's birth place, having been born here April 18th, 1821. He migrated from here in 1827 to West Virginia. He recognized the old log house in which he was born. It was pierced with cannon balls in several places during the battle of Antietam. He met several of his relatives who were loyal and made him welcome, while we remained here.

Maj. Curtis on the receipt of his commission was immediately put in command of the regiment, as the Lieutenant Colonel was still held a prisoner of war, and the Colonel was in command of a brigade. For more than two weeks we remained at this old village, which is indeed, a very old one apparently, there being one or more old-style churches in it gone into disuse, and tumbling down. It is historically interesting too, as being the scene of the bloodiest battle (at the date of it) ever fought on American soil, the battle of Antietam; and is today the site of one of the great National Soldiers cemetery.

On August 4th, we were ordered to Martinsburg, W.Va. We started in the morning and marched to Harper's Ferry, a distance of ten miles, took the cars there which carried us to within two miles of Martinsburg, they being prevented from going any further by reason of the railroad's having been torn up by the enemies, got out of the cars when they stopped and marched the rest of the way to town in the evening and camped for the night.

In the morning we moved our camp to a pretty lawn of some five acres at the edge of town, filled with fine young shade trees, the property of the Hon. Chas. James Faulkner, who held in all about 800 acres of valuable land adjacent to town. As the weather was very warm we wanted to camp on this lawn to get the benefit of the shade there. No doubt our doing so was not altogether agreeable to Mrs. Faulkner and daughters who still occupied the fine mansion at the rear of the lawn. But as Mr. Faulkner had seen fit to join his fortune with that of the Rebellion, it was hardly any part of our business to be consulting his interests, or the wishes of his household, though Mrs. Faulkner used to claim to be a good Union woman. She protested that she was such, to the Union soldiers, at least, fortifying this claim on one occasion, by saying that she "would not give a cent for a woman that did not have a mind of her own - would you?" Subsequent events seemed to show that the lady did protest too much.

Martinsburg at this time was a thrifty town of several thousand inhabitants, situated in the Shenandoah Valley on the Baltimore and Ohio railroad, and was noted for the general loyalty of its inhabitants. There was always an air of welcome to us about the place.

Chapter Five

Col. Klunk during the time the regiment was straggling about in the Cumberland Valley, sent in his resignation upon the plea of sickness in his family, and while stationed at Martinsburg he received notice that it had been accepted. This left the regiment with Major Curtis as the only field officer with it, Lieut. Col. Northcott being still a prisoner.

Our regiment remained on the Faulkner lawn the 25th, when we moved our camp to the northwest side of the town, where the other troops were encamped. We stayed at Martinsburg about two and a half months. While we were here Quartermaster Gen. Meigs inspected the troops at this place. Also while at this place there was a grand parade and review of the troops on the occasion of the presentation of a flag to the First New York Cavalry. Col. McReynolds of that regiment making on that occasion a short speech.

September 25th, fifty men of the regiment were detailed to cook rations for the troops passing from the Army of the Potomac to Gen. Grant's army at Chattanooga. The next day part of the Eleventh Corps passed through by rail going to join Grant. The next day after that, Gen. Howard, commander of the Eleventh Corps, passed over the railroad following his troops. A salute was fired in his honor as he passed. One day later some more troops from the Army of the Potomac (part of the Twelfth Corps) followed on after the others.

While we were at this point a considerable number of the boys of the Twelfth got furloughs. Pertinent to the subject of furloughs may be mentioned here an incident of the many illustrating the humors of camp life. There were two brothers in Company I, Van and Tom. While we were in Pennsylvania during Lee's invasion of that state, Van became sick and we left him behind on leaving there; and during our stay at Martinsburg, Tom, not having heard from Van, and not knowing whether he was alive or not, became uneasy about him. So he made an application to get a furlough to go to hunt his brother up; but he failed to get it. Some days after this Tom, it seemed, had been in too close proximity to some fellow who had been looking on the wine when it was red (or something of that kind) getting a sniff perhaps of his breath, and Tom's sensibilities were somewhat aroused. In this condition Tom got to thinking about the case of Van, and becoming somewhat desperate he said that he was going to apply again for a furlough to hunt him up. Adding that if he did not get one he would go anyhow. "I'm going by thunder," said he, "I don't care if the war stops!"

It happened that Tom's second application failed. He thought better of it, and concluded that he would not go without a furlough and the war went on. It should be said that in due time Van returned to the regiment.

Referring to a diary kept by one of the boys of the Twelfth, it is seen that a number of prisoners was captured "near North Mountain" on October 16th. These are doubtless the prisoners referred to by Maj. Bristor, then Captain of Company H, in the following account, after his first telling about the capture of a Rebel captain, a spy.

I was in command of the post at Kearneysville, Jefferson county, West Virginia, for about two months during the summer and fall of '63. While in command at that post a loyal citizen came to my headquarters about 11 o'clock one night and informed me that the Rebel spy Capt. Anderson was at a farm house some three miles distant, and near Col. Porterfield's house. I at once had sixteen of my men wake up, and called for two men to volunteer to go on a very hazardous expedition. To my surprise the entire sixteen volunteered to go. I was not much surprised, however, for my men were always ready for duty when called upon.

I selected two of the youngest of the sixteen, whose names I believe were James P. Murphy and William Watkins, I then started these two men directing them to follow the citizen to the house where Anderson was, about a mile beyond our outer pickets. The men were told by their guide that he thought Anderson was in a certain room. The two brave young soldiers carefully and quietly worked their way into the room, up to the bed where Anderson was sleeping, and demanded his surrender, before he knew a Union soldier or a soul was near him. They forbade his speaking a word above a low whisper, at the risk of his life. They took him out of the house without ever waking the family, and brought him to my quarters about 3 o'clock in the morning.

When they awoke me I questioned the prisoner who was represented to me as a Rebel spy, and he claimed to be a private citizen from London county Virginia, and said that he was coming the next day to give himself up. I asked him why he would give himself up if he was a private citizen. He replied that he had got a Yankee suit from a friend and he thought that he had better come and tell me about it for fear that he might be taken for a spy or something.

But he was identified by citizens of that county (Jefferson) as a spy, whose name was Anderson. I sent him to Martinsburg, and turned him over to Col. McReynolds, who was then in command at that point. He sent him to Fort McHenry where he (Anderson) was tried, and, I have been informed hanged.

A few nights after this, one of the "Louisiana Tigers," who had been disbanded on account of their officers not being able to do anything with them, was strolling about through the country foraging and etc., and finally got caught in the dark, and when at a house near that of Col. Porterfield, in which neighborhood Maj. Gilmore was camped, he inquired the way to his camp. The lady being a Union woman, directed him right towards my camp. He came to my outer pickets, and one of them came into camp with him talking all the time as if he, the picket, was a Rebel. A corporal by the name of A. H. Hull, brought him in.

As soon as the Rebel came to my quarters, everything being rather gloomy and dark, he thought he knew my voice, calling me Captain, taking me for a Rebel captain. I talked to him and asked him if he had not been lost, and he said he had and impressed his delight in getting back to camp, for he wanted to go the next night on that expedition to blow up Back Creek bridge "and send a lot of Yankees to hell," expecting by blowing up the bridge to cause the Baltimore and Ohio railroad train to pitch headlong into the creek, as it thundered along, with all on board unconscious of their danger, and thus cause great loss of life. I told him that I would see that he should go.

This Rebel was somewhat intoxicated and gave the whole thing away. Just as I finished telling him that he should go along with the party, the 4 o'clock train from the east blew its whistle. The prisoner laughed, and said he knew he was in the hands of the Yankees, but thought he would see how much he could fool them or draw them on, I said, "all right my good fellow you have drawn us on and we shall draw Maj. Gilmore on."

He told me during the conversation that Gilmore was to take thirty men and he was to be one of them and blow up Back Creek bridge. I placed him under close guard, and soon as daylight came I sent a message to Col. McReynolds giving him all the essential details of the foregoing account, and asked him to send a detachment of men sufficient to capture Gilmore's men; requesting him also to send an officer of the Twelfth West Virginia regiment in charge of the detachment; and if my memory serves me rightly, he sent Capt. Moffatt, of Company G.

Our men got to the bridge about two hours before Gilmore's band came and were secreted or in ambush, when they arrived and began to drill holes in the abutments of the bridge. At this our men hollered out, "What are you doing there, you Rebel sons of b----h's?" They surrendered to our men. The captures were four lieutenants, twenty-five men, and thirty-one horses. Major Gilmore it seems, had stayed at a neighboring house to get something to eat, and his orderly or adjutant was there also. So we captured all that were at the bridge. Lieut. Billings of Shepherdstown, W. Va., was one of the prisoners.

The First New York Cavalry reported this capture, and their regiment got the credit of it, when not a man of that organization, except one, who went along as a messenger or orderly, was in the party making the capture.

During the latter part of September going back a little, the Eighty-Seventh Pennsylvania, the One Hundred and Twenty-Second and the One Hundred and Twenty-Third Ohio regiments, at this point, were ordered to join the Army of the Potomac. The Eighty-Seventh had been in the same command with the Twelfth for about a year. There had always been a friendly feeling between the two regiments, so the night before the former left for the Army of the Potomac, some of the boys from it came over to bid our boys good-bye - and it was good-bye forever for some in either command.

The election for governor of Ohio was soon to take place, and the Eighty-Seventh boys having learned that a considerable number of the above named Ohio troops, say a tenth, were going to vote for Vallandigham for governor, were not at all pleased that they should do so. One of the Eighty-Seventh apparently having been indulging in a little strong drink, was especially vehement against those Ohio boys so disposed to vote. He threatened what the boys of his regiment would do in case they were to remain here, and those Ohio boys should so vote, not knowing that the Ohio troops alluded to were, as well as his own regiment ordered to the Army of the Potomac. He urged our boys to use violent means against any of the Ohio boys at this point, who should vote for Vallandigham for governor. This hostility toward those disposed to vote for him, was because of his political cause with respect to the war and its prosecution.

Our boys by this time had become substantially a unit in sentiment so far as the political war policy of the administration was concerned. All wrangling concerning it had ceased. And right here may be given a strikingly significant and truthful observation, made perhaps not far from this time, by Lieut. Blaney, of Company D, showing the rapid evolution of ideas, the swift progress and revolution of the sentiment of the time and more especially the potent virtue of the knock down argument, to which class of disputation, war preeminently belongs. Because of the justice, truth and significance of this remark, it should not be omitted from this record, imperfect though it must necessarily be.

In conversation Lieut. Blaney observed: "I have noticed that our boys have never objected to the Emancipation Proclamation since being in a battle." This remark was true, it is believed, without an exception.

If the war had never come these soldiers, many of them, would doubtless never have been convinced of the justifiableness of emancipation in that contingency. But being brought into battle, and thus required to do as best they might, what they could do to settle the issues involved by the knock down argument in its last and dire extremity - the employment of the bludgeon of war; and seeing their comrades falling around them, light quickly struck in on their minds with a telling force. The conversion was as sudden it seems, as that of Paul spoken of in the scriptures. They suddenly saw, in this death struggle, that anything that the enemy was opposed to; that whatever would tend to weaken or cripple him; that any means justified by civilized warfare to conquer the enemy they should favor and employ; and hence the prejudice, the tradition and the education of years were swept away as if by a flash of lightning, when the ordeal of battle came. There was no longer on the part of the boys any considerate regard for the interests of the enemy, nor any further objection to the emancipation of the negroes.

Another incident of the war illustrating how fast men learned during the war, may as well as not be given here, although it occurred at a later period. Adjt. G. B. Caldwell, in a conversation one day regarding the employment of negroes as soldiers said: "When I went into the service at first I thought that it would be a humiliation and disgrace to me if I had to serve in an army where negro soldiers were employed;" but now, said he, "I have come to the conclusion that they have as good right to be killed as I."

It is very probable that Adjt. Caldwell might have spent all his days, if the times had been peaceful, without ever having changed his views in regard to the matter of making soldiers of negroes, although he is a man of quick perception. But just as it is said of men in a drowning condition that all the events of their past lives come quickly before them; so in time of war and the peril of battle, men's minds are quickened, common-sense asserts itself and men perceive quickly the wisdom or unwisdom of that which in the piping times of peace, they would not see at all.

On September 28th, we were paid two months' pay, this being $13 per month for the privates, or $26 for the two months. This was always a welcome event with the soldiers. They had money now to spend with the sutler, but their money did not go far in buying from him. Canned peaches were, if not just at this time, later in the war $1.25 and tomatoes $1.00 per can.

While we were here at Martinsburg, the boys or many of them, who were taken as prisoners at Winchester, a few months before, were returned to the regiment, being ordered by the government to take up arms again, although they had been let out of prison only on parole, and not exchanged. This action was taken by the authorities at Washington in retaliation for the conduct of the Rebel authorities in putting the prisoners taken and paroled by Gen. Grant at Vicksburg, back into the field again, without their having been exchanged.

While the boys of the Twelfth, who were captured at Winchester, were held as prisoners they were kept at Richmond, Va., and although they were not held long until they were paroled, their experience of prison life was not such as to invite another trial of it. In the language of the west they had "got all they wanted of it." Before any of our boys had ever been prisoners, some of them used sometimes to threaten, when it was difficult to get furloughs, that they would, when a chance offered allow themselves to be taken prisoners, expecting in that case to be soon paroled and then sent home from the camp, as paroled prisoners on furlough. But after the prisoners returned to the regiment, having had a taste of prison life among the Rebels, and related its hardships to their comrades there was no longer any talk among the boys of allowing themselves to be captured in order that they might in that way get a furlough.

As before written Lieut. Bengough, of Company F, was killed in the battle of Winchester on Sunday, June 14th, 1863. Shortly after this his widow in company with another lady, went to Winchester to recover the body. The two women were arrested as spies. The interesting story of their capture and release, is thus related by the then Mrs. Bengough, now as then, living in Pittsburgh, leaving out her preliminary sketch of a trip from Fairmont, W. Va., to Pittsburgh in March, 1863:

TWO WOMEN OF THE WAR

Some months later, I learned of the death of my husband, Lieut. J. T. Bengough, who was killed during the three days fight at Winchester. F. P. Pierpont, Adjutant General of West Virginia, sent me a telegram to that effect and accompanied by my sister-in-law, Miss Celia Bengough, principal of the High School in Toledo and sister of the present pension agent at Pittsburgh, Harry Bengough, left Pittsburgh for Winchester to recover the body. My late husband had been a lieutenant under Gen. Milroy and during the battle the firing having ceased in his direction, being tired, he with his command lay down to rest; as he slept he was killed by a sharp-shooter.

Arriving at the headquarters of Gen. Mulligan on New Creek, Va., we were assigned quarters in a big building, which we subsequently discovered was occupied as a barracks by the soldiers, and we awoke during the night to find the room filled with men. Celia was greatly excited, but I calmed her fears and tucking our heads under the quilt we weathered the storm until the soldiers filed out in the morning. Mulligan furnished us with a pass into the rebel lines, and assured us he had personal friends among the Confederates, who would see that we were properly treated.

After walking a few miles night overtook us, and we put up at a house, the proprietor of which agreed to take us to Winchester for $20. In the morning we got into a buggy. I drove the horse he following on horse back to bring back the rig. It was a long hot ride, and with nothing to eat but cherries we were almost starved. Our escort would not approach the town nearer than three miles. He was afraid of losing his horses, so we footed it.

I had been in Winchester before, and boarded opposite the government corral, and we thought if we could find the place, we might be accommodated for the night. But alas, for human hopes, and happiness, we discovered there were many roads leading into Winchester; that we had lost our bearings and were at sea. What should we do? We dare not make inquiry, and it being about 7 o' clock in the evening we had to conclude quickly. Entering the town we found it full of rebel soldiers. They paid no attention to us, so we wandered about for some time without success. Finally we met a boy about 10 years old, and asked him the name of the street on which the corral was situated, "Where the Yanks used to keep their horses?" he interrogated, "Oh, that's away up yander" and pointing with his index finger out into the right he showed us the way. We were a long time finding the place, and when we did, how changed; the corral was tenantless, and the house we expected to lodge in presented a deserted appearance. With fear and trembling we knocked at the door and were admitted.

The lady knew me but was uncommunicative. She gave us lodging and a supper and breakfast of salt junk, for which we paid a fancy price. In the morning we pursued our mission. We found our way to the headquarters of Gen. R. E. Lee, who gave us a pass to the fortifications for the purpose of disinterring the body and one to the hospital for a squad of our prisoners to rebury it in the cemetery. The General told us the body could not be shipped as the railroad between Winchester and Martinsburg had been torn up.

Having obtained the passes (which I still have in my possession) the General required us to report at his headquarters after our work had been accomplished - disobedience in this respect caused us much suffering and imprisonment in Castle Thunder, Richmond.

We buried the body in the cemetery and went to our boarding house. It was evening and a sad one for us; our hostess had changed considerably since morning - she refused us anything to eat, saying there was nothing in the house. We had money, but were afraid to go out to purchase, so in lieu of anything better, we went outside and sat on the doorstep. We sat there for some time, when we observed a man across the street, close to the corral, dressed in surgeon's uniform. We thought he tried to arrest our attention, but were afraid to encourage him; he disappeared for a time around the corner, and as suddenly appeared this time on our side of the street and passing close, dropped a note, which we read in our room, by a light of a rag burning in a saucer of grease. He stated in the note that he was Lieut. McAdams of a Pennsylvania regiment, the number of which I cannot recall, that he was a prisoner, but not a surgeon, having borrowed the uniform in order to serve us; we were prisoners and would be treated as spies. "I will bring you tea and hard-tack from the hospital about 9 o'clock tonight." He kept his promise dropping the tea and crackers as he had the note. We never saw nor heard of McAdams since. He was a man between 30 and 35 years of age, heavy set, with sandy hair.

Between 12 and 1 o'clock that night, we stole out of the house, climbed the back fence and made for the Romney Road. It has been said we should always hope for the best, and at the same time be prepared for whatever presents itself. When we found ourselves out in the open country terror seized us and brought us to a realization of the situation. The chill of the night, caused us to shiver, so we quickened our steps in the direction of the hill and the fort.

We could see over the misty landscape, the Confederate flag floating proudly from its battlements. We knew the Romney Road lay back of the fort, so we climbed the hill, which was littered with the bodies of horses, mules, cannon balls and unexploded shells which had fallen on the soft hill side and lay in pockets made by the feet of the artillery horses in drawing Early's guns into position.

The haze subsided and one constellation after another appeared - that bright luminary, the moon, waded her way through now and then gliding behind a cloud, leaving the stars on duty, there appearing with new lustre, covered the battle field with a silver sheet. All nature seemed to be opened to our eyes, and in harmony with the surroundings. The night was painfully quiet. The only audible sound we heard, was the lullaby sung by a little stream that meandered down the hill - the night birds were silent, and we fancied we could hear the dripping of the dew. We seemed to wander in a charmed atmosphere, and would not have been surprised if Mab and her Peri's had come forth.

A little to the left stood the guns like so many sentinels with their yawning black mouths - we intended to pass them but they looked so devilish that we were afraid and took the longest route to avoid them. We passed the fort and descended the hill, often looking back to see if the guns were following. The moon neared the shore of the sky, the shadows deepened and Celia declared the trees were walking, she being a good elocutionist declaimed - "Night showeth knowledge unto night. There is no speech nor language, their voice is not heard; yet their sound goeth forth to all generations."

We sat down and huddled close together - we fancied a mythical presence and thought we saw forms coming out of the recesses of the mountains. The wind stirred the dying embers of distant camp fires into flame, and a lurid glare lit the heavens like a flash, and then all was dark. It was near morning and the soft faint streaks of daylight glimmered through the right. We arose and drew near the base of the hill - in the distance we could see the long, narrow but extremely picturesque Romney road, with its widely scattered, antiquated houses. We sat down behind a clump of bushes, and almost scared the lives out of a flock of birds - they flew out in the myriads, circling our heads in mingled confusion, chattering wildly, but soon flew away leaving us in possession of the field.

As the day advanced, the sun rose, penetrated the mist, dried our dewy clothes, and evoked from the flowers their morning fragrance; we strolled about gathering bunches of white and purple larkspur - as we culled we neared the road. We were on the lookout for pickets, when a rifle shot rang out clear and sharp followed by other shots in quick succession; as they ricocheted in and out of the mountain passes, reverberated over the hills and through the valleys we thought a whole regiment was firing. Then we heard the shrill but musical notes of the bugle, and knew there was infantry and cavalry at a distance.

We retraced our steps following a cow-path that wound round the hill, thinking to gain the road indirectly, but were mistaken, and taking a more direct route, found ourselves in the presence of three pickets, playing cards. We were not much surprised as they had been uppermost in our minds for we had wandered the hill all night to avoid them. With renewed courage, bonnets swinging on our arms and carrying our posies, we passed by acting as unconcerned as possible. We were not interrupted - at least we were on the Romney Road.

We walked about five miles and being hungry approached a white house enclosed within an open fence with a long line of trees in front, loaded with blood-red cherries. This was the home of Betty Jenkins, a pleasant faced motherly woman of about 40 years. She welcomed us, and we examined a large wheel, that stood in front of the mantel, with a hank of white yam around it, there was a smaller one in the corner, which was used for spinning. These wheels were a novelty to us and we exhibited so much ignorance as to their use, that Betty became suspicious.

When we told her we were northern women, she was nearly frightened out of her wits and was afraid to give us any help. We told her we were almost starved; she then told us to go up stairs to a retired room and she would find food. Betty managed to get us a good meal and we remained there that night. With the first glimmer of dawn we were on deck. Betty prepared breakfast, and we all three parted crying.

When we were at a distance from the house, we looked back, and there stood Betty, leaning over the gate, shading her eyes with her hand waving farewell. Dear, friendly Betty, we never heard of her again. The beauty of the morning raised our spirits, the fresh and invigorating air gave us strength. The sun rose in all his majesty and gilded the mountain ranges. In the distance we saw glittering water walled around by hills. The scenery was surpassing in grandeur and sublimity. The trees were full of buds, and their liquid notes filled the air; spotted lizards and little squirrels ran along the fence rails; brown rabbits scurried across the meadows; the partridge called "Bob White" and the perfume of the honey-suckle scented the air. The fields were covered with wild flowers, tall red poke-berry stalks ornamented the fence corners, and berry bushes were white with blossom. The ravines were covered with dark velvety moss, and silver streams of murmuring water ran zigzag through clumps of willows.

We had walked about 12 miles, when we met a man riding on a big bay horse, lank and lean, with a bulged out pair of saddle bags - he seemed friendly but we paid no attention. As we rounded a bend in the road we heard dogs barking at no great distance, and knew we were near a farm house. The house was situated below the level of the road, with a running stream in front, the bosom of which was covered with ducks, geese and goslings. We descended the long stairway leading down from the pike, and entered the house. There we found a very old man and a tall woman, the latter playing deaf and dumb, afraid to say anything to strangers. We asked for food; the old man brought out a piece of table linen, in which he tied up meat, bread and cheese. Our Evangelist carried the bundle to the top of the steps, and told us how far and what way we must go before we would meet Mulligan's scouts.

Turning off the road we sat on a log and ate ravenously. Resuming our journey we found our commissary stores a burden and threw them away. The heat was oppressive and the dust suffocating, so we turned off the high way and sought the cool forest, but we were afraid of snakes and the sharp twigs cut our blistered and swollen feet. We tried to wear our shoes but could not. We clambered over rocks, logs and low thick brush, which made it tiresome, and again were forced to take the high way. We limped painfully while we tramped, ankle deep in dust under a burning sun.

We waded the north and south branches of the Potomac. The water was low but transparent, and the river bed stony. We amused ourselves, while laving our blistered feet, gathering beautiful stones of many colors, which we afterwards threw away - they grew burdensome. Twice we came to where roads or paths converged, and were at a loss to know which one to take, but Celia, remembered the scriptural injunction that the straight path was the right path - therefore we turned neither to the right nor to the left.

We saw a house in the distance and a few matronly cows and sheep in a field, whose acquaintance we tried to make, but they would have none of it, and throwing their tails in the air ran off bellowing - the poor frightened sheep scattered and hid in the bushes. We entered the house and found an old man plaiting a straw hat and a woman making cherry pies. They had little to say, but gave us milk and pie. The pie had neither shortening nor sugar - the top crust was burned while the bottom was dough. We drank the milk and went on.

About 3 o'clock we encountered a heavy rain storm, accompanied with thunder and vivid lightning, and were wet through, but fortunately the storm did not continue long and the sun coming out in all his heat, soon dried our clothes. We were, now about 18 miles from Winchester, four miles from the Cacapon bridge and nine miles from Mulligan. We hobbled along as best we could for about two miles, when we came to a house on the roadside, enclosed by a dilapidated fence. A pump and wooden drinking trough stood in front, but there was no appearance of horses having quenched their thirst at the trough for some time, the ground being unbroken around it. A clucking hen strutted noisily about, and a tribe of guineas set up a fearful cry of alarm, as we approached. A man and woman were hanging over the garden gate quietly chatting, but as soon as they saw us, they seemed alarmed, particularly the woman. She eyed us carefully and impudently whispering something to her companion. We noticed the agitation and felt uneasy.

We had walked about 20 miles but the meanderings of the road added a greater distance. It was late in the day, and the absence of cattle and fowl noticeable. We anticipated trouble and shied into the woods. We did not make much headway on account of the dense growth of trees, but we persevered and at last came to the Cacapon water. We made a detour and found a tree fallen across the stream. It was high from the water and Celia could not cross it. I coaxed and entreated, but all to no purpose. The river was full of water snakes and the banks lined with villainous looking frogs. We found fault with each other, and Celia resisting my entreaties, blamed me for the escapade, and she quoted scripture to fit the crime, for she was full of texts - "He that cometh not in by the door, but climbeth up some other way, the same is a thief, and robber." I saw the point and we laughed and crossed the bridge.

We were 22 miles from Winchester, and five miles from Mulligan scouts. We had proceeded about 50 yards on the other side of the bridge, when we were halted by a handsome young cavalry officer, Lieut. Bell, nephew of Gen. Bell of the C.S.A. He touched his cap and accosted us - "Good evening ladies, have you got a pass?" Travel-stained, foot-sore, faces blistered, hungry and utterly wretched, we hung our heads, but gave no answer - we were too miserable.

The daylight faded slowly, the night grew chilly and the wind stirred the bending grass. The setting sun shot slanting spikes from the golden west, through the trees and across the road. The cavalry horse stood at a distance pawing the dust, and clanking his equipments, every now and then lifting his head with a majestic air, looked toward his rider, who stood with bowed head rubbing the buttons up and down with his fingers, which adorned the front of his cavalry jacket. It was June - the sun had set, the shadows deepened, and the katydids had almost ceased their rasping.

There we three stood, in the gloom of approaching night, with no sound to break the silence, except the lonely quavering notes of the forest birds. Bats flitted to and fro and circled. Over our heads - the owl hooted, and fire flies lit the ravines. We buried our feet in the dust that he might not see their nakedness, and with heart-rending sobs, cried as we had never cried before. We were captured and we knew that meant on to Richmond.

Lieut. Bell told us we had been arrested as spies by order of Gen. R. E. Lee. We begged we should not be made walk back, for we thought we would have to tramp the whole road over again. He assured us such would not be the case, that he would take us to a house in the woods, owned by a Mrs. Smith, where Miss Bell, his sister, would search us. Having walked about half a mile, we came to a defile in the mountains, which rose very high on either side, with an opening at the top large enough to see a patch of sky, studded with misty stars. Our captor told us these mountains were covered with perpetual snow and ice. In this gap lived Mrs. Smith, with whom we were to remain for the night.

The house was two storied, painted white, and backed close to the mountain. The windows were vine-covered and here and there a glimmer of light shone through making the green look greener. Opposite the house and on the other side of the gap, close to what had once been a barn, stood a lot of unsheltered wagons, buggies and stage coaches in a dilapidated condition.

At the sound of approaching foot steps Mrs. Smith appeared in the door, with a grease-saucer light, and behind her an old aunty, with her head bound up in a yellow bandanna. Dinah was greatly agitated when she saw us approach in the shadows, and throwing up her hands exclaimed. "Fo de Lord, misses, dey is de Yanks!" We knew by aunty's remarks, we had been anticipated.

Mrs. Smith was a neat little dark-eyed woman, with hair and complexion to match her eyes. She wore a gray flannel dress of her own weaving, cotton material being out of the question. She was greatly impoverished, and told us her husband used to run a line of stages, but the Yanks had taken their horses - there was not a man about the place, they were in the Confederate Army; that aunty and she had rolled the snow into big balls during the winter, and dumped them into the ice house - that ice water was the only luxury she had. We drank some of it and were refreshed. After supper we were assigned to a comfortable room, with a good bed in it, of which we stood in need. In the morning we were furnished with water and other necessary toilet articles. After making ourselves presentable we wet a lot of letters in the basin and rubbed them into pulp, that they might not be found in our possession, when Miss Bell would search us - we mixed the pulp with wood ashes on the hearth, until all trace was obliterated. We were searched, but nothing was found upon our person. We got the letters from wounded Union soldiers in the Winchester hospital.

Next morning after breakfast Lieut. Bell and a lot of troopers, made their appearance with a squeaky wagon, drawn by two half-starved mules. He apologized for the conveyance, saying nothing better could be had. After bidding good-bye to Mrs. Smith and Dinah we got into the wagon and were soon on our way back to Winchester. We had not proceeded far, when a wheel slid off, almost throwing us out of the wagon. Our driver with a hickory linch pin and some assistance repaired the damage. We traveled all day and at night put up at an inn, where the roads divided in different tracks.

Our cavalry picketed their horses in a field nearby, that they might eat grass, there being neither oats nor hay to give them. Our guard told us their horses were starving and had already become too weak for effective duty.

After supper we were given a comfortable room furnished with an old-fashioned bed, decorated with high-colored hangings; a picture of Washington relieved the wall; three chairs, a rocker and a dragon-legged table completed the furnishment. A purple wisteria covered the window and climbed to the roof. Our guard slept on the soft side of the porch, first exacting a promise from us that we would not try to escape. We promised, and being as tired as they, slept the sleep of youth.

In the morning, furnished with conveniences, we made our toilet, while our gallant cavalrymen made theirs at the horse trough. After a scanty meal of corn bred, rye coffee and sorghum molasses, the lady of the house announced all was in readiness for our departure. She bade us a friendly good-bye and we took the road again. We traveled slowly, and as we neared Winchester we found fence, bush, and tree limbs ornamented with old clothes, which had been taken from the battle field and dyed butter-nut. The scenery was not improved by the accession. Finally we reached Winchester and Gen. Lee's headquarters. The General was not in, but the room was filled with officers of all grades and rank. Uninvited we seated ourselves and listened to a tirade from Maj. Bridgeford on spies in particular and Yankee women in general. We were too miserable to reply. Celia reminded me that we were in the hands of the Philistines, and might as well hang our harps on the willows, for how could we sing in that strange land.

We waited an hour or more, when we heard the clatter of horses hoofs outside, a dismount and Gen. Lee entered, tall, graceful, refined and haughty. Touching his cap and bidding us "good morning" he reprimanded us for our disobedience, ending with the announcement that we must go to prison. Major Bridgeford made out the necessary papers, Gen. Lee signed them, and then, on to Richmond, guarded by cavalry.

Chapter Five

We passed a hapless night and in the morning took the stage for Staunton, Va. We traveled up the Shenandoah Valley and saw Gen. Lee's whole army, as they marched down the Shenandoah, and on to Gettysburg.

When we got hungry, our guard picked cherries for us, and begged slap-jacks and bonny-clabber from the surrounding farm houses, some of which we exchanged with a wounded rebel, riding on the top of the coach, for maple molasses.

When we came to Mount Jackson, the coach stopped at a tavern, kept by a brother of the man, who shot Col. Ellsworth. It was a beautiful spot. The inn was old but picturesque, and built on a little rise. A couple of wide-spreading trees espaliered across its front. At the side of the house, a row of oleanders contracted their bloom with the green of the foliage, and a cypress vine, trained on strings, covered the windows. A gourd vine clambered up and over the wood shed, almost concealing the door, and compelling, Julius, himself to double himself when he went in and out for wood. Our host was a long-jawed, dark-skinned man, and had little to say, but his wife made up for the deficiency. She flew at us in a rage, called us names and likened us to a lot of thieving Yankee soldiers, who she said, had stolen her chickens and robbed her onion bed. She refused us anything to eat, and said we should not sleep in her house that night. We made no answer, allowing her to have her way. We went out into the orchard and sat on a bench under an apple tree, where a robin perched on the top-most limb cheered us with his sweetest evening song.

A genuine southern mammy with her kinky hair, plaited and tied in wads and knots, stood over a big iron kettle stirring soap. She looked askance at us, not daring to speak, but we knew by her actions that we had her sympathy. Having sat there about an hour, Mrs. Jackson remorseful and relenting asked us in to supper.

When bed time came we were given a large square room (with a bare floor) lighted with a tallow dip. A low post bed, two chairs and a looking glass completed the furnishment, with the exception of two pictures, lacking resemblance to anything we ever saw, hung upon the whitewashed walls. In the morning we breakfasted and then set out for Staunton. It was a lovely day, the blossoms of summer and green of the foliage were very attractive. The beauty of the valley was beyond description, with its silvery pools and trickling streams, moss covered rocks and hedges of wild roses. The song birds whistled and thrilled, and the unceasing notes of the insect tribes filled the woods.

At Staunton we were comfortably housed, but had nothing to eat. We should have gone supperless to bed, but for the shrewdness of a colored chambermaid who, under pretense of making the bed, got into our room, and without a sign of recognition began to beat the pillows, spread the quilts and make a fuss generally. She attracted our attention by the unusual length of time it took her to perform the work. She gave us a significant look and passed out.

The guard who paced up and down the hall way looked in to see if all was right, locked the door and we were alone for the night. We examined the bed and found about a dozen biscuits under the quilts and pillows, and a quart bucket full of tea under the bed.

In the morning we informed our guard of the inhospitable treatment, and he sent the provost marshal to look after us. He immediately ordered the hotel keeper to bring us down to the table, which he did, but he took revenge by putting us at a little table in the centre of the dinning room making us the cynosure of all eyes. When we had eaten Celia wrote with a piece of crayon, "Yankee Table" on our table, which was considered audacious by the regular boarders.

Before leaving the hotel, we gave the chambermaid, who had befriended us, a $1 greenback, the ribbon off our hat and a pair of gloves. We traveled by rail from Staunton to Richmond. When the train stopped at different stations, we were almost suffocated by the crowd that scrambled up the sides of the car and poked their heads through the windows to see what Yankee women looked like.

When we arrived at Richmond, we were obliged to walk some distance from the station to Castle Thunder, being followed by the curious of both sexes. We were taken into the Provost Marshal's office where we found the prison authorities selecting nine captains to be hung, in case the Federal government hanged Fitzhugh Lee. Capt. Rowand of the Virginia cavalry was one of them. The Captain came down with us, and when we entered the Provost Marshal's office, he was greeted by Maj. Turner of Libby prison, with the cheering announcement, "Well Captain you are just in time to draw your death out." Whether he drew it or not, we do not know, for we were marched out into a tunnel-like passage and up a rickety pair of stairs into a cell, 12 by 15 feet, with no furnishment. There was one window of many small panes, with a large sill, which we used for a seat.

Maj. Alexander, commander of the prison frequently cautioned us to keep our heads inside the window for fear we might be shot. There were other women prisoners in the Castle, but they were waiting to be sent through on the next truce boat, there being no charges against them. Among them was Mrs. Surgeon McCandless, of Morgantown, W. Va.

We were searched by an old white headed man, whom the prisoners called "Anti-Christ;" he did not take our money some $75 or $80. We afterwards heard the old man was hung with the Wirz gang.

Chapter Five

An order came from the Confederate authorities to send the other women home. Major Alexander told them to be ready to leave early next morning at the same time asking for the Bengough women. We answered to our names, when he informed us we were held as spies and would be forwarded to some place in South Carolina, for safe keeping. We cried bitterly when the other women left.

Towards evening the Major bettered our condition; he sent us a mattress, pillows and covering, and two colored women to wait upon us. We slept little that night, feeling horribly alone. The moonlight flooded the room; we got up and looked out over the James River; we wondered what our friends were doing at home; if they thought of us, and if we should ever see them again. We asked permission to burn the gas all night, and it was granted. Then the lapse of time had its effect, and we adjusted our lives to suit the situation.

The food we got was not nourishing. It consisted of bread and coffee made of porched rye. We paid $14 in green backs for a pound of tea. It was poor in quality, but we preferred it to the rye.

A Chaplain visited us every day, and always left Bibles. We asked him if he could not find some other literature; in a few days he returned bringing a beautifully illustrated volume of "Don Quixote." He must have given us up for lost souls for he never came again. We read the book over and over - criticized it and quarreled over the criticisms.

One day we saw a long line of rebel soldiers driving a large drove of cattle along Cary street; each soldier had a hoop-skirt about his neck, and everything conceivable in shoes, dry goods, and notions tied to each hoop. Then we learned the battle of Gettysburg had been fought, and the captured cattle belonged to Pennsylvania. After that our fare was varied with fresh beef - once we got a dried apple pie, baked without shortening, on a saucer, but it tasted better than any pie we had ever eaten before or since.

Shortly after the hoop-skirt brigade had passed, about 1,000 Yankee prisoners were marched up the same street and housed in an old building opposite Castle Thunder. They were given meat and bread. One of the men after eating his meat threw the bone out on the pavement, the guard instantly fired into the crowd, taking the arm off a fine looking man, without provocation. We saw him carried to the hospital on a stretcher, the blood streaming through canvas on to the pavement. John Brown, of Allegheny, present post commander of 128, was among that crowd of prisoners.

We received frequent visits from people of note. Our greenbacks were borrowed to show to Jeff Davis, Gov. Wise, Judah P. Benjamin and Maj. Turner - they were promptly returned.

One day Maj. Alexander told us he had been ordered to go on active duty. He was a sea captain and had been put in charge of the prison on account of having had his leg broken. When the war broke out the Major run a cargo of ammunition into a rebel post, instead of turning it over to Uncle Sam. He was imprisoned for it in Fort Lafayette, where he broke his leg by jumping from a port hole; he finally got into the Confederate lines and was placed in command of Castle Thunder. The Major told us there was to be a clearance of prisoners and said, "I should like to have you both put on the exchange list, Gen. Winder, called 'Hog' Winder by the prisoners, gives a feast tonight, and before the festivities are over he will be in a very moist condition. Now, if we can give him the exchange list at this juncture, he will sign it without reading and you shall be ready for the truce boat in the morning." The scheme was a success, and we slept none that night. About 2 o'clock in the morning 1,000 of our prisoners were marched from Libby en route for City Point and halted in front of the Castle. While they stood there Lotta Gilmore, a southern girl, imprisoned in Castle Thunder, sang the "Moon Behind the Hill," and was answered by one of the prisoners in line who sang, "When This Cruel War Is Over." We encored the minstrel, and asked what name and regiment. He called out "Massachusetts," and we replied "Pennsylvania," and immediately received three rousing cheers.

Lotta Gilmore was imprisoned because her lover had counterfeited Confederate currency - he had shown the money to her, but she refused to testify against him and was imprisoned for contempt of court.

Belle Boyd, of rebel spy fame, visited the prison in male attire, and was introduced as Lieut. Warry.

There was a Col. Dunham of some New York regiment, imprisoned opposite to our cell, but at a distance. We could see him through the chinks in the board partition. We sent him a note written on one of the fly leaves of "Don Quixote," and gave Washington, the colored hunch-back one dollar to deliver it; he rolled it in his shirt sleeve, and when he swept Dunham's cell, gave it to him. Dunham left Richmond the same morning we did.

About 3 o'clock in the morning Maj. Alexander made his appearance, we had not retired that night, and told us to make ready, as soon as possible to take the train for City Point. We made ourselves as presentable as our limited wardrobe would allow, but realized that we were laughing stocks. Celia's hat was faded and battered and out of shape; mine had been gray, but now it was no color at all, and without a particle of trimming, having given the ribbon to the colored chambermaid at Staunton. Our shoes, bearing the name of "Schmertz

Pittsburgh" were down at the heel and out at the sides; our stockings minus feet, and our hands bare; we had traded our last pair of gloves for a piece of pie. Our faces resembled boiled lobster in color, never having recovered from the tramp along the Romney Road, nor the long ride up the Shenandoah.

The colored women brought us four fresh laundered skirts. We each took one giving the others to the women, and a $2 greenback apiece. We wrote good-bye to the Chaplain on the fly leaf of "Don Quixote," also thanked him for the book and the comfort it had given us. We inscribed a farewell stanza of our own composition, (Celia composing one half and I the other) in Major Alexander's log book, placing both books with care on the window sill - that seat we had so often sat upon and looked out on the James, in our loneliness. We bade the colored women an affectionate adieu, for they had comforted us to the best of their ability, and we were attached to them, then passed down the dark and gruesome rickety prison stairs, out into the culvert, and freedom. When the fresh morning air wafted over our faces, we staggered against the wall - we were dreadfully weak, but visions of home and friends gave us renewed strength and we soon revived.

Maj. Alexander escorted us to the train, bidding us god-bye, and gave us a letter to be delivered at City Point, where an exchange of prisoners took place. We embarked on a U.S. vessel, and sailed down the Chesapeake. We passed Hampton Roads, and Fortress Monroe and saw the masts of the sunken Cumberland, above the water, in Hampton Roads.

We landed at Annapolis, stopping at a hotel there about a week, boarding being furnished us without price, and thence to Baltimore.

The morning after our arrival in that city, we started out to deliver Alexander's letter. We were instructed how to find the man; given a description of him, and told to give him the letter and ask no questions. We were to remain in the place designated until we found a man answering the description in the middle store of a block on a certain street. We went to the place and paced back and forth through the store, asking no questions; finally when about to despair, we noticed a man answering the description in every respect, seated on a chair on the edge of the pavement, in front of the store. He was evidently a Hebrew. We delivered the letter and the man took it, read it attentively, changed color several times, but made no comment. He finally wrote a brief epistle and handed it to us and directed us to present it at a certain place. We did so and at the place were given transportation to Pittsburgh. We stopped for refreshments at different places, and nowhere were we asked for money for services rendered.

We arrived at the Union depot in December, before Christmas, and reached home by a round-about route; we did not care to face the public in our city, as we were ashamed of our appearance. We sent no word that we were coming, but walked in unannounced. Father and mother were panic-stricken and could not believe their own eyes. Our friends and neighbors, for miles around came to see us and ask questions. The "fatted calf" was killed and a general rejoicing took place. We were the lionesses of the day. Once again in Pittsburgh, I received work as a compositor at Haven's under James M. McEwen.

Two years after leaving Richmond, Alexander walked into Haven's care worn and penniless. He said he had been included in the sentence against Wirz, but had escaped. I had a difficult time in getting Mr. McEwen to make peculiar promises, before I should introduce Alexander; finally he promised, and the introduction took place. A look of astonishment overspread his face when he found out who his new acquaintance was, but they were "Masons" and Alexander was introduced, during his stay in Pittsburgh, to other members of that order, and found means to get to England. In the meantime amnesty being granted, he came back to the states, and resumed his former calling.

LOTTIE BENGOUGH M'CAFFREY.

Chapter Six

During our stay at Martinsburg up to October there was little, if anything, of importance in a military way took place. We spent our time in doing duty, drilling and etc. On that day however, Imboden attacked the Ninth Maryland Infantry at Charles Town, killing the Adjutant and capturing a considerable part of the command.

An attack was somewhat looked for at this point in this same day and Col. Pierce in command here, made every preparation to meet it, but none was made. In the evening our regiment and a battery were ordered to Harper's Ferry. We marched to Shepherdstown, about half way, and encamped for the night. We bivouacked on the streets of the town. A little incident occurred here showing the beauties of soldier life. One of the boys in lying down for the night, placed the strap of his haversack under his head, so that if anyone should try to steal his haversack, he would likely know it. In the night he was awakened by a jerk of something from under his head, and he found that his haversack was gone. It was a very dark night, and an object could be seen scarcely any distance; but he heard something rattling on the pavement. He followed this sound, and found that a hog was making an attempt to confiscate his rations, the rattling being made by the tin cup fastened to the haversack. By a vigorous charge on the enemy the rations were recovered and the soldier went back to renew his nap. It needs hardly be said that if there were any hogs in America that were d---d hogs, that was one of them.

Shepherdstown, situated on the bank of the Potomac was at that time a dull, sleepy old town, the quietude of which was quite suggestive of the proverbial saying, "All quiet on the Potomac." This saying was applicable to the place at that particular time; though no doubt, it had been often awakened before, and was afterward, from its wonted drowsiness by "the cannons' opening roar" being only three or four miles from the Antietam battle ground, the center of a region of battlefields, and itself the scene of one or more fights.

We continued our march in the morning through rain and mud, and arrived at Harper's Ferry at 3 o'clock p.m. We crossed the Potomac here on the railroad bridge and camped on Maryland Heights, which are close to the Potomac, not leaving but little more room than enough between its base and the river, for the canal and the Baltimore and Ohio railroad (which latter in going east crosses into Maryland from West Virginia at this point) to pass.

Just opposite these heights nearby, looking south on London Heights. The Shenandoah river on the southeast side of the valley skirts these latter heights and forms a junction with the Potomac at Harper's Ferry. The Potomac then flows on east through the defile between the two heights. The Maryland Heights command, in a military sense, Harper's Ferry, which lies between the two rivers at their junction. From these heights is a fine view up the Valley for many miles. At this time there was a company of Massachusetts heavy artillery stationed on them. They had a siege gun planted there, throwing a hundred pound shell, pointing in the direction of Harper's Ferry, which was capable of shelling an enemy coming down the valley, and approaching the town anywhere within three miles of it.

These Massachusetts boys were true to the traditions and preferences of their section in thinking that a dish of baked beans was the very cream of good things. The following little incident illustrates this fact. It shows that they looked forward to the stated time when they should have their favorite dish with joyous anticipation: One day one of the Twelfth boys overheard one of the artillery boys talking to a comrade. The talk had been of no especial interest to him, the one talking, when suddenly a thought seemed to strike him, which aroused him to considerable enthusiasm. He said: "Let me see - this is Wednesday, tomorrow is Thursday, and the next day Friday, when, by gahge! we are going to have baked beans."

Gen. Sullivan commanded the troops here. We were brigaded with the Thirty-fourth Massachusetts. This regiment was under very strict regimental discipline. Each officer's tent when in camp, had a sentinel placed in front of it; and no private soldier was allowed to enter his tent without first getting permission. No intercourse was held between the officers and privates, only on business. They had not seen any service only guarding the railroad. They were finally equipped with arms and etc. and neatly uniformed; and the style displayed, soon convinced the boys of the Twelfth, according to Col. Curtis, then major, that they, the Thirty-fourth, considered them, the Twelfth boys, a lot of rude mountaineers that were not their equals. But an opportunity was soon given to test that matter, so far as fast marching and roughing it generally were concerned, to their entire satisfaction.

No disparagement of the Thirty-fourth, is intended by the foregoing remarks. The men of that command were brave soldiers, and their colonel, Col. Wells, was a brave, capable and careful officer. There was probably little or no difference in bravery between the Eastern and Western soldiers. Gen. Sheridan thought, after seeing both European and American armies in action, that while the latter were no braver than the former, they, the American soldiers were the most intelligent, resourceful, and efficient soldiers in the world. And because the Western soldier was more used to the handling of arms, and for the reason that the hardships and varied experience of frontier life had produced in him a ready adaptability to necessities, he was perhaps a little more distinctively American in the quick resourcefulness, in the rough and rugged requirements of war, than was her more delicately reared Eastern brother.

No doubt those Massachusetts boys thought their colonel was too rigid in maintaining the exclusiveness he did on the part of his officers. Gen. Grant says of Gen. Buell: "He was a strict disciplinarian and perhaps did not distinguish sufficiently between the volunteer, who enlisted for the war and the soldier who serves in time of peace." This seems to have been the trouble with Col. Wells. "One system," says Grant, "embraced men who risked life for principal, and other men of social standing, competence, or wealth and independence of character. The other includes, as a rule, only men who could not do as well in any other occupation."

The Twelfth remained on the Heights, with the exception of a movement up and down the Valley, for about two and a half months, doing picket duty and working on fortifications there. At least this was the work of part of the regiment. However, on November 5th, we marched across the river to Harper's Ferry to hold the camp of the Thirty-fourth Massachusetts one day and night while that regiment was on a scout to Charles Town and back. We moved onto the Heights again the next morning, the Thirty-fourth having returned to their camp.

Gen. Sullivan having been ordered to make a demonstration against Staunton, Maj. Curtis received orders on the night of the 9th to have the Twelfth furnished with three days' cooked rations, and forty rounds of ammunition to the man, and be ready by dawn on the next day to march up the Valley to make the demonstration.

This movement was apparently made with a view to drawing troops from Richmond to protect Staunton, and as a diversion in favor of Gen. Stoneman, who started December 8th, from Knoxville, Tenn., with three mounted brigades, led by Burbridge and Gillem, and moved along the Virginia and East Tennessee railroad to Marion, Va., where Gillem struck the Rebel Gen. Vaughn, the Sixteenth chasing him 30 miles into Wytheville; capturing 200 men, eight guns and a large train; then moved on along the railroad as far as Max Meadows, Va. Our force and that of Stoneman would thus, in our movements tend toward each other. On this expedition Stoneman captured in all 500 prisoners, destroyed the lead works 15 miles east of Wytheville, destroyed on his way back to Knoxville the valuable and costly salt works at Saltville, Va., and made other material captures, and destructions, including destruction to some extent of the railroad.

At the appointed time the Tenth, our regiment marched from the Heights across to Harper's Ferry, where we joined the Thirty-fourth Massachusetts with four pieces of Indiana battery under command of Capt. Minor. The force moved early in the morning of this day under command of Col. Wells, he being the senior officer in the command. The route was through Charles Town at which place we were joined by the First New York, the Fifth Maine, the Twenty-First Pennsylvania and Cole's Maryland Battalion, which reinforcements were all cavalry. In addition to this, there were added to the artillery strength at this place, two 12-pound brass pieces.

A rather short march was made that day, as the Thirty-fourth had started with heavy knapsacks of clothing, blankets, and etc., to keep them comfortable, as the command had neither tents nor shelter of any kind to protect the men.

Camp was made that night between Charles Town and Berryville. The next morning the advance was given to the Twelfth. They started off whistling "Yankee Doodle" and keeping step to the music at a lively gait. Berryville was passed through, and coming to the Opequon Creek beyond, Col. Wells ordered the command to halt until a temporary bridge should be made. The boys of the Twelfth, who had frequently had such obstacles to overcome, soon set the Thirty-fourth boys an example of how to get on the other side of a creek, by plunging into this one and wading across. Col. Wells exclaimed to Major Curtis, "What kind of men have you? They don't seem to care for water or anything else." The Major replied: "They are used to that kind of work."

The Twelfth boys marched on rapidly, in order to give the Massachusetts regiment a lesson in marching and about 12 o'clock the wagon master came galloping up to the front and requested Col. Wells to slacken up the speed, as the men of the Thirty-fourth were all giving out, emptying their knapsacks of blankets and extra clothing, and climbing into the wagons and artillery carriages to ride. The order was given to proceed on a slower march, which was done.

This plan of rather slow marching pursued by Col. Wells, going as he did at the outset at the rate of about sixteen miles a day, is to be commended. It showed him to be considerate and careful of his men. Men ought not to be marched from twenty to thirty miles per day, unless there is some special urgency for so doing. But it often happened that the various commands to which our regiment belonged, would march considerably over twenty miles a day, when no apparent reason existed for so doing. Those responsible for this hard marching being mounted did not seem to realize what a heavy drain it was on the energy of the men to carry about thirty pounds, including arms, equipments and etc., all day on a hard march, or to appreciate how heavy this weight would become before the end of a day's long march.

Surgeon F. H. Patton, in charge of the Soldiers' Home at Dayton, O., in a recent interview said that most of the inmates there were afflicted with heart trouble, and he attributed this fact to over exertion during the war. Assuming this to be true, it is believed that much if not most of this heart trouble is attributable to unnecessarily hard marching.

On this second day's march the command passed through Winchester from which place the regiment, being in Gen. Milroy's army, was routed in the preceding June, by Lee's army and camped two miles from town. While here some of the Twelfth boys took the opportunity of looking over the battle field, and saw where some of their comrades had fallen and been buried, with only a little earth thrown upon them. The third day the command marched to Strasburg and remained there four days.

Some of the comrades tell of a trick one of the Twelfth boys played on a citizen at this town, during this stay here. He, the soldier, somehow had got hold of a watch chain made of imitation gold dollars. The chain was formed by linking these dollars together. He separated them by removing the links. No doubt with a view to catching a victim, this soldier one day was carelessly toying with his gold dollars in the presence of a citizen, when the eye of the latter caught a sight of the seeming coin. The citizen immediately asked the soldier what he would take for it. The latter played the indifferent dodge - seemed like he did not care whether he sold his coin or not; but finally said that as he would spend his money anyhow, he would exchange it dollar for dollar, for "greenbacks." The citizen promptly handed over the required treasury notes, putting the bogus coin in his pocket with the remark that he would "salt that down." Very probably he would discover later that it was the man instead of the money that was "salted."

Cheating tricks, such as this are not to be approved of course; but a faithful though imperfect record, demands that incidents of this character as well as those of a more creditable kind, should be given.

On the night of the 16th, while still at Strasburg, it began raining. In the morning, the command marched to near Woodstock, the rain still falling. In the evening the rain turned to sleet. Camp was made in the woods where part of the timber was pines or cedars and in the night some of the men, who had put up their gum blankets to partially protect themselves from the falling sleet, had to move their quarters on account of the sleet breaking the limbs of the trees above their heads, making it unsafe to stay where they were. Of course, this disagreeable weather was very trying on the endurance and patience of the men. Having relation to this trying severity of the weather this story is told. There was a soldier in the Twelfth, who was familiarly known as "Kid." He, it seemed got very much disgusted with the bad weather, prevailing at this time; and by reason of his patience and endurance being sorely tried, he began to curse the war in general; and wound up with saying in a mainly jocular and slightly serious manner, that so far as he was concerned the Johnny's might have their Confederacy.

The next day, however, the sun came out bright and the day was comparatively beautiful; and some of the boys remembering what "Kid" had said the day before reminded him of it saying, "Kid, how do you feel about it today? Are you willing today to give the Johnnys their Confederacy?" "No," said "Kid." "I'll be damned if I am; I'll try them a hustle for it first." "Kid" was a good soldier. He faithfully performed his duty to the end of the war. He was in at the final "hustle" at Petersburg and Appomattox, and saw the flag of treason go down before the flag of our country, to be hoisted no more forever, it is hoped.

On the 18th, the command continued its march going short distances each day until the afternoon of the 20th, when Harrisonburg, about 100 miles from Harper's Ferry was reached. At the bridge across the North Fork of the Shenandoah, which was crossed the day before, the 19th, forty men of the First New York cavalry were left to guard it. In the evening of the day Harrisonburg was reached, the command was formed in line of battle, on account of a report that the Rebels were coming, but no attack was made. However, Gen. Early, with a division, a force many times that of ours was near and the object of the expedition (the drawing of the Rebels' attention and the withdrawing of troops toward us from Richmond, to enable our troops in other fields to successfully accomplish their purposes) having been gained, the command after dark that night started to retrace its steps down the Valley, reaching New Market by 4 o'clock next morning, distance 18 miles.

Here is an incident which it may be thought should have a place here: On our return down the Valley, perhaps at New Market, a woman stuck her head out of a house and shouted, "You're running again are you?" It appears that the boys received this taunt good-naturedly no doubt thinking, that it was a pretty good joke. The average American is proveriably good-natured; and can often enjoy a sarcasm or joke at his own expense. Perhaps there never was a man before in which there was less of hereditary clannish or personal hate involved than in this. This was true especially of the Northern soldier. This lack of personal enmity was often shown by the good-natured sociable chats the soldiers of the two armies would have when they would get together, those of the one side being prisoners, for instance.

So the boys in the case of the above incident showed no sign of cherished hate or any ill-natured personal resentment toward the Rebel woman for the taunt. Sharp thrusts like this coming from Rebels, were sometimes met, however, with more than counter balancing thrusts. For instance, one time while our regiment was at Winchester the winter previous, a rather large guard having gone out some three or four miles with some wagons to get fire wood, a woman sarcastically said to the boys, "It takes a good many Yankees to get a little wood." "Yes," replied some one, "it does, but it would take a whole army of Rebels to get wood up North."

After remaining five hours at New Market the march was resumed and continued till evening, when the force camped. Just after dark the rear guard was fired on from across the Shenandoah by some bushwhackers, causing the troops to be ordered into line; but it was soon learned that there was nothing serious. There was no further disturbance during the night. The next day on the way down the Valley, 400 Rebel cavalry charged on our rear guard at Woodstock but some well-directed shots from a section of artillery sent them back flying. Camp was made that night at Strasburg.

Starting from here the next morning the command reached (in two days) Harper's Ferry, the 24th, a distance of 48 miles. The command on its retreat averaged about 25 miles per day. This was hard marching, but there was reason for it. Col. Curtis says that Gen. Early was in close pursuit; as far as Winchester and that it needed no rear guard to keep up the stragglers.

Col. Wells managed this expedition skillfully, choosing a good position every night for his camp. Besides making an effective diversion in favor of Gen. Stoneman operating along the Virginia and Tennessee railroad, the command captured 68 prisoners. This march up and down the Valley in severe winter weather, was very hard on the men, they having to sleep on the ground, without tents or shelter of any kind, but they stood it fairly well.

Early remained at Winchester till the 31st, when he advanced upon Harper's Ferry threatening an attack upon that place. Our regiment by daylight that morning crossed over to Harper's Ferry, Maj. Curtis having received orders the night before to move his command from Maryland Heights to that place early in the morning. We marched to the camp of the Thirty-fourth which was stationed on that side of the river, where we remained all day. There was no attack however. It rained all of this day. At night we camped with the Thirty-fourth.

On the morning of January 1st, 1864, which will be remembered by all old soldiers as the cold New Year's day, the mercury being 23 degrees below zero at Harper's Ferry. Maj. Curtis was ordered in connection with the other troops at this place to form the Twelfth in line of battle on Bolivar Heights, just back of Harper's Ferry, to protect it from the assault expected to be made by Early. The regiment was placed on the top of the Heights. It being so very cold, it was impossible, for the men to stand in line without freezing; and they were allowed to stack arms, break ranks, build fires and stand around them, or run backward and forward to keep from freezing.

The entire day was spent in this position and night coming on without the enemy's appearing, the command was withdrawn to within our works. The Twelfth returned to the camp of the Thirty-fourth, some of our companies quartering in vacant houses, in which fires were built making it decidedly more pleasant than standing in line in the bitter cold air. When early in the morning, information was received that Early had concluded that it was too cold to fight, and had withdrawn his army from our front and gone back up the Valley, our regiment returned to its quarters on Maryland Heights. It was so cold that New Year's night that, it was so reported, six of the First New York cavalry's teamsters were frozen to death. This same night a part of the Sixth corps passed by Harper's Ferry on the railroad on its way from the Army of the Potomac to Martinsburg, and through the day (the second) a brigade of the same corps got off the cars here and went out to Halltown, some four miles distant. No doubt, Early's movement down the Valley had caused these troops to be sent to his department.

On the 4th, Maj. Curtis received orders to proceed immediately with the Twelfth by the Baltimore and Ohio railroad to Cumberland,

Md., and report to Gen. B. F. Kelley, who was in command there. He, Kelly, fearing that Early would make a movement against Cumberland, had requested that the Twelfth be sent to him to assist in defending the place in that contingency. Six companies got off on the route during the afternoon of that day, and arrived at Cumberland in the early part of the night. The other four companies did not get started from Harper's Ferry till 10 o'clock that night, being delayed in getting their baggage from camp. They had only one car to the company, (freight car) and they were so crowded that there was scarcely room for the men to sit. They reached Cumberland at 10 o'clock the next day. The regiment was furnished with very comfortable quarters, such as it had not had before during its service. One-half the companies was quartered in what was known as the old Shriver Mill, and the other half in a large hospital. There being plenty of room here in this latter building, the boys had free swing to work off their surplus energy, and some of them for a day or so after being quartered in it, spent part of their time trying their skill in dancing.

Major Curtis, on our arrival here received an order from Gen. Kelley to have the Twelfth furnished with four days' cooked rations, forty rounds of ammunition, lie upon their arms and be ready to move at a moment's warning. The order was complied with and the boys expected every minute to hear the bugle call to fall in; but none came and no further orders were received from Gen. Kelley to prepare for battle. Early having concluded, no doubt, the weather being so very cold to go back to his winter quarters, and wait until it moderated before engaging in further field operations.

The Twelfth remained here doing guard and picket duty during the months of January, February and March. On January 23rd, we received two months pay, and the same day the officers of the regiment met and by a formal vote recommended the appointment of Major Curtis as colonel of the Twelfth, and on the 26th, he received his commission as Colonel, to rank as such from this latter date, vice J. B. Klunk, who had resigned, Lieut. Col. Northcott still being a prisoner of war. Capt. R. H. Brown of Company I, on February 6th, was commissioned Major of the regiment, in accordance with the recommendation of the officers of it.

Many of the boys still cherish tender recollections of the old mill and the hospital we were camped in at Cumberland and the good times we had at that place. Many agreeable acquaintances were formed here by the boys, which in some instances ripened into enduring friendship. The gay Lieutenant away from scenes of strife turned his attention to more peaceful and congenial pursuits, while some of the boys were not slow to imitate and emulate his example, in endeavoring to reduce the Confederacy to submission by arts long known and long practiced - those by which the hearts of the fair Rebels were attempted to be captured.

Paper collars, soft bread, soft drinks, some not so soft, soft interviews and a large correspondence were some of the luxuries enjoyed at this place. Occasionally some enterprising member of the Twelfth fired with zeal, or something else, would interview the provost guard and inspect the interior of the old depot, used as a guard house; which diversion taken with the picnics had with the canal boatmen, served to vary the monotony incident to a soldier life.

At this point may be given a story told by J. H. Haney of Company K, about a trick played by some of the boys of his company upon a landlord of this city during our encampment there. The story as well as is remembered is about as follows: Some of the boys of the aforesaid company, persuading themselves that the water of the place did not agree with them, or that their stomachs needed a stimulus in order that they might be able with some relish to partake of their usual ration of salt pork and hard tack, concluded that they would go early one morning to a hotel near the railroad station, kept by a man named Kelly, and try the virtue of his tangle foot. When the boys got to the hotel the landlord was still in bed. One of them suggested that they be patient and not wake him. In the meantime this same soldier reconnoitered to the rear of the building and discovered a string of mackerel there on a porch. He came back and told what he had seen, suggesting to a comrade that the fish might be made available for the drinks. He acted immediately on the suggestion and went and got them intending to try the experiment.

It was not long till the landlord was out of bed. The boys walked into the bar-room with the fish saying that they had had for some time mackerel issued to them, and that they had got very tired of them; and wanted to know if the landlord would not treat the crowd for the string they had brought. The landlord, being a clever Irishman promptly said that he would, setting out the bottle, and throwing the string of fish out on the porch. They took their dose of corrective when looking out of the door, they saw another boy, with whom the water did not agree directing his steps toward the hotel.

One of the boys in the bar-room went out and met him, telling him of the mackerel on the porch and wanted to know what was to hinder their being traded for the drinks. That was hint enough. It was not long until the first were in possession of the new comer, and pretty soon he walked into the bar-room with them. The rest of the boys assumed an air of surprise, and said, "Hello! you are here are you? and got fish too?" Yes their mess had more of them than they wanted and he thought that he would see if the landlord would trade him a drink of "red-eye" for this string. The landlord obligingly agreed to do so; and the drinks the second time were gotten for the same fish, the landlord again throwing them out on the porch without discovering the trick.

This trick was played successfully three different times that morning when the boys concluded that they would go to camp. They started but had not got far when the landlord called out, "Hello! boys." They thought, "Now we are in for it - now we will get a blessing!" But the landlord saw the humorous side of the matter, and so he said, "Come back boys. Any man that is darned fool enough to buy his own fish three times ought to stand treat." So they went back and got the fourth drink as the result of their fish deals.

Coming as the story does from Hen Haney, it is not by any means to be regarded as a "fish story." He avers that the boys who took in "the landlord were not bummers, but rather genteel fellows who did what they did in spirit of fun rather than otherwise; that they all had been, since the war, well doing and prosperous men. After the paymaster paid them, they went back and paid the landlord for the drinks; and he being a jolly Irishman looked upon the Company K boys after that as being 'the broths of boys.' "

While the regiment was at Harper's Ferry some officers and sergeants were detailed and sent to their respective sections of country to recruit. A number of the recruits obtained, came to us while we were at Cumberland. The older soldiers in some cases called these recruits in a jesting way "conscripts." Though the recruits, as a rule had not seen any service, the time was not far off when they were to see plenty of it, and all distinction between themselves and the soldiers longer in the service should be lost. Gen. Grant was soon to be placed in command of the armies of the United States; and instead of the lack of unity or cooperation and persistency of effort, that hitherto had characterized the operations of our armies, there was destined to be, as far as possible, a cooperation of movement and a vigorous, persistent "hammering away" on the part of all our forces. The fighting of the present year was to be bloodier than ever, especially in Virginia. While heretofore, for instance, one or two considerable engagements were as many as took place in the Valley during a year, the present year was to witness six or eight hard battles there. And the Twelfth had in store for it four or five times as much fighting, during the coming fifteen months, as it had it in all its previous service.

Going back a little, on January 27th, Gen. Milroy arrived in the city putting up at the Revere House, and the next day the Twelfth was marched to his place of stopping when he made us a short speech.

In the forepart of February, Col. Curtis received orders to take the regiment and go into camp on a hill west of the city, which was done, and while remaining here having very light picket and guard duty to perform, and working on fortifications, the Colonel found time to thoroughly drill the regiment in battalion drill, the manual of arms, and dress parade. It became very efficient in drill and in the manual of arms.

February 2nd, the Rebels made a dash in on the railroad and burned a bridge seven miles east of here. A few weeks later McNeil's and Woodson's men under the command of Jesse McNeil dashed into Cumberland at night and captured and brought off Generals Crook and Kelly, and Capt. Thayer Melvin, Gen. Kelly's adjutant general. This was a very daring feat.

Chapter Seven

March 12th, Maj. Gen. Franz Sigel arrived here and took command of the department. During this month the arrangement was made for the raid against Lynchburg, Gen. Sigel to command the force in person, to be moved it was first intended from Webster, near Grafton on the Baltimore and Ohio railroad but as finally decided from Martinsburg up the Valley. He carefully inspected the troops here intended to go on the expedition. In his inspection which was minute and almost individual in character, he passed closely along the lines of men, looking sharply into their eyes, apparently to see if there was fight there.

On a Sabbath day shortly after Sigel's arrival here. A few weeks later McNeil's and Woodson's men parade, he and his staff rode up to the camp and quietly took position behind the Colonel, and witnessed the efficiency with which the men executed the orders given them; and when the parade was over Gen. Sigel rode up to the Colonel and complimented the regiment on its high attainment in drill, stating that he had no idea that there was so well drilled a regiment in that department.

Lieut. Col. Northcott, having recently rejoined the regiment, from being a prisoner in Libby prison, on the occasion of a dress parade on the 27th, gave us a short speech. Gen. Sigel was also up to the camp at the time and spoke briefly to the regiment. Officers and men were all pleased to see the Lieutenant Colonel once more with the regiment; and he no doubt, was no less glad to exchange life in a Rebel prison for his accustomed duties with the boys.

Adjt. Gen. Pierpont, our former Major between whom and the Twelfth, there had always been a strong, mutual attachment came from Wheeling on April 2nd, to pay the regiment a visit and greet his late comrades again.

The next day, the 3rd, the regiment was ordered to Webster, W. Va., by the way of the Baltimore and Ohio railroad, where a force was concentrating to start the expedition against Lynchburg, by the way of Beverly to Staunton, Va., at which place it was to form a junction with Gen. Crook's forces, moving from the Kanawha Valley. Gen. Sigel ordered the Twelfth to start in the advance with 250 head of cattle in their charge for the soldiers to subsist upon. The regiment succeeded in getting the cattle through to Beverly 42 miles from Webster. This being the first opportunity the members of the regiment had of playing the part of "cow boys" they performed the task with the zeal of novices and had a jolly time of it. We found the Tenth and Eleventh West Virginia and the Twenty-eighth Ohio infantry at Beverly.

By the time the Twelfth had arrived at this place with the cattle, Sigel was convinced that it would be impossible to get his artillery through on this route; and he changed the plan of moving against the enemy, to marching up the Valley. We stayed here two nights and one day, when the regiment was ordered to return immediately to Webster with the cattle. We, on the return, reached Philippi, the 11th. Four companies C, E, G and I, remained here a few days under the command of Maj. Brown. The rest of the regiment went to Webster with the cattle, in the morning. This was a hard and worse than useless march of 84 miles from Webster to Beverly and back. The weather was very rainy and we had to march through deep mud well mixed, by the driving of 250 head of cattle over the road. The boys talked sarcastically about it, saying that they did not understand it, but that they supposed this movement was strategy.

On our return in passing through Belington, a small town between Beverly and Philippi, a lieutenant, who was in command of the post there asked Col. Curtis where he intended to camp that night. The Colonel informed him that in coming out he had noticed a farm that was supplied with a long high fence of new rails; and that was the point he intended to make as it would give the boys an opportunity of conveniently getting good fuel to keep up ample fires. The Lieutenant replied, "That is the very place you should go into camp. You can't punish them half enough, they are the meanest d-----d Rebels in the state. They assisted a gang of Rebel soldiers in capturing a large train of wagons loaded with commissary and quartermaster stores, on their way to Beverly taking all the goods and horses, and burning the wagons."

Chapter Seven

The regiment proceeded to the point designated and went into camp along the line of fence. One of the young men of the family came to us while arrangements were making for camping. He looked as though he had just left Mosby's gang of guerrillas. The Colonel approached him and inquired if he could procure some straw for the men to sleep on, stating that the ground was damp and cold, and he would like to make them as comfortable as possible since they had no tents or shelter of any kind. He replied: "No, we have nothing of the kind on the farm. Everything has been taken from us, and we have been compelled to cut the limbs from the trees to browse our cattle on to keep them from starving." Of course, the young man expected that this statement would be accepted as the truth.

However, the Colonel concluded knowing the capacity of the Twelfth boys to make themselves comfortable, that they could be trusted to take care of themselves and that there was not much likelihood that they would sleep on the bare ground that night. This conclusion was justified about one hour after the camp was located. At that time a line of men could be seen with great bundles of straw coming into camp.

Before this the Colonel had walked to the house to get quarters for himself and Surgeon Bryan. He procured a room from the old lady. She appeared to be boss of the ranch. He inquired of her if she would sell him some meat, as he had been informed by the cook of his mess, that the supplies of meat was about exhausted. She replied: "No, we have not a bit of meat for our own family."

About 8 o'clock at night there was a racket out at the chicken roost. The chickens were fluttering and squalling as though the owls had attacked them. The old lady's daughter ran out to learn what had caused the disturbance, and returned very shortly saying: "Mam, them Yankees are stealing all our chickens." The boss of the ranch ordered the Colonel to go out and stop the men from stealing her chickens. He, very obediently complied with the orders, and returned pretty soon - reporting that he failed to see anyone about the chicken roost and took his seat. About an hour afterwards, the same racket of fluttering and squalling was repeated. The girl ran out again, and after making a general inspection of the chicken roost ran back and exclaimed: "Mam, them infernal soldiers have stole every chicken we have but old speck." And then the old sharp-nosed thin-visaged Boss, with a tongue apparently loose at both ends, rattled her slang at the Colonel at a terrible rate, calling him and his men all kinds of vile names. But her troubles did not end here.

The next morning just at day break the Boss rushed into his bed room, and seizing him by the shoulders and shaking him shouted:

"Get up, your men have stolen all my meat." He replied: "Why, Madam, you told me you had no meat about your house." "Yes," said she, "but I had, and your men have undermined my smoke house and took all I had." He informed her that she had done wrong in telling him a falsehood in saying that she had no meat. She should have asked for a guard to protect it. She then demanded that a guard be sent to search the regiment to see if it could be found. This was done, and the guard returned in due time, reporting that he had thoroughly searched the camp and no meat could be found. He may have made a correct report; nevertheless, when the Colonel joined his mess for dinner that day, he found a very fine roast of ham prepared for the meal. But he could not learn where it came from.

While the four companies before named were at Philippi, there was a considerable amount of government revenue stamps stolen. It seemed conclusive that some soldier had done the deed; and Maj. Brown had a careful and earnest search made of every man of the four companies, but the stamps were not found. The officers and men generally of the detachment were indignantly that any one of the Twelfth had committed such a crime, feeling that it brought dishonor upon the whole command. They would have been pleased if the guilty one should have been found and properly punished. Many months afterward, it is said, it became pretty generally known who had done the deed.

The detachment, on the 20th, marched to Webster, joining there the rest of the regiment, and the next day, in accordance with orders, the regiment marched to Grafton, taking the cars there to go by the way of the Baltimore and Ohio railroad to Martinsburg, arriving there the 22nd, in the evening, and camped near the First Virginia infantry camp. We remained at Martinsburg several days, and there were inspections and a general review of all the troops here. In the meantime there was organized in the second brigade, consisting of the Thirty-fourth Massachusetts, the Fifty-fourth Pennsylvania, the First Virginia, and Twelfth West Virginia under command of the gallant Col. Joseph Thoburn.

We had now got started on a season of hard campaigning which was the run into the late fall. We were about to start up what had hitherto been in the main and what was to continue to be for a time, with some bright exceptions, the Valley of defeat and humiliation; but which was in the end to be the Valley of glorious victory for the arms of the Union.

The 28th, the command received orders from Gen. Sigel, commander, to be ready to march at 8 o'clock in the morning with five days' rations in our haversacks. We set out on the march in the morning at the appointed time on the Winchester pike, and marched to Bunker Hill, ten miles distant, and remained there till May 1st, when we marched through and to a point about two miles beyond Winchester. All along the pike from Martinsburg to Winchester on the march between the two towns, could be seen the graves of soldiers of the one or the other side who had fallen as victims of the cruel, bloody, wicked war. There was perhaps not a mile of the whole route over which we passed along which there could not be seen a soldier's grave; and at Winchester there were thousands buried. Everywhere could be seen the destructiveness and paralyzing effects of the war. Fences were torn down, farms were stripped of live stock, high grass was growing up to the edge of the towns, and it seemed as if the country was deserted by its inhabitants. Everything and the condition of things generally were object lessons teaching of the baleful effects of war.

On this day we passed through the historic and memorable old town of Winchester and camped about two miles beyond the town. The next day we had brigade drill under the supervision of Gen. Sigel. We remained here about a week during which time the organization of the army was completed. Our stay here afforded the boys of the Twelfth an opportunity to walk over the old battle ground of the Winchester battle fought on our side under Gen. Milroy. The boys examined the scene of the battle with considerable eager curious interest.

While we were at this point, there were extra precautions taken against a surprise. Strong picket forces were kept out, five companies being sent out on some of the roads, at least, and orders were given to keep one-third of the men up at night all the time, showing that Gen. Sigel was a vigilant careful commander. This alertness and these precautions indicated that we were drawing near the enemy, and gave a hint of coming clash of arms, which indeed was not far in the future.

The command on the 9th, moved up the Valley, our brigade in advance under Col. Thoburn. We marched 13 miles on this day and camped in the evening at Cedar Creek. The bridge across this creek had been destroyed, and it had to be rebuilt before the command could proceed farther. The bridge being rebuilt, we resumed our march on the 11th, passing through Strasburg, and camped one mile short of reaching Woodstock, the distance marched being 14 miles.

It perhaps should have been noted that when the command reached Fisher's Hill after leaving Cedar Creek, it was halted and the men were ordered to load. Those who had been under fire before, felt the gravity of the outlook, and it was noticeable that more than one brave man looked very serious as he tore the paper from his cartridge.

We remained at our camp near Woodstock one day with nothing unusual occurring, when on the next day our regiment with two pieces of artillery was ordered up the Valley about seven miles, one mile south of Edinburgh, as an advance picket. Some Rebel cavalry were seen here at a distance. Company S, was deployed across the road leading south with orders to allow no one to pass. Soon two young ladies, in passing from home to town discovered the pickets, a member of the company relates, and turned to run. They were captured after an exciting chase and sent to town, and ordered to remain there till the next morning. There was a pouring rain that night and the soldiers got a taste of the beauties of soldier life, getting thoroughly soaked with rain. Some tried to sleep; others preferred to stand or sit around roaring fires. In some cases those who tried to sleep found the water collecting in pools around their bodies.

It was at this place and time or near it, it is believed, that an incident occurred which shows, as far as it goes, that a soldier would better obey orders. The writer of this was for the night, assigned to Company C, to go with it on picket, there being only one commissioned officer of the company present at the time. All was quiet at the picket post in the night and in the morning John W. Crow and another soldier asked Capt. Bartlett of the company, if they might go to a house several hundred yards distant to get some bread. He said that they might go, but told them to not go any farther. It was a spider-and-the-fly-case - they did not come back again. At all events we did not see them for several months afterward, when they came back as exchanged prisoners. They then told that when they went to the house mentioned, the mistress said that she had no bread, but she thought they could get it at a house a little farther off, probably knowing what would happen if they went there. They went and were captured. No doubt they often deeply regretted their disobedience of orders.

The Twelfth was relieved from picket in the morning by the One Hundred and Twenty-third Ohio and the Eighteenth Connecticut, and we returned to our camp near Edinburgh, the rain still falling. On our way we met the First Virginia and the Thirty-fourth Massachusetts going up the pike. It began to look as though things were approaching a crisis. In the morning at 2 o'clock May 15th, Companies A, B, F, and I, were ordered back to Edinburg to take the place of the regiments that had relieved us the morning before, in order that they might go to reinforce the First Virginia and the Thirty-fourth Massachusetts which had met some of the enemy, and had had considerable fighting with them the evening and night of the 14th.

About 8 o'clock A.M. the rest of the force came up and we rejoining our regiment, all pushed on to Mount Jackson about 14 miles from our camp at Woodstock.

At Mount Jackson we went into camp, but were ordered to move out in less than thirty minutes. The four regiments in advance having engaged the Rebels at New Market six miles farther up, we marched in the direction of the fighting.

The morning had been clear, but soon after crossing the Shenandoah at Mount Jackson it began raining. Cannonading could be distinctly heard in our front, telling of serious work going on there and pre-saging a share of it for us, the regiments moving to the assistance of our comrades. We crossed the North Branch of the Shenandoah about one mile from Mount Jackson, The marching after leaving this place had been rapid and laborious through rain and mud, but soon we were ordered to double quick which we kept up for a few miles, till at about 2 o'clock P.M. we reached the field of battle, and were hastily formed in line of battle under the fire of the enemy, their balls at this time, however, passing harmlessly over us.

Our entire brigade under Col. Thoburn was formed on the right of the pike, the two regiments which had been with Col. Moor at the front having returned to their own brigade, Thoburn's, Col. Moor with two regiments of his brigade, the Eighteenth Connecticut, the One Hundred and Twenty-third Ohio infantry with a small body of cavalry was left something in advance. The two other regiments of his brigade were a considerable distance in the rear with the wagon train.

The Twelfth as best can be gathered from a M. S. by Col. Curtis, was first formed in line at some considerable distance in rear of the three other regiments of our brigade; but this was scarcely more than done "when we were withdrawn" as Col. Curtis says, and formed close in the rear, say within 60 yards of the Thirty-fourth Massachusetts, and the First Virginia, except two companies, A and B, which were sent to the right to support Carlin's battery.

The eight companies had scarcely thus formed in line when we heard in our front for the first time the much mentioned Rebel yell. Gen. Breckinridge in command of the Rebel force had moved to the attack with about 5,000 men, and overlapping Moor had soon driven him to the rear. With scarcely a halt he moved on to the attack of Thoburn's brigade, the main line, but was repulsed by a gallant charge made here.

Just where the Rebels raised the yell in making their charge, Gen. Sigel rode up to the eight companies of the Twelfth and ordered it into column by division to resist the charge; but when the charge was repulsed, we were put into line again, and ordered to lie down. The Twelfth had a bad position. We were placed where we could do no good and yet where we suffered seriously, a more trying position on a soldier than where he has a chance to return the fire. There are no data at hand showing the loss of the regiment, but the compiler's own company lost in killed and wounded seven men in this engagement.

The battle was short, sharp, the losses heavy on each side and for a while the result doubtful. It was quite generally said by our men after the battle that at one time just before our line gave way, the Rebel line was breaking. The Rebel account goes to sustain this statement. Col. J. Stoddard Johnston of Breckinridge's staff says, according to Pond's *The Shenandoah in 1864*, that "when his (Breckenridge's) line had reached within two hundred yards of the enemy, the position was very critical, and for a time it seemed doubtful as to which would be the first to give way." It is thus seen how near we were to gaining a victory. Had Moor's two regiments been drawn back and formed in line with the rest of the infantry and not left where they could do little or no good; and if Sigel had formed his infantry in our line as the enemy were, according to the authority mentioned, it is no violent presumption to say that the victory would probably have been with our troops.

The doubtful struggle was finally decided by our line giving way in some confusion and Sigel ordered a retreat. We fell back slowly. Imboden's official report confirms this, saying: "Sigel's entire line retired slowly." The enemy did not press us much; for if we had suffered severely they had also. The Lexington cadet battalion of 250 lost more than one-fourth their number in killed and wounded. That one fight seemed to do them; they were not present at the battle of Piedmont, three weeks later, though it was nearer home. In fact, they were never heard of in battle again. It is remembered that a Harrisonburg newspaper obtained as we went up the Valley, two weeks after the battle of New Market, under Hunter, lamented the heavy loss of the Cadets in that battle; and urged that they should not be put into another engagement, saying that the young men or boys should be saved for the next war.

Then we had retreated as far as Rude's Hill, a mile or two, we met the two regiments, the One Hundred and Sixteenth, and the Twenty-eighth Ohio infantry that had been in the rear and were not in the engagement; and they covered the retreat from this point to Mount Jackson, where we crossed the river, halted and formed in line of battle. The Rebels came close enough to throw a few shells but not close enough to be within musket shot. After dark we resumed the retreat and continued it, with stops for rests and meals, until we arrived at Cedar Creek the next day, the 16th, when our retreat came to an end.

There is nothing so successful as success; but it seems that there is no excuse taken for failure in war, neither by those in or out of authority. Col. Curtis records that the boys of the Twelfth in going up the Valley were constantly singing "We Fights Mit Sigel" but on the retreat their song was changed to "We Fights no more mit Sigel." One of the things that the officers and men of the Twelfth were displeased with and which they criticized severely was the fact that we were so placed in that battle that we could not fire on the enemy without firing into our own men, and yet so close to the front line that we suffered severely from the enemy's fire.

It will be seen, however, from the following letter from Gen. Sigel which tells why the battle was fought just when and where it was, and other details which the survivors of the Twelfth will read no doubt with eager interest, that he disclaims responsibility for the regiment's final bad position on the field of battle. And it is inferred from Col. Curtis M. S. before mentioned wherein he speaks of our being "withdrawn" from our first position and placed in our final one, that he supposed this was done by competent authority. It appears that no one knows who was responsible for the blunder. Sigel's letter is given nearly in full:

New York, August 19th, 1891.
Lieut. Wm. Hewitt, Linton, Ohio.

Dear Sir:
The advance of my forces up the Shenandoah Valley was made for the purpose of assisting Gen. Crook's movement from the Kanawha Valley, by inducing Breckinridge, who commanded in southwest Virginia, to detach a part of his forces against me. To attain this object we advanced as far as Woodstock. From this place Col. Moor was sent forward on a reconnoitering expedition in the direction of Mount Jackson to ascertain the movements of the enemy, as from the telegraphic dispatches at Woodstock, we found that Breckinridge was down the Shenandoah Valley against us.

In the evening and during the night of the 14th, it was ascertained that Col. Moor had passed Jackson and had met a part of Breckinridge's forces; I, therefore, moved forward to Mount Jackson, to be nearer him (Moor) and for the reason that I intended to await Breckinridge's attack at that place. We arrived at Mount Jackson on the morning of the 15th, and found that Moor had gone as far as New Market, seven miles from Mount Jackson; that Breckenridge was near him, and had made an attack on him during the night of the 14th, which was repulsed.

Made aware of the exposed position of the little force of Moor, I immediately sent orders for him to return to Mount Jackson, and to Gen. Stahl to move forward with the main force of our cavalry to cover the retreat of Moor, and retard the movement of the enemy. But this movement was executed so slowly and the distance from Mount Jackson to New Market was comparatively so great, that I resolved to move forward with my whole force, after having waited over an hour for an answer to my orders sent to Moor and Sullivan.

While the troops were in motion I rode forward myself, accompanied by an aid, as far as Rude's Hill; and on my way was met by Capt. Alexander, who had been sent by Col. Moor and he reported that his (Moor's) troops were in an excellent position and that I should come to their assistance. Under these circumstances, I sent back to our troops to hasten their march towards New Market; while I went forward to meet those (Moor and Stahl) I arrived near New Market about noon, and before the enemy began his attack.

It now became clear to me that all the troops could not reach the position close to New Market; I ordered Col. Moor to evacuate his position slowly, covered by cavalry, and to fall back into a new position, which was selected about three-quarters of a mile north of New Market right and left of the turn pike leading to Mount Jackson. During this time I sent two officers, Captains McEstee and T. G. Putnam back to Gen. Sullivan who was in command of the infantry division, with orders to bring forward all his troops without delay, and at the moment when Col. Moor was approaching the new line from his position in advance, it was reported to me by Capt. R. G. Pendergast, commander of my escort, whom I also had sent back to hurry the troops up that all the infantry and artillery of Gen. Sullivan had arrived (the head of the column being in sight) and that they were waiting for orders.

Supposing this report to be correct, I formed the line of battle, Col. Thoburn's brigade and two batteries on the right, while Col. Moor was ordered to form on the left of Thoburn. The Twelfth West Virginia, and Dupont's battery took position behind the right of Thoburn's brigade as a reserve, and two companies of the Twelfth West Virginia were posted behind the batteries on the right for their support. Von Kleiser's battery was in the center of the line, Ewing's on the left, and the cavalry behind the extreme left and some behind the center. My own position during the battle was in the line between the batteries on the right, and the Thirty-fourth Massachusetts (Col. Wells) as on the right the principal attack of the enemy was directed. With me was an orderly, a young man of 17 years who held bravely out during the whole fight. My staff officers were some distance behind the line, near Dr. Rice's house.

The battle which now followed has been described in "Battles and Leaders of the Civil War," and therefore, I need not go into details. I simply desired to show that I was neither surprised, nor did I accept the engagement without good reason and full deliberation. But in accepting it on the place and ground it was I was misled by the report of Capt. Pendergast whom I trusted, as he was an efficient and brave officer.

He reported two regiments the One Hundred and Sixteenth and the Twenty-eighth Ohio present and awaiting orders, while we found them, after the battle, at Rude's Hill, one and a half miles back from our line. I am ignorant up to this day of what was the unfortunate cause which kept them back, as I was relieved soon after the battle, and had no opportunity of investigating the matter.

There were some other disadvantages against us in this battle, but after all, our troops fought bravely and so did those of the enemy. We lost 93 in killed and 552 in wounded, the enemy 42 and 522 respectively.

After the battle we retreated to Rude's Hill, formed line and remained about half an hour, whence we withdrew to Mount Jackson, which was done slowly and in perfect order. We remained there for two hours, during which time as Lieut. Col. Lincoln says in his "Life with the Thirty-fourth Massachusetts Regiment," the men ate their supper, the injured were looked up, their wounds examined and dressed and the slightly wounded placed in ambulances for transportation. Those more severely wounded were disposed of in the hospital buildings of Mount Jackson, and left under charge of Asst. Surgeon Allen of the Thirty-fourth. These arrangements completed at about 9 p.m., the column was again put in motion, the Thirty-fourth bringing up the rear.

It will be seen from these statements that we did not "flee in disorder" from our position at Rude's Hill to Mount Jackson and Cedar Creek, nor lose or burn any wagons, nor "forsake" our sick and wounded, as was publicly proclaimed at the time, nor did the enemy capture any muskets except those of our killed and severely wounded, left on the field.

We were beaten but not disheartened. We went back to Cedar Creek, because all our ambulances were filled with the wounded whom we could not transport without a strong force of protection, and for the purpose of disengaging ourselves of a train of 200 destined for Gen. Crook. We reached Edinburg at 7 o'clock in the morning and Strasburg at 5 in the evening of the 16th.

On the 17th an ambulance was sent to Mount Jackson by flag of truce loaded with supplies for our wounded. On the 18th, a detachment of infantry, cavalry and artillery, under Col. Wells of the Thirty-fourth Massachusetts, was sent to Strasburg and the cavalry advanced to Fisher's Hill, the pickets of the enemy retiring before them. On the same day reinforcements were approaching from Harper's Ferry, and I sent a telegram to Gen. Crook on the Kanawha to prepare for an advance. On the 20th, Gen. Hunter arrived and on the 21st, I was relieved from the command of the department and by the request of Gen. Hunter took command of Reserve Division, with headquarters at Harper's Ferry.

As to the Twelfth West Virginia, it consisted of good and brave officers and men. It was very well drilled in the manual of arms; but as was natural, considering the little time they had practiced it, deficient in battalion drill; so that it was difficult for me at the commencement of the battle to bring them from line into column and vice versa. This created considerable trouble at the beginning of the fight when they left their position in reserve, came forward and fired over the heads of the Thirty-fourth Massachusetts. I do not believe that Col. Curtis gave them the order to do so. * * * But such things happen sometimes with inexperienced troops, and I am very glad to know that the regiment, under its same brave commander, fully redeemed its honor by its gallant conduct in the battle of Piedmont and on other occasions.

Our whole campaign and especially the battle of New Market, were a wholesome lesson for them and prepared them to become what they afterward were.

I think I have now given you the most important facts and features of the case; and assure you that I shall always remember with kindness and gratitude the services of the Twelfth West Virginia.

Very Truly Yours,
SIGEL,
Late Maj. Gen. of Vols.

According to Pond before cited, General W. S. Lincoln, of the Thirty-fourth Massachusetts infantry shows that the aggregate of Breckinridge's infantry the day after the battle was 4,047. We therefore must have had about 4,500 infantry in the battle as according to Rebel authority (See Pond) they had no reserves. It would appear therefore that we were out numbered, we having only five regiments of infantry so disposed and handled as to be effective; while the enemy had three brigades and the Cadet battalion of infantry. Our infantry and artillery had to stand the brunt of the battle and it is no disparagement to them under the circumstances that they were worsted in the engagement.

Whatever may be said of Sigel's generalship regarding the battle of New Market, it must be said that he acted bravely, was right in the thick of the fight all the time and after the battle began did the best he could to save the day. And in view of the heavy losses sustained on each side in the battle, and our slow and orderly retreat to Cedar Creek, the following message sent to Grant by Halleck: "Sigel is in full retreat on Strasburg. He will do nothing but run; never did anything else," is markedly untrue and undeserved, and so far as it seems to imply that Sigel was cowardly, is grossly unjust, as his entire command at New Market would testify.

A day or two after Sigel's command had fallen back to Cedar Creek. He called on the Twelfth to furnish a squad of volunteer scouts to go up the Valley and learn what the strength of the enemy in our front was. Corporal De Bee, of the regiment and six or eight men volunteered to go. They went to Sigel's headquarters for instructions. He told them to go into a house and put on citizens cloths and go right into the enemy's camp and learn their strength. The boys answer "Yes," as if to say that they understood and would do so; but at the same time there was an unexpressed conclusion that they were not anxious to wear citizens cloths on that trip and they would forego that pleasure.

The scouts started out on that expedition traveling nearly all of that day, along on North Mountain, it is believed. After they had traveled a while, three or four of the squad concluded that they would turn back, which they did, but the rest of the boys being more plucky kept on, and in the evening they came in sight of the Rebel camp. In the morning the boys found such a position as from which they could view the entire camp of the enemy, and they carefully counted the number of tents they had, and then started on the return to Cedar Creek, arriving there sometime during the day. When they reached our pickets they (the latter) not being of the Twelfth and not knowing the scouts, sent them into camp under guard. The scouts reported to Sigel that they had found the Rebel camp, giving its locality and said that they counted the number of tents in it, telling the number. Sigel complimented Corporal De Bee and his comrades for what they had done saying that they had given him more information than he had got from all the cavalry that had been out scouting.

Here is a humorous incident of the battle of New Market that was current among the boys afterward. As well as can be recalled it was told thus: Col. Wells of the Thirty-fourth Massachusetts was a strict disciplinarian, but in defiance of this fact the boys of his regiment would sometimes fire off their guns in camp. In such cases he was want to say, "Orderly, orderly go and ascertain who fired that gun and report him to me immediately."

This order of the Colonel's having been repeated in the same stereotyped language at different times impressed itself upon the minds of the boys of the Thirty-fourth and became a matter of remark and jest among them. Well at the battle of New Market when the battle was opening and the first gun or so was fired, some fellow of that regiment with characteristic American humor, who was bound to have his joke if it was to be his last on earth yelled out, "Orderly, orderly, go and ascertain who fired that gun and report him to me immediately."

Comrade Jas. N. Miller of Company A, taken prisoner at the battle of New Market tells of an incident of the battle, and his prison experience as follows:

The first man killed in Company A, if I remember rightly, was John A. Chrismond. He was a recruit who came to us at Harper's Ferry, in the winter of 1863-64. He was a light hearted fellow, somewhat reckless, who carried a fiddle often playing and singing. At the battle of New Market as we were going into the fight, Chrismond and I were in file together. The battle had begun and the cannons were booming. He said to me in his jovial way, "Hickory" - that was the nickname the boys gave me because I was "tough" physically - "I hope I will be killed to day." I said to him as calmly as I could for my heart was up in my throat like a great lump. "Chrismond, you oughtn't to talk that way." "Well," he replied, "I don't care."

We lay down along side of a battery which was firing and I saw Gen. Sigel on his horse giving orders to "fire percussion!" The fortune of war threw Chrismond in the front rank and he being a large man, and I a slender boy, I crouched down behind him. The Rebels were charging upon us, and about the first ball that came near us struck Chrismond in the breast; and he died without a sound. After the fight in which I was captured, I helped to carry his body off the field into a little stable or some kind of an out building. I supposed it was buried by the Rebels.

After the death of Chrismond and before we got a chance to return the fire of the Rebels our company was ordered to the right of the line to prevent a flank movement. This threw us over a hill into a woods, and we did not notice that the main line was being driven back until it was quite a distance away. Then when we discovered this we "skedaddled" as fast as our legs would carry us.

Becoming exhausted I fell behind. Seeing three fellows in blue cloths in a field to the right, I supposed they were some of our boys, and got over a fence next to them. They aimed their guns at me and yelled out to surrender. I first thought I would jump back over the fence and try to escape, but I saw it was no use, and held up my hand. They had on homespun cloths of bluish color. One of them, a sergeant of a Georgia regiment, took me to the rear, and treated me very kindly allowing me to pick up a haversack and a blanket, and this latter probably saved my life.

I reached Andersonville the 29th of May, and endured with others the oft-told horrors of that place. I took the scurvy and the diarrhea but on the 10th of September I managed to "flank out," in company with Sergeant Rogers and Col. Cook of the Eighteenth Pennsylvania cavalry, who had known me at Waynesburg in their state. Instead of being exchanged I was sent with others to Florence, Ala. Here there was no prison ready for us, and by getting some of the pure air of that place and also some vegetables I got better of the scurvy. Sergeant

Rogers ran the guards here and got away, and I would have gone with him, but my leg was bent nearly double with the scurvy, so that I knew that I would hinder him and we would both be captured.

On the 8th of December, I was paroled with the sick and sent to Charleston Harbor, transferred to our lines. I never was exchanged so I suppose I am still a prisoner of the Southern Confederacy.

The hardest thing in all my prison life was to feel that as a soldier I was practically useless except to aid in keeping some Rebel soldiers out of the field. While our regiment was winning its first victory at Piedmont and enduring the terrible march from Lynchburg and helping the peerless Sheridan to send Jubal Early "whirling" up the Valley, I was lying in the sands at Andersonville and Florence, missing all the glorious record of the regiment. But it was the fate of war. So far as the chances of death were concerned, however, the percent of mortality was greater in prison than in the field.

I could write many pages of incidents in prison life but one must suffice. At Florence there was some clothing sent through the lines to us by our Sanitary Commission. It was given out to the most needy, and there wasn't much choice. I tore my only shirt (which I hadn't washed for three months) up into strips so that it barely hung together, in order that I might get a new one. The first day of the distribution I gave it to one of my companions - I think it was Freeman Younkin - and he went up to where the clothing was being distributed, and came back with a new shirt which he got on the strength of his (my) old one. The next day my detachment was called and when the distributing officers reached me he asked me if that was my only shirt. I replied that it was. "Well," he said, "you'd better get a needle and thread and sew it up, for you can't get another new shirt on the strength of that one." So I got left.

Private W. C. Mahan of Company I, tells the story of his being taken prisoner and his prison life as follows:

At the battle of New Market Private Wm. Thompson of my company was badly wounded, his leg being broken by a musket ball. Another man of the company and I started to carry him off the field. We were told that we would find the ambulances at a certain place, but we failed to find them; and having to carry the wounded man we fell behind, and were captured. At night, we the able prisoners, were allowed to go under guard out over the field to hunt up our wounded. A Captain of the Thirty-fourth Massachusetts, who was himself wounded, found his brother on the field wounded. I recall to mind that I saw the Rebel Gen. Breckinridge talking to this Captain. Some of our wounded were put into an old house that night and our unwounded carried water to them.

We, the prisoners, were taken via Staunton to Lynchburg. We were kept at this latter place for a few days. Here one day two of our men got to talking about somebody with whose conduct on the way here, I believe they were displeased, using some pretty severe terms about him. The guard who was nearest them, a quite young fellow, thinking or pretending to think that they were talking about him though they were neither talking to nor about him, shot one of the men, killing him. It seemed as though this young Rebel thought that he had done a great thing in killing a Union soldier, for he, insisting on doing so, followed the box with the corpse, to the grave. Some of the other Rebels condemned the conduct of this young fellow as being barbarous and brutal.

We were taken from here to Andersonville by rail. We got along very slowly, being detained on the way by the enemy's use of the road in carrying their own soldiers and etc. We were perhaps a week or ten days on the way. At one time, we were two days without food. During one of our delays on the route the Rebel women brought food for their own men, but none for us. They had a little darkey boy with them, who waved a Rebel flag at us. Both he, and the women seemed to enjoy the demonstration very much, he grinning and they laughing as he waved.

The prison camp at Andersonville was enclosed by a stockade about 16 feet high of heavy timbers set on end, and so closely fitted together that you could scarcely see between them. Inside of this was the "dead line," 40 feet distant perhaps. It was marked by a row of posts and stringers of timber extending along on top of them from post to post. On top of the stockade of intervals there were sentry boxes placed, in which the sentries or guards stood. Outside this stockade, at a suitable distance there was another stockade, commanding the first with loop holes in it through which to fire at the prisoners, in case they should try to scale the inner one.

The prisoners were formed into companies of 90 men each. Three of these companies were formed into a division, and the companies were subdivided in squads of 30 each. At first I believe it was not the case that they were thus formed; but the necessity of having a divide of the scant rations, approaching somewhere near fairness, demanded some sort of organization among the prisoners.

It was necessary for a prisoner to know to what company and the number of the squad to which he belonged in order that he might get his rations, or even get out to be exchanged. When a lot of prisoners was to be sent out of camp to be exchanged or supposedly so, if a prisoner were not present to answer his name, someone else would answer for him and get out, and the prisoner named would be left. Getting out in this way was called "flanking out."

Whenever a lot of prisoners arrived they would right away be organized as above, each division, company, and squad having a chief chosen. When the rations were to be divided the chief of a division would divide into three lots, one lot for each of his companies. He would then have the chiefs of the latter turn their backs to the ration; when he would ask each, "Will you take this lot?" and they would choose without seeing which lot was indicated. The companies and squads divided in the same way, the latter dividing among the individuals. The squad chiefs were frequently changed, because they would often inform a friend before hand which ration to choose.

We got raw rations (corn meal) and cooked week about. The flies here were very bad, and when the cooks would make up a batch of dough and lay it down, the flies would gather thickly on it, then they would slap another batch on the first to kill the flies. In this way our bread got full of flies and looked like bread currants or raisins in it. The same wagons that were used to haul our dead were used to haul our bread.

The trading instinct was not altogether devoid of exercise here. Enterprising soldiers would trade bread for meal and get more meal than made the bread. Sometimes a soldier would be heard asking, "Who will trade a bone for meat?" Those who wanted bones claimed that by breaking, boiling and making soup of them they got more nourishment from them than they could get from the meat. Some of our men would even make bargains with a sentry, although, of course, it was not allowed. They would give him money to buy something which he would perhaps do and give it to the prisoner furnishing the money, the next time he, the guard was on duty. Sweet potatoes got in this way would sell for 25 cents each.

There was a stream of water which ran through the camp, and as a matter of course it got very dirty, there being so many thousands of men in the camp. The prisoners would therefore sometimes reach under the dead line where the stream crossed it for water. One would reach under one foot, another two, someone else a little farther in order that they might get less filthy water. Perhaps the sentry on duty nearest the stream would permit this crossing of the dead line; but when another came on duty there he might fire upon the prisoner over the dead line without a word of warning. Many were killed in that way.

Everybody knows something of the many deaths daily occurring in prison here. Our men used to be anxious to get to carry the dead out of camp, in order that they might thus get some fire wood. This privilege was permitted for awhile, but when the Yankees began to play the trick of carrying out late in the evening a comrade assuming death, and the Rebels would go out in the morning to bury him and find him gone, this privilege was stopped, commandant Wirz declaring that he would have to get to putting ball-and-chains on the d---d dead Yankees, as some of them would run off after they were dead. Another scheme of the prisoners in order to draw the rations of a dead comrade, and thus add to the aggregate, of the scanty supply of their squads, was to not report his death. The Rebels learning of this practice of the prisoners in order to prevent it, resorted to frequent counting of them.

One of the prisoners with whom I became acquainted was a member of the Ringgold cavalry, which was from Washington County, Pennsylvania. He was of a jovial disposition and was called "Happy Jack." He used to stand at the gate where the dead were taken out, count their numbers for a day - the great mortality seems to have suggested this idea - and from the total he would calculate when his chances for being taken out a corpse would come.

For a time there was much stealing in camp, incited no doubt largely by the dire necessities of the men; but after awhile we got police appointed to stop the stealing, which they did, and to attend to other matters. For instance the "Hundred Days Men" seemed to not endure the hardships here so well as the old soldiers. They would mope and set around. They died relatively much faster than the old soldiers. When the police would see one of those dispirited fellows they would fasten on his back a wooden contrivance that they called a "spreadeagle" to keep him from sitting down, and they would make him move about for his health.

We were kept somewhat informed as to the progress of the war by the arrival from time to time of some of our men who had been recently made prisoners.

There is no tragedy so dark but it has its relieving features. And one of the comic ways the prisoners had of beguiling the time was this: One of them would run his hand into his shirt bosom and say inquiringly to another, "Grey back or no grey back?" as if he were playing "Odd-or-even." The addressed would perhaps answer "No grey back," when the propser of the guess would likely say, "You have missed it," pulling out one.

After being kept here for some months, though I did not get so like a skeleton as some, my flesh became in so unhealthy a state from having the scurvy, that when I would press my finger on it, the print would remain for a long time as if my flesh were putty. I got to be one of the very sick.

At the end of my imprisonment here of about four months, the sickest of the prisoners, or a part of them, were taken out to be exchanged. I came very nearly not getting out that time, for my name was close to the end of the list of names called. We were taken first to Millin, Ga., and we stayed here a few days, the sicker part of us on one side of the camp, and the others on the other side. The prisoners would while here sit around fires all night, and in the morning many of them would be found dead where they had sat.

Once while here I went after some water. I was so weak that I had to use a cane. Coming back I fell and spilled the water. I was too weak to go for more, was discouraged, felt like giving up, and do not know what I should have done if an artillerymen of a Wheeling battery had not brought me the water. He and I parted promising to write to each others friends when we should get home. A part of us myself included, were taken to Savannah where we were exchanged, changing our clothes here.

We were taken from here to Annapolis where we again changed clothing. Once more we were in God's country! At Annapolis we were restricted for a few days as to the amount of food we got. One day at my meal I did not want my meat and a comrade nearby eyed it eagerly. At last he inquired, "Are you going to eat that meat?" I told him that I was not when he snapped it up quickly.

When I got to Annapolis one of the first men I saw was "Happy Jack." He was much changed by his hardships but I knew him by his black curly hair. His buoyant spirits had brought him through.

I got home after the frosts of the fall of the year had come. I wrote according to promise to the Wheeling artilleryman's friends. His sister answered my letter that he was killed on board of a government steamer on his way home up the Mississippi by its explosion.

Thus ends my story of prison life at Andersonville. No attempt is made to give anything like an adequate account of it - that could not be done - but rather I have tried mainly after 27 years have passed to recall some of the matters concerning it, that I do not remember to have read about in any account that I have seen.

Chapter Eight

On the 18th of May, our regiment and the Thirty-fourth Massachusetts with two pieces of artillery moved from Cedar Creek, five or six miles up the Valley to Fisher's Hill, and occupied it as a picket. Gen. Sigel came out to our camp there. The next day the two regiments fell back two or three miles to Strasburg and occupied an old fort there built by Gen. Banks. We received today mail - always a welcome receipt to the boys, the first since leaving Winchester, ten days before. In the evening the Thirty-fourth band came to the headquarters of the Twelfth to give us a serenade. Speeches were made by Col. Curtis, Adjt. Caldwell, and Capt. Smiley of our regiment.

On the 2nd, Gen. Sigel was relieved from command here and Gen. Hunter assigned to his place. Three days later we were reinforced at Cedar Creek by three more regiments of infantry, the Second Maryland, the Fourth Virginia and the One Hundred and Sixtieth Ohio, and about this time, or a little later we were further reinforced by the Fifth New York heavy artillery.

On the 25th, we drew ten days' rations of coffee and sugar and three days' rations of hard bread. The troops from Cedar Creek came up, all having had marching orders. We were now about to start on the memorable campaign against Lynchburg. Hunter had issued his famous order announcing to his troops that they were about to enter on an explosion of hardships, in which they would have to live off the enemy, and if need be to eat mule meat. The infantry were required to carry each man 80 or 100 rounds of ammunition. A little after noon of this day the great march began of what was known as Hunter's raid.

We camped in the evening near Woodstock. On the way the cavalry burned a house and barn, by orders of Gen. Hunter, the owner having been engaged in bushwhacking.

On the 29th we resumed our march passing through Edinburg and Mount Jackson, crossing the Shenandoah here on a bridge newly built by the Rebels to replace the one burnt by Sigel and camped near New Market and the ground of the battle of two weeks before. Some members of the regiment looked over the battle field. They found that our dead had been buried in a heap where some stone had been quarried out. The dead of the enemy that had not been taken to their homes, had been buried in the cemetery at New Market. The enemy had left 31 of our wounded at this town and vicinity, who it had appeared had been quite well taken care of. This night our regiment went on picket on the bridge over the river in our rear.

The second day after our arrival here, two companies of the Twelfth, I and K, were detailed to fill in with stone the wooden abutments of the bridge, and the Thirty-fourth Massachusetts went out foraging; thus making a beginning of living off the enemy.

We remained here until June 2nd, when we marched at 5 o'clock a.m., our regiment in the rear of the wagon train, arriving at Harrisonburg in the evening, our advance having driven Imboden out of town. The Rebels left some sixty of our wounded and thirty of theirs here, brought up from New Market. Distance marched this day 24 miles.

On the 4th, we marched from here taking the pike leading to Staunton, but Hunter finding Imboden posted about seven miles ahead at Mount Crawford after examining this position, turned to the left taking a side road leading via Port Republic. Seven miles from Harrisonburg we came to Cross Keys where the forces of Fremont and Jackson fought on June 8th, 1863, and a little farther on to where the Rebel Col. Ashby was killed. At Port Republic on the south branch of the Shenandoah our pioneers put a pontoon bridge over the river on which we crossed and marched about one mile on the road leading to Staunton.

Early in the morning of the 5th, we resumed our march, but did not go far until our cavalry began skirmishing with the Rebels, driving them and capturing a number of prisoners. It may be well to say here that an Irish woman, who accompanied the First New York cavalry was noticed helping tenderly to bury some of the killed "my (her) boys" of that regiment that morning.

Seven miles from Port Republic we found the Rebels in force, consisting of the commands of Generals Vaughn and Imboden, and a number of militia, numbering in all, as learned from prisoners, between 8,000 and 9,000 men, all under the command of Gen. W. E. Jones. Hunter's command consisted in all of 8,500 men, the infantry in two brigades the First commanded by Col. Moor, and the Second by Col. Thoburn. The cavalry were under command of Gen. Stahl, the infantry, under Gen. Sullivan.

The enemy were posted on either side of the pike their right drawn back somewhat. They had breastworks of rails extending at least from the pike to the Middle river on their left, several hundred yards distant. Hunter made disposition for battle at once, and the engagement that followed is known as the Battle of Piedmont. The First Brigade was formed on the right of the pike, and the Second Brigade on the left. The opposing forces faced each other from either side from the edge of woods, with several hundred yards of cleared land between.

The battle began. It was opened by the artillery from each side. The Twelfth and the Thirty-fourth Massachusetts of Thoburn's brigade were ordered forward through the woods, on the left of the pike, with a view to charging some of the enemy's artillery; when, being discovered they were vigorously shelled by the enemy. After awhile they were brought back to the point where they had entered the woods. While waiting here for the coming of the balance of their brigade Colonels Thoburn and Curtis and Adjt. G. B. Caldwell with their orderlies, rode out into the open ground forming a group, for the purpose of watching the effect of the artillery fire. They were discovered by the Rebels, who threw a shell right into their midst, which exploding took off the fore-leg of the Adjutant's little mare. That group immediately dispersed.

The other regiments having come up, Col. Thoburn moved his brigade forward in the open ground into a slight hollow, within 200 yards of the enemy for the purpose of making a flank charge upon him. While the infantry were moving forward into this position, the artillery on each side opened up a heavy fire, and the Rebel band played "Dixie," while ours played "Yankee Doodle." Just before the charge that gallant young officer Capt. Meigs, of Hunter's staff rode backward and forward along the line encouraging the men to do their duty on this charge, and the day would be ours; that they must not hesitate or falter but go right through, that we were now a hundred miles from our lines, and that defeat would be disastrous. The First Brigade had made three charges right in the face of the Rebel front and had been repulsed. But we will let Adjt. G. B. Caldwell of the Twelfth tell the story of the battle in his graphic and enthusiastic way, as it came red hot from his pen a few days after for the Wheeling Intelligencer. Or more particularly of the part taken in the engagement by the Twelfth. The letter was written from the headquarters of the regiment at Staunton and is as follows:

This regiment moved from camp at Port Republic at 6 o'clock a.m. June 5, 1864. Our forces marching forward towards Staunton some four miles, our cavalry became engaged and drove the enemy a distance of one and a half miles, suffering a loss of thirty, killed and wounded, Capt. Imboden a brother of the general's was taken here. The ball then opened by the loud mouthed artillery bellowing forth, both Union and Rebel in hellish dialogue of the death answering each other's thunderous salutations. Post the crackling and roaring of Rebel woolen factories, consumed by flames kindled by the hand of Union retributive justice; past the roaring batteries; past Carlin's braves stripped to the shirt sewing out iron vengeance to traitors, the Second Brigade, our fearless, cool, and sound-judging Col. Joe Thoburn commanding, marched a mile to the very front, forming the left of our force. The position was 150 yards from the Rebel lines drawn up behind a fortification of fence rails, so arranged as to make perfect protection against musketry. Here for one hour and a half in a woods at one and one-half miles range, the two twenty pounder Parrott guns of the enemy were served entirely against us with all possible rapidity and great precision, amid the tremendous explosion of shell, the profuse of rain of case shoe the fall of trees and limbs, amid wounded and dying among all these combinations of horror, with not a gun fired by us and no excitement to cause a wild carelessness of danger, our line never wavered.

The First Brigade (our right) being heavily pressed moved us in retreat perhaps half a mile undetected by the enemy. This maneuver was admirably masked in the woods like our advance before in the morning. A wide hollow whose descending sides were open fields stretched between the First and Second Brigades. Across this we must go. Our batteries open their fiercest fire, from hill to hill leap the ponderous black messengers of destruction, the reverberations of half a hundred guns on both sides, brought into action by the endeavor our batteries make to attract the attention of the enemy's ordnance, make earth tremble, and the air roar while we run the fiery gauntlet to reinforce our right. With unbroken lines we march over with steady tread.

The Rebels occupy a woods in whose edge they have as on their right, an admirably impromptu fence barricaded. Up we go to within 100 yards, lie down, fire and draw the Rebel fire. Men are struck all along the line. Most of the enemy's rifles are empty. Springing to their feet and cheering wildly the men rush forward and over the parapet. Our color bearer plants that banner of holy hopes and hallowed memories right where the sheet of Rebel flame runs crackling along, and mounting up cries, "Come on boys here's where I want you." Gloriously forward we go right into the woods our flag the first our regiment the foremost, the Rebels contending in a hand to hand struggle. Prisoners stream to the rear by the hundreds. Other regiments come to our support.

The character of the conflict is attested by bayoneted Rebel dead. The emblematic rags of treason their battle flags, a few minutes before planted in the dirt. They flee in utter rout and one wild shout of "Victory is ours!" runs along for more than a mile through infantry, artillery, cavalry, through stragglers and wagon trains, till the very wounded in the hospitals cheer again and again. The conduct of the men cannot be too much praising. Often a soldier would press forward so furiously as to be enclosed single-handed among a mass of Rebels, surrendering to be recaptured instantly by his advancing comrades. The whole Rebel force having fled, we camped for the night in the woods among the Rebel dead, too numerous to be buried till the morrow.

Thirty ambulances constantly running with the attendants, cannot collect all the wounded into hospitals, even in the long hours of this summer afternoon and evening. They have from two to three to our one in killed and wounded, and 1,000 able-bodied prisoners, 60 officers, four or five colonels, Brig. Gen. Jones, their commander killed, 1,700 stand of arms, four or five stand of colors and last and best Staunton grace our triumph.

And here let me pause to pay a tribute to the memory of one of our own country's martyrs in our holy cause, our color bearer Corporal Joseph S. Halstead. A braver spirit never bore the banner of beauty and glory forward amid the bursting shells and the leaden rain of death. With comrades falling all around him he went ahead of the bravest, ahead of his brigade. The head and front of that terrific charge into the jaws of death, he rushed forward and planted our flag on the very parapet sheeted with flames from the enemy's rifles. Then over and forward again goes our banner into the hand to hand conflict in which that glorious day's fate was decided. He falls at last, but if there be consolation in such an hour, and to a Christian and one so wholly a soldier as he, he has it to the full a knowledge of his country's glory and his own. In the moment of victory with a broken and dispirited enemy flying before us with the shouts of comrades drunk with the enthusiasm of the hour rendering the very sky, with the valor of our arms attested by the piles of grey-clothed dead and hurt around him with the deep heart-felt admiration of all, attracted by his surpassing daring, with his comrades standing around him in speechless and tearful sympathy, with prisoners streaming or crowding to the rear, colonels and subordinates in traitor regalia, their perjured leader stricken dead by loyal vengeance, he fell at the very acme of our triumph, battling the flag which he had borne so royally to glory and to victory, with blood as noble as ever coursed through patriot veins. Poor Halstead among the brave the choicest spirit of them all, long will his memory be cherished and his valor in that hour of carnage and triumph be the theme of the bivouac talks of his comrades.

Col. Curtis had the pleasure of receiving the sword of a Virginia regiment's colonel, whose surrender he demanded. One of our Marshall county boys had the honor of bringing a Rebel colonel "to time." He, the Marshall county boy, is a young fellow of about 17. Another from Hancock county, I. N. Cullen, (Comp.) had a grey headed Confederate bring a musket to his breast with an order to surrender. He threw the musket aside and twisted it out of the old fellow's hands, then kicking him over the parapet and out of the woods saying, "Old man you're too old for me to bayonet." Another Ohio county boy mounted the parapet in the charge and looking down on the Rebs, says "Lookout Johnnys we're coming down on you like a thousand of brick." That was funny at such a time - it was "in the cool."

In the morning before the fight, Gen. Jones drew his men up and told them that we were going to avenge Fort Pillow, that to surrender would be to die and such stuff for an hour. If anything was wanting to prove the superior humanity of the Union soldiers or the barbarism induced in the South by slavery here it might have been found. First Sergeant Hart Marks, of Company K, accepted the surrender of a Rebel lieutenant and passed on to the front. The Rebel drew a revolver from under his coat and shot him, fortunately slightly, in the back, yet our boys spared him. I know of more such cases, several. Marks shortly afterwards received two wounds, one in the side, and one in the shoulder, the last having passed through a twisted blanket, while charging the woods, the Rebels being behind the trees. Another of our regiment, the eccentric Barney Wyles, pressed ahead too far and was surrounded; he surrendered but his captor shot at him after surrender, with a revolver, cutting his clothes. Our men rushed on him, wrested the revolver from him, and then spared him. All evening could you see Union soldiers feeding wounded Rebels, and food was scarce with us then, having to come all in the shape of forage. In every regiment a number of instances can be given of such treachery as above. Could any contrast be greater?

The day after the fight we came to this place. I wish that some of our copperheads, who have "nigger on the brain" could come here. You have heard that southern people are darkened by their sun. One can hardly tell which are the whites - not that the whites are so black, but that the blacks are so white. Miscegenation is played out. At this place 1,700 rifles were captured and therewith a government armory; cotton factories, commissary stores, railroad buildings and bridges were burnt. A brass field piece was found here all right. Two 100 pound guns were rendered useless, by the trunions' being broken off. But I cannot enumerate one-half the damage, and will leave that to more general correspondents.

I append a list of killed and wounded in this regiment. In addition to this list David Severe, Company G, was killed. I have just heard on picket this morning, that Corporal W.L. Herbert and Frank Metz were captured, both of the same company as Severe.

Returns of killed and wounded and missing of the Twelfth regiment, West Virginia Volunteer Infantry in the battle of Piedmont, Virginia, on the 5th of June, 1864.

COMPANY A.

KILLED - First Sergeant Wm. H. Leach, Privates Lewis Manning, Geo. L. Jones and Reuben G. Boyd.

WOUNDED - Capt. Hagar Tomlinson, left leg flesh wound; Sergeant John G. Jones, fourth finger, left hand off; Corporal George Orum, head slightly; Private Thos. M. Turner left thigh, severely; Private Wm. F. Magers, right hand, slightly.

COMPANY B.

WOUNDED - James B. Manning, left thigh, flesh wound.

COMPANY C.

WOUNDED - Corporal Benjamin Chambers, left arm, flesh wound; Corporal Wilson Chambers, upper part left breast, not dangerous; Wm. H. Ambercrombie, shot through both cheeks, severely; Francis M. Gray, left thigh broken, dangerously; John Dacon, left breast, dangerously; Geo. Barnes, right arm, flesh wound; Isaac N. Fisher, second finger right hand; Harmon Crow, right hand, slight.

COMPANY D.

KILLED - Sergeant A. R. Gilmore, Corporal Joseph S. Halstead, color bearer. Privates, C.W. Hamilton, and Robert J. Anderson.
WOUNDED - Corporal Daniel Maxwell, top of head, severely, but not dangerously; Corporal E. M. Adams, left shoulder slightly; Jno. W. Murray, right arm, severely.

COMPANY E.

KILLED - Corporal Jno. H. Wildman.

WOUNDED - Privates Jno. H. Bennett, right leg, severely; and James Bachus, shot through cheeks, dangerously.

COMPANY F.

WOUNDED - Privates Henry Fortney, left leg, severely; Robert Heiskill, right fore finger; Ezra Wallace, left thigh, severely; Abia Wamsley, left fore arm, severely; A. M. Shroyer, left fore arm severely; and Calvin L. Flemming, right thigh, slightly.

COMPANY G.

KILLED - Private Wm. H. Garrittson.

WOUNDED - Private Alpheus Wyer, abdomen dangerously.

COMPANY H.

KILLED - Corporal Ed. O. Haymond.

WOUNDED - Privates Archer Wood, left elbow, severely, and left side slightly; Jacob Nose, right ankle, severely; Adam Price, shoulder, seriously; James W. Thomas, left thigh, slightly; Frank McVicker, left side head, slightly; Jno. R. Wolfe, side head, slightly.

MISSING - Henry Bircher.

COMPANY I.

KILLED – Joseph R. Lyons, Wm. Beal, Andrew Daugherty, Joseph B. Durbin.

WOUNDED – Wm. H. Moore, right side, severely; Wm. B. Campbell, left shoulder, severely; Jno. R. Baxter, right breast, slightly; S.H. Minor, left thigh, flesh wound.

COMPANY K.

KILLED – A.W. White.

WOUNDED – First Sergeant T.H. Marks, flesh wound in side and shoulder, slight; Joseph Macks, left hand, not dangerous; Wm. H. Hallbritter, right side, (shell) mortally, died; Alex. McConneha, left arm and wrist, flesh wound.

MISSING – Corporal J.E. Fleming.

Total – Eighteen, killed; 41, wounded, and two missing.

In addition to the foregoing letter from Adjutant Caldwell, a few further details and observations regarding the battle may not be unworthy of mention. A member of Company D, in a manuscript history of the company says that "early on the morning of June 5th, we were ordered into line before some of the boys breakfasted. After marching a short distance, we were halted, brought to a front and ordered to load at will. We were then informed by Col. Curtis that the enemy was near and that every man was expected to do his whole duty. The file-closers were ordered to take their positions in the rear of their companies. In looking along the line a determined expression on the countenances of both men and officers was notable, which boded no good to the enemy; and Adjt. Caldwell remarked, "The boys are full of fight today."

This fighting spirit manifested by the regiment is perhaps explainable in part by the belief confirmed by information got from the citizens in coming up the Valley that we came near whipping in the New Market battle, and the consequent resolution, having come so near it then, to whip altogether this battle. And there the fact that our cavalry were driving the enemy's cavalry this morning, doubtless had something to do in working up the fighting mood of the men.

Col. Curtis having been mounted all day on a very fine horse wanted to try him in battle and see if he would be manageable under fire. When the order was given to charge he mounted him and looking over into the Rebel works he discovered that something had occurred to raise great excitement among the enemy. He repeated the command just given by Col. Thoburn to charge and shouted "Go in boys they're whipped." The position of the brigade, from which the charge was made was such that in making it the Twelfth would strike the right flank of the Rebel breast works extending from the pike to the river, at about the center of the regiment, compelling one-half of the men to climb over the breast works. But they went on cheering and shouting as they went, lighting among the Rebels when a hand to hand struggle for victory ensued for a few minutes when the Rebel line gave way, falling back toward the river, which was fordable at that point. The Twelfth followed the Johnnys briskly, capturing prisoners and killing those who refused to surrender.

About midway between the pike and the river, the Forty-fifth Virginia infantry under command of Col. Brown held its position at the breast works until the Twelfth attacked it. Col. Brown was a graduate of West Point; but after being educated by the government was now trying to destroy it. A private by the name of Shinn, of Harrison county, it appears, ordered him to surrender; which he refused to do, because the order came from a private, but the private had the drop on him and was about to shoot him when he, Brown, observed Col. Curtis mounted on his horse which he had jumped over the breast works, moving along the line with his regiment. Brown threw up his hands giving Curtis a sign which the latter understood, exclaiming, "I will surrender to you." The boys were ordered to take him to the rear with the other prisoners, and on his way back he took a very fine revolver from his belt and handing it to the boy said, "Give this to your Colonel with my compliments." The boy was honest and gave it to him and it was still in the possession of Col. Curtis at the time of his death.

After the surrender of Col. Brown and his regiment the rout became general. Col. Halpine, Hunter's chief of staff is further authority for saying that the forces engaged in this battle were about equal, counting of the Rebels about 1,500 militia. Halpine says:

"The fight though not large in numbers was singularly obstinate and fluctuating; the enemy beating back repeated charges of infantry and cavalry under Generals Sullivan and Stahl, and it was quite late in the afternoon after a long and sweltering day of battle, when the movement of the gallant Col. Thoburn's division across the narrow valley and its charge up the hill upon the enemy's right flank decided the contest in our favor. But for the coming on of night and the broken heavily timbered nature of the country, the famous feat of "hagging" that army - so popular with congressional orators and enthusiastic editors - might have been easily accomplished; for a worse whipped or more utterly demoralized crowd of beaten men never fled from any field."

Gen. Jones, the commander of the Rebel force, was shot in the head and fell dead upon the field. This was what caused the apparent excitement among the Rebels, noticed by Col. Curtis, as before mentioned. The Rebel leader was shot just as he was getting his troops ready for a charge. He fell in front of the Twelfth, and it was supposed that some member of it fired the fatal shot. Among the prisoners captured was Capt. Boyd Faulkner, of Gen. Jones' staff. The demoralized and routed Rebels, many of whom ran into and across the river, making their escape in that way, reported on their retreat, so we learned the next day, that the Yankees before the battle had been dosed and mad drunk with whisky and gun powder, so that they fought recklessly and charged upon their works regardless of the slaughter made in their ranks.

A comrade of Sergt. Halstead's company records a striking and touching incident concerning him, showing his devotion to patriotic duty. He was mortally wounded in the battle, falling upon the flag and staining it with his blood just after he had crossed the enemy's breast works. He was carried off the field of battle and cared for by his comrades. He lived until about 8 o'clock that night. Just before he died he sent for Col. Curtis to come and see him. The Colonel came immediately and kneeling by his side and taking his hand, said, "Sergeant, you are badly wounded," "Yes," Halstead replied, "I feel that I have but a few minutes to live, but before I die I desire to know if I have done my duty as a soldier." The Colonel answered, "Yes, you have gallantly sacrificed your life for your country, you could do no more." Halstead said, "Then I am ready to go," and died soon afterward.

This battle of Piedmont was the third engagement for the Twelfth and its first victory. It having been our fortune up to this time to fight our battles in the Shenandoah Valley, in which the Union arms had hitherto met with an almost uniform series of disasters, and which had indeed become a valley of humiliation to us owing to the fact that we had generally out numbered, the Twelfth had hitherto met with defeat. This time the day was ours, and we got to view the battle field instead of having to yield that privilege to the Johnnys; and that the regiment behaved so gallantly as it did in this battle is all the more creditable to it that it did so in spite of the demoralizing tendencies of previous defeats.

Gen. Hunter was a large dark visaged stern man of severe aspect; a man not at all of a sympathetic genial disposition, who was calculated to win the personal attachment of men generally. He was not only severe in appearance but he was really so. On one occasion on the march to Lynchburg, a man was noticed as the army passed by, tied up to a tree by order of Gen. Hunter it was said. It is not remembered that any other general under whom the Twelfth served ever punished a soldier in like manner, by direct personal order. Notwithstanding Hunter's lack of popular qualities, now that he had won a victory, he was at this time popular with the boys; and they were disposed to cheer him when he made his appearance before them. They were thus merely paying a tribute to success.

That night after the battle, we slept in the woods held by the Rebels during the battle, and owing to the great reaction of feeling after the fight - the letting down of the high tension of excitement kept up all the long day of strength, the boys generally slept well, though in some instances the moaning of an enemy wounded beyond relief could be heard nearby. In the morning we marched for Staunton some 11 miles distant, which place we reached that day after an easy day's march. After having gone about four miles on the way toward Staunton, we met an aid who informed us that the enemy had fled from that place, and that we now had communication with Generals Crook and Averell, who had moved from the Kanawha Valley, when cheer after cheer went up all along the line over the announcement.

On nearing Staunton we passed one or more houses where the occupants had hung in front of their homes white cloths as indicative of submission or with a view to securing protection. When we got into the town the women seemed dreadfully frightened; some of them were in the streets wringing their hands and crying as if they were afraid the Yankees might eat them alive. Their conduct was in strong contrast with that of the women of Winchester to whom the Yankee was no new sight; they being not in the least afraid of him, having learned that he was no dread monster. But rather they were, in some cases, haughty, defiant and saucy. If we had stayed awhile in Staunton these women would soon have got over their dreadful alarm, finding that they were as safe as with their own.

We were the first Union soldiers that had ever set foot in Staunton as victors. This early summer of 1864 was marking a distinct advance or progress of the Union cause. Grant was planting himself firmly before Petersburg never to yield his ground. Sherman was moving on toward Atlanta and before long would capture that important point, we of Hunter's command had pushed farther up the Shenandoah Valley, than any Union army had ever done before and we were soon to menace Lynchburg, an almost vital point to the enemy, and a place that had never been seriously threatened before; thus causing the enemy to detach heavily from his force at Richmond to send troops into the Valley and to thereby prepare the way for Sheridan to gain, in the fall of the year, his important and telling victories, and thus make his great military reputation.

After arriving at Staunton in the evening the Twelfth went into camp on a hill east of the town. That night the prisoners captured at Piedmont were confined in the stockade which the Rebels had used for the confining of our men. The next day, the 7th, our regiment was sent on the march for what reason it is not known on the road leading to Beverly, W. Va. When about six miles on the way while we were stopping for a rest, orders came to us to return and we marched back to Staunton. While remaining at this place, the large number of prisoners we held, and our surplus wagons, with some of our not too severely wounded in them, were sent in charge of Major Samuel Adams, a quartermaster, from here to Webster on the Baltimore and Ohio railroad guarded by the Twenty-eighth Ohio infantry, whose time had expired.

On the morning of the 9th, Col. Curtis received orders from Gen. Hunter to proceed with his regiment to a certain point on the railroad leading to Richmond to burn the bridges, tear up the track, and make the road as difficult to repair as possible. In performing this work, the ties and rails were so piled up that when the ties were set on fire, the rails would be so bent it would require much labor to make them serviceable again. The men engaged heartily in this work.

On the morning of the 10th we set out on the march to Lexington our division taking one road and Crook's division, it having joined us two days before, another road to the right of ours. At Staunton large quantities of the enemy's tobacco had been by authority thrown into the streets. Nearly every man had picked up more than he could conveniently carry and for a day the army might have been tracked by the tobacco plugs strewn along the road. When seven miles on the road toward Lexington a courier came to us bearing the news that a large wagon train was coming with coffee and sugar for us, and that Grant had driven Lee inside of his entrenchments around Richmond. The boys, of course, cheered this news heartily. We camped this night at a place called Midway, 18 miles from Staunton, and the same distance from Lexington which place is situated on the north branch of the James river, and is the seat of the Virginia Military Institute. When near this latter town we were rejoined by Crook's force. Before we reached the town the Rebels burned the bridge leading across the river to it. After some skirmishing and a few shells thrown from our side the Johnnys who were still in the town left. But we did not enter the town this day.

The next morning we crossed over the river on a bridge constructed by the Pioneer corps and camped near the town. The Institute, where about two hundred cadets were attending at the time, Governor Letcher's house and some houses belonging to Rebel officers were burned at this place by order of Gen. Hunter. There were also some iron works burned here. Stonewall Jackson's grave is here at the head of which there was a pole, bearing a flag when we entered the town; but the flag and pole somehow soon thereafter disappeared. We remained at Lexington two days and during this time the supply train referred to with rations and quartermaster's stores came up.

At 5 o'clock on the morning of the 14th, we marched taking the road leading to Buchanan in Botetourt county on the south branch of the James river. We passed within two and a half miles of the Natural Bridge over Cedar Creek and arrived at Buchanan a little after dark. The Rebels had burned the bridge over the river before leaving, but the pioneers soon made another in its stead, on which we crossed. According to an account by W. W. Foreman, of Company D, a spy, was taken this day, and after a court martial was shot the following morning.

This past day we had had a long hard march, considering the heat of the weather. Pertinent to this matter of hard marching this anecdote which should have been told sooner, is given. It will be remembered that when Hunter set out on this expedition the men were required to carry from 80 to 100 rounds of ammunition per man. Grant in assuming command of the armies of the United States ordered the heavy artillerymen to be armed as infantry and sent into the field. Some of these soldiers were sent to Hunter. They were given to straggling considerably, not being used to marching, and besides many of them wore tightly fitting boots, which they had worn while in the fortifications, making the matter worse. One day one of these soldiers who was straggling behind as we marched somewhere in the Valley, was accosted by an officer, doubtless with the intent to reprimand him, and asked to what command he belonged. The soldier in allusion to the heavy amount of ammunition he was carrying, answered with a big oath, "I belong to Gen. Hunter's ammunition train."

The next day, the 15th, we resumed our march; but Crook's division taking the advance we did not get started till late in the day and marched only 11 miles this day, camping for the night at the Peaks of Otter. Our route today led over the Blue Ridge on which we saw a dead man in citizen's dress by the roadside, who had been shot by our men. It appeared that he with others had been felling trees across the road in front of us, and had been killed in the act.

Early the next morning we were en route, and a march of nine miles brought us to Liberty, a pretty little town on the Virginia and Tennessee railroad. A great many wounded Rebels from Lee's army were in the hospital here. After doing considerable damage to the railroad, and burning the depot here, we passed on five miles farther, on the road toward Lynchburg and camped. The next day at an early hour we pushed on toward this city. We were now in an apparently fine country. It was this day or the afternoon of the day before, that a fine residence near the road was burned by order of Gen. Hunter, it appearing that our troops had been fired on from it. We passed through the town of New London. About 4 o'clock P.M., when some three miles from Lynchburg, Gen. Crook whose division was in advance, engaged the enemy at an outpost driving him from his entrenchments there to his inner line of defense and captured about 70 prisoners and two or three pieces of artillery. We camped upon the field.

The next morning, the 18th, we moved forward, our skirmishers driving the Rebel skirmishers, until we could see the enemy's fortifications within two miles of the city. Our division, or at least the part of it to which the Twelfth belonged, was on or across the Bedford road. There was no considerable fighting except skirmishing and shelling until about 2 p.m., when heavy firing was heard on our left, Hunter having attacked there in force. There was no fighting on our part of the line just at this time, but soon thereafter, the Rebels being observed to be getting ready to sally out of the works to charge us on the Bedford road, we here, at a brigade were massed on the left of the road in five close lines in the edge of some woods, with clean open ground between us and the Rebel works, some 500 yards distant. Soon the Rebels were ready and charged us; and at the same time they began shelling us. The most of the shells, however, crashed through the tree tops above our heads doing little harm. We opened fire on the charging column before it had come far and kept up a steady and continuous roaring of musketry until the Rebels broke and "skedadled" back to the works, which they did before they got half way to our lines. We repulsed them easily. Some soldiers, who were in the rear during this charge said afterward that they had never before heard so heavy musketry and that they thought from the tremendous roar kept up that we must be getting slaughtered. Hunter failed to capture any of the enemy's works this day, but the Rebels thought best to keep on the defensive. Our loss was about 200 hundred and it was thought the enemy's was heavy.

When the Rebels charged us on the Bedford road a number of men in the front line about opposite the center of the Twelfth, broke making quite a gap a dozen or so of them trying to get behind one tree. A number of the Twelfth boys ran forward to the gap and fired on the advancing Rebels. And here at this point it is desired to pay a tribute to an enlisted man, Sergt. Thomas J. Ormsby, of Company C. The soldier in the ranks has not been without praise but it is doubtful if he has had his full due relatively with the officers. Ormsby ran the gap going perhaps 30 feet in advance of the front line trusting that our own men would not shoot him. He was the one man, it is believed, who thus went forward of the 2,000 or more massed men. He wanted to watch the progress and outcome of the fight. When the Johnnys began to break he turned toward our ranks and said laughing, "They're running boys."

This same sergeant when a battle seemed imminent was in the habit of talking to the men of his company in an encouraging way, telling them to not fear, that we would whip them and all that. He was no bully nor braggart, but simply wanted to inspire the men with his own confidence. A soldier in another company called this peculiar habit of Sergt. Ormsby "preaching." One day when a fight was threatened this soldier called the attention of a comrade to the sergeant's conduct saying, "Did you ever notice Ormsby when there is likely to be a fight? Listen to him preaching to Company C. He's the d-----dst man ever I saw." Sergt. Ormsby seemed almost devoid of fear. The soldier who drew attention to the sergeant, was afterward killed in the Valley of Virginia under Sheridan.

After the repulse of the Rebel charge we were moved from the woods and reformed into line. There was no more fighting except skirmishing. The spirit of the men was still good, as was evidenced by the way they were disposed to expose themselves to the Rebel fire. Hunter, however, was just one day too late attacking Lynchburg, for the very day he arrived before the city, Early's corps arrived in it, and all night thereafter the Rebels were beating drums and cheering over more reinforcements. It seems almost certain that if Hunter had been only one day earlier in his attempt against Lynchburg, the place would have fallen. But after all the result as it was may have been best, for it led to Sheridan's opportunity to establish his great ability as a commander, to his signal victories in the Valley as before written, and thereby, very probably to the hastening of the downfall of the rebellion.

Hunter having satisfied himself that Early's corps had come to the defense of the city started just after dark on the retreat. We marched all night stopping at Otter creek in the morning, the 19th, to rest and prepare something to eat, having marched 18 miles. After breakfast we marched on, passing through Liberty and camped three miles beyond along the line of the Virginia and Tennessee railroad. Now that Hunter had failed in his attempt against Lynchburg he was compelled to abandon his Shenandoah line on account of Early's having the shorter route to it, and retreat to Charleston on the Kanawha by way of Buford's Gap, following the railroad from Liberty to Salem, at which point 36 miles from Liberty the railroad was left.

We left camp near Liberty about 2 o'clock in the morning the 20th, passing through Thoxton's and Buford's stations, at which places some subsistence was obtained and going on after a march of 17 miles we stopped in Buford's Gap in the Blue Ridge to eat of our scant supply and rest. A little after dark we resumed our march. Shortly after the infantry started, our cavalry staying behind for a time captured about a hundred of the Rebel cavalry, in the pass, who had been harassing our rear. We marched all night reaching Salem in the morning. Here we halted to meal, breakfast and dinner. While here the enemy attacked our rear. The attack not very serious, was repulsed. The wagon train and some artillery were sent ahead, some cavalry having gone ahead a while before.

About three miles from Salem the rear of the train which from oversight or want of precaution had little or no guard with it, was attacked by McCausland, capturing or killing a number of horses, cutting down the carriages of five guns so that they had to be abandoned and getting off with three guns. The infantry were hurried up from the rear and he was driven off with a loss to us of thirty men. After this affair with the Rebels we marched on ten miles farther, passing over a mountain and camped for the night of the 21st, to have our first good rest. We had marched in the last twenty four hours 26 miles, and in all for the last three days 70 miles doing most of the marching after night though the nights were short, with little or no sleep. The men were so worn out for want of sleep that when a short stop was made for a rest, they would fall asleep and were hard to waken up. Though our march had thus been rapid the bridges, stations, and water tanks along the railroad as far as we followed it were pretty thoroughly destroyed by our men.

Near the summit of the mountain over which we had just passed on the road in our rear up which the Rebels were expected to come our men had placed in position two pieces of artillery to give them a salute if they should venture up the mountain. In the night cavalry were heard coming and when they were near enough the artillery was opened on them, sending them down the mountain flying. The Rebels followed us no farther.

We remained in camp at the foot of the mountain till 1 o'clock p.m., when the 22nd, we resumed our march. We passed through New Castle, over Middle Mountain, Peter's Mountain, through Sweet Springer, over Allegheny Mountain, through White Sulphur Springs where the men being so hard pressed for something to eat pulled up growing potatoes and ate the old tubers; crossed the Greenbriar River, passed through Lewisburg, over Little Sewell Mountain, and over Big Sewell Mountain, camping at its foot. It was on coming up one of these mountains that many dead horses were seen. So many were they, it seemed that, for a mile or two, there was one to every rod or two. They had given out from want of feed and were shot to keep the enemy from getting them.

It was now the 27th, the 9th day since we had left Lynchburg. We had marched from that time 168 miles. For the last three or four days we had had in the way of subsistence little or nothing except coffee, sugar and very poor beef, of which latter the men became very sick, getting it only partially cooked by roasting it over a fire. We had got to that extremity that we were glad to get bran or raw corn to eat. It was said that an officer in one case at least, offered a dollar for a pint of corn. Here at the west base of Big Sewell, however, the train of supplies which had been promised us for a day or two, finally came up to the great gladness of all. And the race for rations was now at an end.

The next day we pushed on and passed the Hawks nest on the New River, the 29th, an almost perpendicular precipice of rocks, eleven hundred feet high, overlooking the river, crossed the Gauley River the same day at its junction with the former river, the two streams forming the Kanawha river, and camped. We remained here two days, being now within easy reach of supplies, and were mustered for pay while here. July 2nd, we marched to Camp Piatt on the Kanawha ten miles from Charleston, having marched 227 miles from Lynchburg.

Col. Strother, Gen. Hunter's chief of staff in his report of the expedition, gives these results: "About 50 miles of the Virginia Central railroad had been effectually destroyed. The Virginia and Tennessee road had been destroyed to some extent for the same distance, an incredible amount of public property had been buried, including canal boats and railroad trains loaded with ordinance and commissary stores; numerous extensive iron works, manufactories of saltpetre, musket stocks, shoes, saddles and artillery harness, woolen cloths and grain mills. About three hundred muskets and twenty pieces of cannon with quantities of shells and gun powder fell into our hands, while immense quantities of provisions, cattle and horses were captured and used by the army." Col. Strother claims also the infliction of a loss of 2,000 killed and wounded on the enemy, besides the taking of 2,000 prisoners with a total loss of only 1,500 men and eight guns in Hunter's command (see Pond). Hunter, however, lost a great many horses, mules and wagons by reason of lack of subsistence for the horses and mules.

It appears that a far greater result was achieved by Hunter's expedition than any, or it may be, of all those given by Col. Strother, for Jefferson Davis explained to the people of Georgia after the fall of Atlanta that, "an audacious movement of the enemy up to the very walk of Lynchburg had rendered it necessary that the government should send a formidable body of troops to cover that vital point, which had otherwise been intended for the relief of Atlanta."

Hunter regarded the achievements of his command as valuable. He sent a dispatch from Loup creek near Gauley Bridge, June 28th, saying that, "the expedition had been extremely successful inflicting great injury upon the enemy." He added, "The command is in excellent heart and health." Gen. Hunter, who had kept up during the raid a rather luxuriant table, comparatively sumptuously supplied, was perhaps himself in pretty good health and heart; but that his troops in general - who had suffered much deprivation and hardship, having to live mainly on meat for some days inferior no doubt to good mule meat, and having been so exhaustively marched that a few days before we reached rations he ordered those of the command, who could not keep up to keep in squads so that they could defend themselves from bushwhackers - would agree with this opinion is hardly to be believed.

July 3rd, the Twelfth with a considerably portion of Hunter's infantry besides, took steamboats at Camp Piatt on the Kanawha for Parkersburg on the Ohio, to take cars of the Baltimore and Ohio railroad back to the Shenandoah Valley again. We passed down the Kanawha and up the Ohio getting along pretty well till we came to Buffington's Island where we had to go ashore and foot it a short distance on account of the boats not being able to pass the schools there with her load of passengers. After passing the shoals we boarded the boats again. From this point we got along pretty well till we got to Blannerhassett's Island, about six miles from Parkersburg, where we had to go ashore again on account of low water, and march to that city, arriving at a village opposite the 4th, having marched up on the Ohio side of the river and camped for the night.

We crossed the river the next day and took the cars for the Valley. It was five days later when we reached the village of Hedgesville on the western skirt of the Valley, having been detained on the way on account of the Rebels having burnt several bridges east of Cumberland, Md., which had to be rebuilt before the trains could go on. At this village we began to hear reports and rumors as to the nearness and strength of the enemy; but notwithstanding whatever the commanding general may have known the troops generally seemed to have no definite information as to the strength of the Rebels near us.

Chapter Nine

The next day, the 11th, after our arrival at Hedgesville our brigade which was now united, marched to Martinsburg having had to march from near Back Creek, a distance of 15 miles, on account of the Rebels having torn up the railroad east of that creek. We had now got back to the town from which we had started on April 29th, under Sigel up the Valley. Just before we reached the town our cavalry had driven out of it a small force of Rebel cavalry. According to Col. Curtis when we moved from here under Sigel, the Twelfth had 800 men present, while now we were reduced to 250 men present for duty. The five-sixths of this reduction mainly of sick, it is safe to say was chargeable to the Lynchburg raid principally, showing how severe it was on the men, and hardly sustaining Hunter's dispatch from near Gauley Bridge, that the men were in excellent health. But though the command suffered great hardships they could not say that they were not forewarned by Gen. Hunter, that that was what they might expect and so they could not say that they were deceived in that particular.

As before said we were once more in the Valley, once a fair land of peace and plenty, but now a desolate land battle-scarred and laid waste by the conflicts of contending armies; and fated to be the theatre of further bloody battles; when in truth it might be said, "The earth is covered thick with other clay, Which her own clay shall cover, heaped and pent."

The day our brigade arrived at Martinsburg the Rebel Gen. Early, who had marched from the relief of Lynchburg into the Valley and whose troops had burned bridges and torn up the track of the

Baltimore and Ohio road, east and west of Martinsburg, appeared before Washington having gone there to attempt its capture. But he, like Hunter at Lynchburg, was just one day late, the Sixth Corps having come to the relief of the capitol that same day, just as Early had come to the relief of Lynchburg the very day Hunter appeared before that city. The next day the 12th, after some sharp fighting with the Sixth Corps, Early, being satisfied by prisoners captured that Grant had sent reinforcements to Washington, withdrew from before the city. It is possible that Early's attempt to capture Washington might have been successful, had not Gen. Sigel wisely withdrawn his troops from Martinsburg on learning that Early was coming and thus frustrating his (Early's) plan to capture them, and marched to Harper's Ferry gathering up some troops on the way, and occupied Maryland Heights, just where according to Pond he was not wanted by Early, he having been detained there for a day in a vain attempt to dislodge Sigel intending to make that his (Early's) base in his movement against the capitol, and had he not met with further detention by Lew Wallace's stubborn fighting at Monocacy Junction.

The Twelfth remained two days at Martinsburg when the 13th, we marched taking the road leading to Harper's Ferry, reaching there the next day crossing into Maryland, passing down the Potomac and camped about two miles from Harper's Ferry near Knoxville. There were now here about 9,000 troops mainly of Hunter's troops. The 15th, the force here waded the river into Virginia and took the road leading toward Leesburg about 18 miles distant. When about nine miles on the way, we turned to the right and marched to Hillsborough in Londown county and camped for the night. Early's foiled army was now on the way from Washington to the Valley followed by Gen. Wright of the Sixth Corps with a force of about 15,000 men.

The same night that we were lying at Hillsborough, Early was at Leesburg about a half day's march having lain there all the day before; but the next morning the 16th, he moved through Hamilton and to Snicker's and Ashby's Gaps. Hunter's troops might easily have been thrown across Early's route ahead of him, and would have been no doubt, had the follower's strength been great enough, but his force being too small to risk an attack, it was evidently deemed prudent to not make it. However, Tibbets's small brigade of Duffie's cavalry attacked Early's trains and captured one hundred and seventeen mules and horses, eighty-two wagons and 40 or 50 prisoners getting off with thirty-seven loaded wagons and burning over forty others. This attack on the Rebel trains was made near Purcellville as they moved through that town.

On this same day, the 16th, our division under the immediate command of Gen. Crook marched to Purcellville, five miles from Hillsborough, starting at 4 P. M. At the former town it was reported that Wright's command was only three miles east of there. We stayed all the next day at Purcellville; but the following day, the 18th, we marched taking the road leading to Snicker's Gap. On the way while stopping to rest the Sixth Corps came up. Our division now under Col. Thoburn moved through the gap and passed down the Shenandoah River about two miles below Snicker's Ferry, he, having been ordered by Gen. Crook about 2 o'clock to move his division with the Third Brigade of the Second to Island Ford, cross there and move up to Snicker's Ford to hold it for the army to cross.

Thoburn proceeded to execute this order and thus brought on the engagement of Snicker's Ferry. When Thoburn's men attempted to cross, the enemy having a picket behind bushes, opened a brisk fire; but Wells' brigade finding a good fording some distance below pushed across and captured the Rebel picket of 15 men, and the captain commanding them. Thoburn's force now all moved over, when he, learning from the prisoners that there was a large force of the enemy near, sent word back to Crook to that effect, who now ordered Thoburn to not attempt to march to the ferry, but to await a reinforcement of a brigade from the Sixth Corps.

Before long the enemy attacked in strong force. About this time the Sixth Corps came up, halting within close cannon shot upon the Blue Ridge, which here closely skirts the river, but no reinforcements came to us, Breckinridge attacked on the left and centre and Rhodes on the right. Here on the extreme right was a lot of dismounted cavalry from various regiments under command of Lieut. Col. Young of the Fourth Pennsylvania, who soon gave way retreating across the river. Thoburn quickly changed front to meet the flank attack of Rhodes but after hard fighting, our right was forced across the river some getting drowned. Our left held its ground until ordered back, recrossing the river in fairly good order, considering circumstances. The fight was short but severe. Our loss was 65 killed, 301 wounded and 56 missing. Total, 422. Among the field officers our loss was heavy. Col. Dan. Frost of the Eleventh, Lieut. Col. Thomas Morris of the Fifteenth West Virginia Infantry and the Colonel of an Ohio regiment were killed, and Col. Washburn of the One Hundred and Sixteenth Ohio Infantry was thought to be mortally wounded, a musket ball having entered his left eye and come out of his right ear; but he recovered. The loss of the Rebels must also have been severe, and the more so since in forcing our men back they brought themselves within range of the Sixth Corps batteries, on the opposite side of the river, which opened and kept up a hot fire upon them for a little while doing good execution, and thus aiding also our men in recrossing the river. The next day the Rebels were busy burying their dead and removing their wounded, and two days later when the enemy had gone the citizens, living near the battle field told us that their loss was heavy.

At the time of this engagement, Thoburn's men regarded the failure of the Sixth Corps to come to their support as resulting from an indifference on the part of that corps, as to how Thoburn's men came out in the fight. However, the true explanation of the matter may be found in this dispatch from Wright Halleck: "The attempt at crossing was resisted in strong force; and believing it better to turn his position I designed doing so by way of Keyes Gap thus effecting a junction with some of the forces of Gen. Hunter lower down the Valley."

The Twelfth was the last regiment to retreat across the river. According to the account of Col. Curtis, Col. Thoburn having confidence in the pluck and staying qualities of our boys, ordered him to form his regiment in line in front of the ford, and hold it at all hazard till further orders. The position was an excellent one being in a road parallel with the river, the bank of which road made a good breast work. The regiment held its position until ordered to recross the river doing so in the dusk of the evening, the rest of the force having crossed shortly before, one of the noticeable features of the fight here, observed by our men, was a peculiar way the Rebel skirmishers had. They would advance fire and then turn their backs toward us to load, those seen obliquely to our left wore a blue-grey uniform, which at a distance looked blue. This fact together with their having their backs toward us when loading, caused doubt as to whether they were our men or the enemy, and some of the officers gave orders to fire upon them while others, saying they were our men gave orders to not fire; but while it was generally seen which way these skirmishers were firing there was no longer any doubt, and the men were told to let them have it. Here and on our left generally, the Rebels were driven back.

One of the specially sad and lamentable results of this fight was, that some members of the Fourth West Virginia Infantry whose time had expired were killed in it. They had been waiting before starting home until a sufficiently strong force should be going to the rear to make it safe for them to start. In the meantime this Snicker's Ferry fight came on, and the Fourth boys being plucky fellows generally, these discharged men said that they would not stand back while their comrades were going into a fight, and so some of the poor fellows were killed with discharges in their pockets.

The next day after the battle our forces lay on one side of the river and the enemy on the other, our sharpshooters getting a shot at them once in awhile. One division of the Nineteenth Corps came up this day. Generals Averell and Duval were now moving up the Valley toward Winchester from Martinsburg with 2,700 troops, infantry, cavalry, and artillery, getting in Early's rear. In the morning the 20th, his force was gone from our front. Averell's movement no doubt, compelling this withdrawal, and during the day we crossed the river and camped in some woods. Before the troops here crossed the river, however, we heard considerable commanding away to the west of us. There was much conjecture among the rank and file as to what that meant. This proved to be a battle between Averell's force, Duval commanding the infantry and a superior Rebel force, the fight being near Winchester, in which Averell won a complete victory.

That evening the 6th, and the Nineteenth Corps recrossed the river and took the road leading through Leesburg to Washington, Wright thinking it seems that Early was on his way to Richmond and expecting it appears, that he Wright would be returned to Grant at Petersburg. But he had made a mistake in his inferences, for his troops did not go farther than Georgetown, D.C., and it will presently be seen that Early was not yet ready to leave the Valley.

The 22nd, we marched passing through Berryville to Winchester, and camped about two miles beyond the town on the Strasburg road. The purpose of Gen. Crook in this movement was to watch Early's movements and if possible ascertain his purposes. He did not have to wait long to find them out. Early did not retreat farther up the Valley than Strasburg, and learning there that Wright's force had returned to Washington, he concluded to attack Crook, which he did, and this brought on the battle of Kearnstown. The next day after our arrival at our camp near Winchester, the enemy drove in our pickets, but after some skirmishing the Rebels were driven back. The day after this affair with the pickets, Early attacked Crook with his whole force at Kearnstown. The Twelfth had been formed in line that Sunday forenoon, July 24th, for inspection, at least the men had received orders to get ready for that purpose; but suddenly without there being any inspection the men were ordered to load at will.

A half hour later perhaps our brigade was marched toward Kearnstown. Before starting we had heard for some time considerable skirmishing in that direction, and it was still kept up. It was the season then for ripe blackberries, and as we moved toward the firing we passed through fields where these berries were plentiful. Some of the men could not forego stepping a little out of ranks and picking a few of them. Col. Ely of the Eighteenth Connecticut, commanding the brigade, noticing the men commanded them: "Keep in ranks men, it is no time to be gathering black berries." In truth it was not the most propitious time imaginable for that purpose. It seems that anything said or done at all noticeable in a critical and perilous time is apt to make a strong impression and be remembered, and the boys for some days afterward were in the habit of repeating the Colonel's command, "Keep in ranks men, it is no-o-o time to be gathering blackberries."

Our brigade had been moving forward on the right of the pike. Finally we took a position and made a breast work of rails - a thing of little use in an open country like that; for a breast work there can easily be taken in flank. It was not long until we were moved from this position and placed in line, still on the right of the pike with the other troops. About 1 or 2 o'clock in the afternoon Early attacked with his whole force. There are no data at hand showing Crooks strength; but it was much inferior to that of Early, the latter having force enough to fight us in front and to flank us on both flanks. In fact, it was his expectation to cut off our retreat and capture our whole force. Our left was struck in flank and doubled up and at the same time the centre being hard pressed, the left and centre gave way. Crook seeing this and knowing that he had not force enough to fight Early's whole army ordered a retreat at about 3 o'clock, an hour or so after the battle began. The Twelfth changed front once during the battle but did not otherwise give ground until ordered off the field. Col. Ely giving the order, saying to Col. Curtis, "Move your men off the field by the right flank."

The Rebels followed us sharply for six or eight miles. After passing Winchester our brigade, halted at times and skirmished with the enemy. Just as night was coming on while we were in a piece of woods, a squadron of Rebel cavalry came in view riding within close range. They were going in an opposite direction from us at a distance to our right. When near us they halted. It being near night it was hard to tell whether they were friends or enemies; but many of the men of the brigade especially of the Second Maryland regiment began firing on them, being satisfied that they were Rebels; and they retreated toward Winchester, their horses prancing under the fire. Our brigade became separated from the rest of the troops and for some reason instead of following the direction of the pike toward Martinsburg, as did the other troops, we turned toward North Mountain. Part of the way toward the mountain we passed through rough stony woods, and it being a pitch dark night - so very dark that you could scarcely see the man next you - the men stumbled considerably, falling sometimes while in the woods.

By reason of the darkness we had to get a guide to pilot us; and for the same reason Col. Thoburn and Col. Curtis got separated from the command, for some days we did not know what had become of them. We camped at the village of Gerardtown at the base of the mountain. The main portion of Crook's infantry camped at Bunker Hill. Before daylight the next morning we marched for Martinsburg, there meeting the rest of our force. Our brigade was detailed as a guard for our wagon trains. Before leaving with the trains, however, cannonading had begun south of the town. Crook was holding the enemy back till he could get his trains away. We arrived opposite Williamsport, Washington County Maryland, in the evening and camped for the night.

In the morning the 26th, we crossed over to the town and marched first to Sharpsburg, then to Sandy Hook and next, passing through Harper's Ferry to Halltown arriving there the 28th. On this day Cols. Thoburn and Curtis returned to their commands. The boys were all heartily glad to see them, giving them rousing cheers on their return, and they no doubt were no less glad to be once more with their commands. Col. Curtis says that when he and Thoburn became separated from their commands they were surrounded by a squad of Rebel cavalry, who fired upon them, compelling them to abandon their horses and take refuge in a corn field. The next morning they found the entire Rebel force between them and their commands. They made their way to North Mountain. By traveling at nights and sleeping in the day time, living on black berries part of the time they, through the assistance of the colored people and loyal whites at last returned to their commands to report for duty, being four days absent without leave.

Recurring to the battle of Kearnstown, Crook went to that town as before mentioned to learn of Early's movements; but it is believed that a battle there could have been avoided with little or no loss to us; and in view of the fact that Crook knew that he did not have force enough to meet Early's entire army, he should have declined an engagement. The sacrifice of 1,200 men. Col. Mulligan commanding a division was killed in this engagement. Crook's estimated loss was too great simply to get information as to the enemy's purposes, when the knowledge might have been got otherwise. The loss of the enemy has been supposed to be light.

The loss of the Twelfth in this battle was inconsiderable mainly in prisoners taken. It was perhaps twenty-five or thirty in all. At the beginning of the fight Lieut. Col. Brown was ordered on to the skirmish line with two companies. It was from these companies principally that the prisoners were taken. When our main force retreated, these skirmishers received no order to fall back, the order not reaching them, and they being left behind were surrounded and a part of them, mostly from Company K, were captured. Lieut. Col. Brown, then major, and Lieut. John A. Briggs, of Company K, were among the prisoners. These two officers, however, managed to escape at Harrisonburg from their guard while the latter were asleep and made their way from there to North Mountain reaching there about daylight one morning a few hours after their escape. As day was breaking they hid in woods. It was not long till the Rebel cavalry were seen coming in search for them. They came so near that they could be heard talking. Fortunately, however, the fugitives were not discovered. The particulars of how Lieut. Col. Brown and Lieut. Briggs made their way to our lines, are not known, but somehow they succeeded in getting safe through to New Creek on the Baltimore and Ohio railroad. Lieut. Col. Brown says that after his capture he with some other officers was brought before Gen. Breckinridge, who, he says was a fine looking man, thus concurring with the popular opinion. The general questioned the prisoners, as to the strength of Crook's command and so forth, but they gave him no satisfaction in the way of information.

Col. Curtis tells of an incident of Crook's retreat, about a colored boy, his servant. When the retreat began the boy had charge of a mule having all the Colonel's cooking utensils and other camp equipage strapped upon him. After awhile the regiment came to a fence, the men climbed over, the Colonel jumped his horse over and the boy tried to get the mule to jump, but he refused. The case was urgent, as the bullets were flying all around us; but the boy held on to the mule trying to get him to jump. The mule was still stubborn. In the midst of the boy's efforts a ball struck him in the neck, bleeding him freely. This caused him to free his mind. He said: "Well a d----d mule and a nigger are two of the most contrary things in the world." It is not known whether the boy's vigorous expletive had any effect upon the mule, but about this time he jumped the fence and the boy brought off the mule and traps in safety.

Richard W. Mahan of Company K, who was captured in this engagement tells the story of his capture and prison trials as follows:

As soon as our regiment was brought up my company (K) and Company E, were filed out without halting the regiment, and deployed on the right as skirmishers. This was the last I saw of the regiment for ten months. I have always thought that we were sacrificed in this engagement - I mean the skirmishers. We commenced to fall back after it was too late, very slowly too, firing in retreat. Our army by this time had fallen back out of sight; and the Forty-fourth Virginia (Rebel) cavalry was close on our right and in our rear. So after a short, but brisk home stretch we surrendered in the open field and hot sun, with no apple tree near to make the terms under. Seventeen of our regiment, including two officers Maj. R.H. Brown and Lieut. John A. Briggs eight of them being of my company were captured here.

We were guarded the first night in an old school house. The next morning we were taken to Winchester and kept there about two days with nothing to eat until the third day when they started us off on the march for Staunton, one hundred and eighty miles away, We were there loaded into cars that were already loaded with pig metal and taken to Lynchburg, and kept there ten days. Thence to Danville, Va., arriving there on the 11th day of August, having traveled in closed box cars that had been used in shipping charcoal and tar and when we were taken from the cars into the light we were so black that we could scarcely recognize each other.

From the depot here we were marched to the prison. Halting in front while the doors were thrown open, five dead soldiers were brought out in plain pine boxes. This incident opened our eyes as we thought there must be something terrible inside for death to make such a detail at one time from one of six buildings, containing about 600 each. We marched in and up to the garret where there were already about fifty prisoners quartered, who had no clothing on except a blouse tied around the waist, it being so excessively hot from the heat of the tin roof which came down to the floor on each side. The roof was so hot that you could not bear your hand on it while the sun shone.

We were kept here until the 17th of February, 1865, suffering the usual ills of prison life. And the great trouble with most of us was short rations, which was a half pound of corn bread each morning at 9 o'clock. The Johnnys proposed that if we would go out and work on their fortifications, they would give us extra rations. A few accepted this proposition as workers were called for each morning for two or three days; but they were punished severely by the other prisoners for their disloyalty, and soon no one would respond when the call would be made. "All right," said Johnny, "You all will come at the next call." So they reduced our rations to make us yield.

In the meantime an organization was proposed and effected among the prisoners of one hundred members to respond to the next call with the intention of capturing the guard at the fortifications and making their escape. This was in the month of October, and we thought that in the event we should escape we could subsist on the mast of the woods of the mountains on our way north. All arrangements were completed, and the signal word (which was Corn-Dodger) for combined action in making the attempt at escape was to be given at 4 p.m., which was the hour they would form us into two ranks for a ration of soup; then take us back to prison. So in the morning when the call was made we responded liberally, but unfortunately for myself and, twenty-four others the door was closed on the rear of the column and no more than seventy-five would be received. Being greatly disappointed those of us left in prison went back up stairs and gazed longingly across the Dan River at our boys working on the fortifications. As 4 p.m. approached we watched through the garret window in breathless silence to see the boys execute the plan. Sure enough the signal is given, the guards are clinched and their guns taken from them, and every prisoner there takes to his heels due north. The Johnnys fired an alarm from the fort, and their reserve citizens and dogs were soon in pursuit. They were nearly all captured in the course of a month or six weeks and brought back. Some who got near the Union lines and became careless were picked up.

The mortality among the prisoners here during the time mentioned was 1,300 of the 3,500 in all. We were taken from here to Libby prison and kept there three days and exchanged on the 22nd of February - a day for us to celebrate for two reasons.

The next day the 29th, after our arrival at Halltown, the Sixth Corps and one division of the Nineteenth Corps arrived there from Washington having been ordered back to the lower Valley on account of Early's continued presence there. The authorities, it seemed, had now become convinced that he had no notion of vacating that place just then. And a longer army was now concentrating at Halltown for the purpose of attacking him. The Twelfth heretofore had belonged to a small army; and for the past three months had had very hard service generally, and during that time the regiment had been in five engagements; but now for the first time we were to be placed in a comparatively large army, and from this time to the end of the war we belonged to a large one. We found our service much easier from this time on with a large force, than it had been for past three months with a small force. Gen. Hunter was in command of the army concentrating at Halltown.

On the 13th, there being a force of the enemy at this time, of uncertain strength operating in Pennsylvania and there being a belief or apprehension that Early's whole army was north of the Potomac with a general condition of uncertainty as to the situation of affairs with respect to his force and operations, the troops at Halltown soon after receiving the orders, crossed the Potomac at Harper's Ferry on a pontoon bridge and started on what Greeley calls a wild goose chase into Maryland, to head off a possible attempt by the enemy against Washington. The whole force started in the direction of Frederick City, but after marching some distance, our division turned to the left, the Sixth Corps and Nineteenth going toward that city. We marched about, in a halting uncertain way for three or four days when the Rebel invasion proving to be nothing but a cavalry raid, we marched to rejoin our other troops at the Monocacy, near Frederick City. Hunter's headquarters were in this city.

The Twelfth remained in camp at the Monocacy two days the 4th and 5th of August. On this latter day, Gen. Grant, who had left his army before Petersburg, on account of the unsatisfactory military condition in the Valley, arrived at Frederick City to have a conference with Gen. Hunter and to give him orders as to future operations. He gave him an order dated "Headquarters in the field, Monocacy Bridge, Md., August 5, 1864," which embraced a direction to concentrate his forces at Harper's Ferry just where Hunter had been concentrating his army a week before. The order stated with other instructions, "Bear in mind the object is to drive the enemy south." Grant informed Hunter that a large force of cavalry from the Army of the Potomac was on the way to join him.

Hunter began at once to carry out the order. That same night part of Crook's command crossed the Potomac and occupied the old lines at Halltown. As it happened this same day, the day of Grant's order, Early crossed into Maryland from Martinsburg in force. But the next day Early recalled his army to Martinsburg, being influenced no doubt, by Hunter's move to Halltown, which threatened Early's rear. The 6th, the Twelfth marched from the Monocacy to near Harper's Ferry. On the 8th, we marched across the Potomac to near Halltown where the army was massing.

Chapter Ten

It had been Grant's intention to make Gen. Sheridan field commander in the campaign now about to begin. But, for reasons not necessary to name, Hunter wishing to be relieved of command, was accordingly relieved, and Sheridan put in command of the Army of the Shenandoah. He arrived at Monocacy on the 6th, and Grant returned to Washington the same day. The next day by an order from the War Department, a Military Division was made of the Departments of Pennsylvania, Washington, Maryland, and West Virginia under Sheridan's command.

Sheridan's army was now, August 10th, 30,000 strong. On this day he moved from Halltown up the Valley to give battle to the enemy. Passing through Berryville and Winchester, from which latter point the enemy retreated before him, our force arrived at Cedar Creek, forty miles from Halltown on the 12th. At this point the enemy was disposed to make a stand. That evening the Twelfth and First charged upon and drove the Rebel skirmishers east of the pike across the creek. Crook's command did not cross, but the next day the Sixth and Nineteenth Corps crossed the creek on the right of the pike driving the enemy before them for a mile or two.

The next day, the 14th, a detail of two officers, Capt. Prichard and Lieut. Hewitt, and 60 men of the Twelfth was sent under command of Capt. Prichard to Massanutten Mountain just across Cedar Creek to guard a signal corps there. This guard and signal corps had, however, not been on the mountain more than a few hours until they were attacked by a large force of 800 men, a man of our captured, afterward stated, and driven off, with a loss to us of three or four men killed and wounded.

All the next day there was considerable skirmishing between the opposing forces, but Sheridan, having received intelligence from Grant on the 14th, that reinforcements were on the way to Early, began preparing for the Nineteenth Corps starting the night of the 15th. The next day a part of Anderson's force crossing the Shenandoah river on the Front Royal road was met by Devin's and Custer's brigades of cavalry and driven across the river with a Rebel loss of 300 prisoners. This night, the 16th, the Sixth Corps and the Eighth, the latter Crook's command, retreated down the Valley at Winchester, then pushing on to the position taken near Berryville.

The morning of the 17th, Early started in hot pursuit. Our cavalry with our small brigade of infantry of the Sixth Corps, having been left at Winchester, were attacked by the enemy in the afternoon, but the brigade of infantry and a portion of the cavalry held them in check all afternoon. At length, after night, our men were forced back with a loss of 350 to us, mainly of the infantry, 200 of the latter being taken prisoners. On the 20th, Sheridan, having been enjoined by Grant to be cautious, and not desiring to give battle until he should know more definitely the strength of the enemy, fell back to near Charlestown, the lines being formed with the Sixth Corps on the right, the Nineteenth on the left, and the Eighth in the centre.

It appears that Early had planned to attack Sheridan the next day. His forces moved on two different roads with that purpose, Anderson on one road and Early on the other. The latter attacked the Sixth Corps which at first gave ground, but afterward regained it at night fall, with a loss on our side of 260 killed and wounded. The other corps were formed in line ready for battle, but Anderson not getting up, the fight was soon over, Early concluding to draw off, for the present at least. That night Sheridan, desiring to act on the defensive for the present, also to have a better position and to bide his time which was surely coming when the clouds of disappointment and doubt which had hung over this field too long should be rifted, and the sun of success and bright promise shine through, fell back to Halltown forming line from the Shenandoah on the left to the Potomac on the right. We made breast works of fence rails, railroad ties and so forth the next day. In the meantime there was considerable skirmishing and some cannonading between the opposing forces, the enemy having followed us up.

Early demonstrated against us for three days, when the 25th, a large part of his infantry marched to Shepherdstown on the Potomac, and a considerable body of his cavalry to Williamsport. Our forces captured a few prisoners in our front today. The next day the Twelfth went on the skirmish line. And two brigades of the First Division and one of the Second, Crook's command, Lowell's cavalry cooperating, went to our front to reconnoiter. They broke the Rebel skirmish line burnt some stacks from behind which the Rebels had skirmished, and drove two brigades from their breast works, our loss being 141 killed and wounded. That night, Anderson, who had been left in command here, while Early had moved to Shepherdstown and Williamsport, not having sufficient force to hold his ground, fell back to Stephenson's Depot, five miles east of Winchester.

Sheridan's force did not move for two days when, on the 28th, the army marched to Charlestown. The next day from the position of the infantry could be heard cannonading all day. This resulted from the Rebel infantry's driving Merritt's cavalry from Smithfield, some six miles west of Charlestown, which former town was then occupied by the enemy's cavalry and from further fighting when later Ricketts' division of the Sixth Corps drove the enemy's cavalry out and Merritt reoccupied the town. Along about this time the soldiers in camp ate, slept, wrote letters, and did whatever else they had to do within the almost constant sound of cannon or musketry.

The main portion of the army remained near Charlestown for the next five days. During this time the Twelfth was paid six months pay. And now our sutler reappeared upon the scene. It was a good time for him to be on hand; for now, was his harvest season. At the end of five days or on the morning of the 3rd of September, Sheridan desiring to extend his lines to Berryville, ordered the Eighth Corps to that place. We arrived there in the evening, and the boys immediately began making coffee but they had hardly more than begun to do so, when there were a few musket shots to our front toward Winchester. Right away the boys of the Twelfth began to discuss the matter of what the probable cause of the firing was. Some saying that they thought the butchers were killing beeves; others were doubtful about it but, soon, the shots increasing in frequency, they were about making up their minds that a fight was on hand when Col. Ely commanding the brigade hastily gave the order: "Fall in, fall in!" and soon Crook's command was in line to the right and left of the Berryville pike to meet the enemy which was there in considerable force.

The firing first heard was caused by an attack upon the First Virginia, which had only been put on picket about a half hour before, on the Berryville pike. The fight lasted till after dark. We held our ground on the right, while Duval's division on the left drove the enemy capturing about 60 prisoners. Crook's loss in this affair was 166. While the fighting was going on wagons were heard driving rapidly down the Valley on the road crossing the Berryville pike just to our rear. These belonged to a force of our cavalry that had been on a reconnaissance up the Valley. After dark the Rebels threw some shells over our heads which seemed to fall pretty close to the passing wagon train. The next day some of the cavalry said that we of the infantry had saved them from being cut off in their return down the Valley, for the Rebels would have had to go only a short distance until they would have been across the cavalrymen's road. Crook's command held its position till near morning when it drew back toward Charlestown about two miles. And Sheridan's whole force began to entrench.

Just why this fight at Berryville took place, so far as the purpose and movement of the enemy brought it on, was not at the time understood among our men. The impression seemed to be that Crook's force was there to hold the Berryville pike, while the cavalry were making a reconnaissance up the Valley and the Rebels moving on that road with the purpose of cutting off their return had encountered us, and that was the reason, it was thought the fight took place. But the fact is the fight resulted, so far as the enemy was responsible, from a part of his force in the Valley having started on that evening on the return to Richmond by way of Berryville. Something over two weeks before this Early received, as before stated, reinforcements from Lee, consisting mainly of Anderson's division of Longstreet's corps, which corps was now commanded by Anderson, who had come into the Valley with the division. Lee being hard pressed by Grant at this time had called for the return of these troops, and it was they whom Crook had encountered that evening. The fight was a mutual surprise. Crook's men were getting supper when the enemy attacked the First Virginia on picket sending them back precipitately, thus bringing on the fight. This unexpected engagement delayed the departure of this Rebel force for some days.

After the Berryville battle there was no general movement of the Union forces for more than two weeks. On the 8th, however, Crook's corps was moved from its position on the left of the lines to Summit Point on the right. The status of things on our side was maintained in the main, for the next ten days. Maj. Brown, who was captured about seven weeks before at Winchester, and had escaped from the Rebels at Harrisonburg, returned to the Twelfth from home on the 10th.

On the 13th, Gen. McIntosh of Wilson's division of cavalry, reconnoitering on the Berryville road in the direction of Winchester, captured a South Carolina regiment of infantry, the whole of it, however, being only a little over 100 men and 30 other prisoners. The news of the capture spread through the camp and had an inspiriting effect, no doubt upon the army; and perhaps was regarded as presaging further victory.

Chapter Ten

There having been of late great urgency to have the Baltimore and Ohio railroad opened, and a pressure generally to have the people north of the Potomac freed from the menace of Early's army, Gen. Grant paid Sheridan a visit on the 16th to talk over the situation and see what should be done. Just two days before this, Anderson's division had again started to return to Richmond; this time moving through Chester Gap far south, and thus the condition, the withdrawal of a part of Early's force, that Grant and Sheridan had been waiting for, had come about. So when Grant asked Sheridan on that Friday if he could be ready to attack Early on the next Tuesday he did not want, like McClellan, to delay awaiting reinforcements, or plead lack of means of transportation or supplies, or some other difficulty, but he answered, like a man who meant business, that he could be ready the following Monday thus showing so far as this instance would indicate, not that "There is luck in leisure," but rather that there is a bright promise in promptitude. For by attacking on Monday he took the enemy somewhat at a disadvantage, his forces then being scattered along the Martinsburg pike, thus rendering victory certain for Sheridan, while if the attack had been delayed till Tuesday Early's forces would have been concentrated, they being on the move on Monday for that purpose, and the result of the battle might have been otherwise.

Sheridan having decided to attack Early on the memorable 19th of September, had sent his unnecessary trains and the sutlers to the rear the day before; and accordingly on the eventful Monday he moved to the attack before day. Our brigade consisting at this time of the First, Fourth and Twelfth West Virginia Infantry, then under the command of Lieut. Col. Northcott marched at 5 o'clock p.m., the body of the troops having started earlier. The serious character of the work that the men of the Twelfth believed to be before them had a sobering effect upon them; but they marched bravely forward that morning willing to do their part in the coming struggle. Nearing the Berryville ford of the Opequon, over which all the infantry had to pass, and between which and Winchester, five miles distant, the battle was fought, we heard heavy skirmishing. The battle was opening. The Twelfth and, in fact, our whole brigade, was lucky that day, if it may be regarded as fortunate to escape the chance of being killed or wounded. And, it may be said, the regiment was rather favored by fortune in this regard from this time to the end of our service.

When we reached the ford to our not very sorrowful surprise - for the boys had got over being eager for a fight - it was announced to us that our brigade was detached to guard the wagon train and field hospital to be established at that point. Lieut. Col. Northcott was mortified and vexed that his brigade should be left out of the fight, and he inquired of Col. Thoburn, commanding the division, the reason of it. Thoburn answered that he, Thoburn, had no choice in the matter, his orders being to detach his smallest brigade to be left as a guard at the ford. And thus we were left out of the battle. However, it is not always safe to be in the rear as is shown by the fact that Sheridan intended to attack Early in the rear that morning, but changed his plan when he learned that the enemy's forces were then strung along the Martinsburg pike. As it was, we had to be on the alert, for there were guerrillas hovering about us ready to pounce on any small squad that might become detached from the command.

It was nearly noon before the battle, because general, and for four or five hours thereafter we could see, from our position at the ford, the smoke of the conflict rolling up beyond the woods in our front, and hear the roar of the battle. There we stayed and during all this time we were unable to determine from the sound how the battle was going. In the meantime the men and officers were debating as to the probable result. Adjt. Caldwell of the Twelfth saying that Sheridan had about 40,000 men and the enemy presumably not so many, thought that we would win the day. At length toward evening the Eighth Corps (ours) struck the enemy on their left flank and soon their rout became general. They were sent through Winchester on the run. And the news of our victory soon reached us at the ford.

This was a bloody battle. The total Union lost being about 5,000, there being 4,300 killed and wounded. The total Rebel loss from the best obtainable data was about 4,000. Of this number about 2,000 were prisoners. If the data are correct, there was a great disparity in the losses of the two armies in killed and wounded. Early's losses in these lists being less than half of Sheridan's. This fact may be explained by reason of the enemy's having the protection of trees, rocks and other shelter during most of the battle. Besides the prisoners, Sheridan captured five pieces of artillery and seven battle flags.

At the time of this battle of Winchester or the Opequon, Sheridan had in the Valley an army of 4,300 men, in round numbers; while according to Pond's Shenandoah Valley, "the Rebel records show Early's force in that battle to be less than half that number. However, there are some facts which point to the conclusion that the Rebel force was under estimated. Grant puts Early's strength at the time Sheridan was put in command of the Union forces in the Valley, August 7th, at about 30,000; and he was somewhat stronger at the time of the battle with Anderson's division absent, than he was at the date to which Grant refers. Greeley says in his American Conflict that, in a newspaper controversy between Sheridan and Early in 1865, Sheridan stated "that the prisoners taken by him from Early (during the Valley campaign) exceeded the number to which that general limited his entire command."

Sheridan was a dashing, rushing, and seemingly reckless kind of man, with no pretense of pomp or polish so when he sent his dispatch to Washington announcing his victory, he did not say, "Winchester is ours and fairly won," as the illustrious Gen. Sherman would perhaps have said, or that "Victory had perched upon our banners and we have sent the traitor hosts vanquished and vanquishing up the Valley," or anything of the kind; but he simply said: "We have just sent them whirling through Winchester." The following dispatch was received by Sheridan:

"Have just heard of your great victory. God bless you all, officers and men. Strongly inclined to come up and see you.
LINCOLN."

Here is a characteristic incident showing somewhat the style of man Sheridan was: In his first movement up the Valley in August, when we had reached Cedar Creek where the enemy was, the First and Twelfth, it will be recollected, were ordered to charge some Rebel skirmishers, one company of the Twelfth having previously been put upon our skirmish line. Just as the two regiments were in the act of charging, Sheridan and Crook, passing from the right to the left along the skirmish line to take in the situation, had come opposite the charging troops; when Crook seemed inclined to stop and watch the result. Sheridan, however, appeared to be in a hurry, wanting to pass on; so he said: "Come on Crook, never mind, they'll give them h-ll." Perhaps because of the character of Sheridan as indicated by this incident, and as shown by his dispatch to Washington as given, and the observations in connection therewith, he was popular with the soldiers. But by, more than all else in gaining the victory at the Opequon he gained their abiding confidence and admiration; which fact gave promise of future victory.

The Twelfth with its brigade remained at the Berryville ford till the 22nd, when we marched, following the army up the Valley. We passed through Winchester. From there we guarded a wagon train of supplies up to Cedar Creek reaching there about sun down, just as our army was driving Early's from Fisher's Hill, in sight from the creek. Sheridan employed the same tactics in this battle that he did in the battle of the Opequon, sending Crook's (the Eighth) Corps to attack the enemy on the flank. Sheridan's loss in this battle was only about

400, while Early's was between 1,300 and 1,400 mostly prisoners. This time the enemy's loss was much the heavier making the losses in each army in the two battles about 5,400. Sheridan captured 16 cannons at Fisher's Hill.

After Early's rout his army retreated up the Valley, followed by Sheridan's after night for 12 miles to Woodstock. It was perhaps an unprecedented thing in the annals of the war for one army to follow another opposing army after dark on the same road, as was done in this instance. Our men had been dropping out of ranks all along the road to rest or sleep; and as the Twelfth passed along, it looked as though there was a string of those dropped out soldiers all along the 12 miles from Strasburg to Woodstock. When our regiment reached this latter town there was not more than the equal of a company left in the ranks, the most of the Twelfth having fallen out of ranks too. Those of the regiment remaining in ranks, marched 35 miles that day and night. The Rebels were followed so sharply, that many of them, to escape, took to the mountains. It was said also that, in this right pursuit of the enemy, in some instances, a Union soldier becoming tired and sleepy and seeing some one lying by the road side, would stop there for company; and in the morning he would discover a Johnny by his side, who of course, would be made a prisoner.

The Twelfth remained at Woodstock one day with its corps, then pushing on after the bulk of the army to Harrisonburg, about 25 miles from Staunton, arrived there the 25th, the cavalry going as far as Staunton and Waynesboro destroying arms, ammunition and so forth at the latter place and, in accordance with Grant's orders, all the mills, barns and stacks of hay and grain were burned, and the stock driven off in the Valley from Staunton down to Harrisonburg. The Sixth Corps and Nineteenth marched up to Mount Crawford on the 29th, and back to Harrisonburg the next day in support of the burning operations.

The army remained at Harrisonburg till October the 6th; when the whole force marched down the Valley, arriving at Strasburg the 8th. All the way down to this place as we marched, the smoke could be seen rolling up behind us from the burning barns, mills and so forth. It was said that in many instances, in burning barns, reports of fire arms hidden in them and discharged by the heat were heard. Early reinforced by Anderson's division and Rosser's cavalry followed us down the Valley to Strasburg. The cavalry styled themselves the Saviors of the Valley, and were particularly aggressive. Sheridan got tired of their annoyance and determined to dispose of these new found "Saviors of the Valley." He directed Torbet accordingly to start out at daylight on the morning of the 9th and "whip the Rebel cavalry or get whipped himself." Our cavalry promptly to time attacked Lomax's cavalry on the pike and Rosser's on the back road and after a fight of about two hours routed them on both roads, capturing about 330 prisoners, 11 guns - all they had but one - and 47 wagons - "everything on wheels." The Rebels were run about 26 miles up the Valley on the jump. After the battle for the rest of the day, about all the saving the Johnnys wanted to do was to "save their bacon." Sheridan was very enthusiastic over this victory offering, it is said, $50 for the other piece of artillery.

The second day after this battle of Tom's Brook, as it is called, the 11th, our brigade started from Cedar Creek for Martinsburg as a guard, with a wagon train and the captured property. Near Newton, which is about eight miles from Cedar Creek, we met two or three cavalrymen coming at a headlong rate. They belonged to a party of 26 that had been guarding an ambulance conveying some officers and mail matters, which had just been attacked a little farther on by Mosby. This was a very bloody affair with our men nearly half of them being killed or wounded. Lieut. Col. Northcott stopped the command, and scoured the woods nearby, to see if there were any Rebels about; but it was too late. Mosby had got off with nearly all the unwounded and the ambulance. We camped that night at Winchester where we met Col. Curtis returning from a leave of absence, who now took command of the brigade. The next morning we marched for Martinsburg arriving there after dark.

We remained at Martinsburg two days. During this time Mosby captured a train of cars at Kearnyville, a town between former town and Harper's Ferry. On the afternoon of the 16th, we started to the front again with a wagon train arriving at Winchester the next day, at which place we were told to pitch our tents, as we were likely to remain there for a few days. Accordingly the tents were put up.

As before stated Early had followed Sheridan down the Valley from Staunton to Strasburg but it was only the cavalry that came all the way, his infantry having halted at New Market. Sheridan believed the enemy would not again attempt to come down in force and therefore he had ordered the Sixth Corps to return to the Army of the Potomac in accordance with Grant's desire to have a part of the Valley force sent to him as soon as it could he spared. This corps had started to return about the time we had left Cedar Creek for Martinsburg. But there was an unexpected turn in affairs. Early, on the 13th, had arrived with his whole army, at Fisher's Hill, and, without halting, sent a reconnoitering force to Cedar Creek, which threw some shells into Thoburn's camp while the men were at dinner. Thoburn's men were almost as much surprised as if the shells had dropped from the clouds; for a reconnoitering party had been up the Valley the day before, ten or twelve miles, and reported that no enemy had been seen. Thoburn's division was soon formed, and he undertook to capture the Rebel artillery, the command crossing the creek to attack it but, the enemy being in strong force, he failed. Thoburn's loss in this engagement was 200 or 300. The gallant Col. Wells of the Thirty-fourth Massachusetts was killed in this fight. After Early's demonstration in Sheridan's front, the Sixth Corps on its way to Grant by way of Washington, having got as far as the Shenandoah beyond Front Royal, was ordered back, arriving at Cedar Creek, the 14th.

The next day Sheridan received a message concerning the desired destruction of the Virginia Central railroad from Grant about which he, Grant, had been anxious for some time, and accordingly Merritt's division of cavalry was sent that night as far as Front Royal with the intention of reinforcing it by another division, the design being to employ these troops to break the road just referred to and also the James River Canal or at least to threaten them. Sheridan went with the cavalry to Front Royal, being on his way to Washington, going there at the urgent request of the authorities at the capitol to have a conference with them. But just before leaving Front Royal for Washington he received the following dispatch from Wright, copied from the Rebel signal flag on Massanutten Mountain in sight of our camp: "To Lieutenant General Early. Be ready to move as soon as my forces join you, and we will crush Sheridan. Longstreet, Lieutenant General."

Sheridan suspected this to be a trick of the enemy, which it was, but in order to be on the safe side, he ordered the cavalry back to Cedar Creek. In this instance the enemy, in his strategy, over-reached himself, and three days later on account of this trick, he had to fight two more divisions of cavalry than he would otherwise have had to do. Sheridan continued his journey from Front Royal to Washington, stopping on the way some hours at Rectortown to telegraph to and get an answer from Halleck as to whether he had any information that Longstreet was or was not moving as indicated by the Rebel dispatch. Finally Halleck, after communicating with Grant at City Point answered: "General Grant says that Longstreet brought no troops with him from Richmond," adding some less important intelligence. After getting the telegram from Halleck Sheridan again pushed on toward the capitol.

Coming back to our brigade with the wagon train at Winchester, we remained there just two days, when by orders we were to guard the train on up to Cedar Creek, to start on the memorable morning of the 19th of October, 1864. The soldiers generally of Sheridan's army by this time had settled down to the conviction that the campaign of severe fighting was ended in the Valley for that year. And we at Winchester were at that time ignorant of the changed condition of things at the front; so we lay down to sleep the night before we were to start for Cedar Creek, little dreaming of what was in store for our army there, or of the pregnant events of the coming day. But the dawn of another day has come, and hark! what thunderous sound from the south is that? "Tis the cannons opening roar." The fair Valley is to be the scene of another day of blood and carnage; the last battle for its possession.

Notwithstanding there was fighting going on at the front as we started for Cedar Creek some 15 miles distant but we had not gone far when we met, at about 9 o'clock, some stragglers and wagon trains retreating from Cedar Creek. Col. Curtis then ordered his train to be parked. And now there was about to take place one of the most marked, extraordinary, and dramatic incidents or events, taken in connection with the outcome of it, in the annals of our country. Indeed it may be said it is unparalleled in the history of American warfare. It was Sheridan's Ride from Winchester to the army in front "to save the day." He rode up the pike past our brigade on his famous black horse at a brisk trot with a small escort following, at or soon after 9 o'clock in the forenoon, and every soldier of the brigade had a chance to witness the immortal scene.

When the stragglers were met, Col. Curtis threw a line of men across the road to stop them, and put them under guard. There have been statements saying, or leaving the impression, that the number of stragglers getting back to or near Winchester was quite large, but as well as is remembered, there were not more than 100 or 200 of them. Col. Curtis says that when Sheridan, passing to the front, came to where our brigade was, noticed the demoralized stragglers, he rode up to them and standing straight in his stirrups and gritting his teeth as he looked at them, shouted at the top his voice: "Boys if you don't want to fight yourselves, come back and look at others fighting. We will whip them out of their boots before 4 o'clock." He then ordered Col. Curtis to organize the stragglers into a battalion, put officers in command of them and move in to the front with his entire force. This the Colonel proceeded to do, bringing up his wagon train. He had gone but a short distance, however, when he received another order from Sheridan to return to Winchester and protect that place from an apprehended attack by Rebel cavalry. Accordingly the command returned with the train to the town.

Our army at Cedar Creek had met with a surprise attack mainly against its left flank. The Eighth Corps (Crook's) being farthest to the front and left, was struck first, just at break of dawn, before the men were all out of their tents, and being attacked almost simultaneously in front, flank and rear, it was soon routed, losing heavily in killed and wounded and prisoners, the loss in prisoners being quite large. Our army was forced back by the suddenness and vigor of the Rebel attack and principally by the necessity of having to give ground, in order to clear its flanks about four miles from Crook's camp by 11 o'clock a.m. It gave no further ground. And it appears that from about 9 o'clock, it being that time before all our previously unengaged infantry had been engaged, the attacks of the enemy were feeble. This fact may be explained by the reason that they had been marching and fighting from near midnight, and because many of them had fallen out of ranks it seems, to plunder our camps. When Sheridan came up at about half past eleven a.m., the only parts of our force engaged were one division of the Sixth Corps and the cavalry, and they not heavily. There was a lull before the counter-storm.

Sheridan came upon the field about half past eleven o'clock a.m. As he was approaching our army, tremendous cheers were heard in the rear. The cheering came from the stragglers that, though there were not many of them far in the rear, were two or more thousand in number, from all the corps a mile or two in the rear. They were cheering the returning commander. And one of the singular and surprising incidents of this remarkable battle was that the stream of these stragglers now turned toward the front. It is not probable that any other commander in the Union army could have inspired so telling moral effect. When Sheridan reached the line of battle along which he rode swinging his hat, he was hailed by the men with throwing their hats and tempestuous cheering. While his arrival had an encouraging effect on our men, it would tend no doubt to have a discouraging effect on the enemy, causing them to think that our army was getting reinforcements it may be.

Just before Sheridan came upon the field, the Rebels had been repulsed in an attack upon our left made to seize the pike. As soon as he observed the situation he resolved to drive the enemy from the field; and he rode along the lines telling the men that they would sleep in their old quarters that night. He at once set about reforming his lines and strengthening his left. At about 1 o'clock p.m., Early made an attack upon our left, but it was easily repulsed. Three hours later our lines being formed mainly on the northwest side of the pike, and at right angle to it, Sheridan ordered an advance upon the enemy by a left half-wheel which was gallantly responded to by the whole line. The left of the enemy gave way first: the rest of their line did not stand long, and soon their whole force was a flying mob. Our army pursued the routed Rebels capturing 1,200 prisoners, 24 guns, and much other property, besides retaking 24 guns lost in the morning. The field was won; the day was saved; our army had retaken its old camps; Sheridan had made good his promise that the men should sleep in their old quarters that night, and thus was made the single instance in our history as a people of an army being thoroughly worsted in the morning, gaining a signal victory in the afternoon. Sheridan will go down to history as a unique and illustrious warrior.

Our loss in men in this battle of Cedar Creek was 5,764 in killed, wounded, and prisoners, 1,429 being prisoners. Col. Thoburn of the First Virginia Infantry commanding a division, a gallant and highly esteemed officer, and Capt. Philip G. Bier were among the officers killed in this battle. This latter officer was enlisted by Col. Curtis as a private in Company D, of the Twelfth and appointed Orderly Sergeant of the company, January 17th, 1863, he was promoted to Second Lieutenant and assigned to Company A. On the recommendation of Gen. Sullivan and others he was, in January, 1864, commissioned as a Captain and A. A. G., and assigned to duty on Gen. Hunter's staff. He remained on his staff during the Hunter raid against Lynchburg and until Hunter was relieved, when he was transferred to Gen. Crook's staff. Acting in the discharge of his duty in trying, during the battle to save the wagon and ambulance trains, he was mortally wounded, and died the following night. The officers of the Twelfth, for the high regard which they had for their gallant dead comrade, had his body embalmed and sent to Wheeling where it was buried.

According to Early's account of his loss in this battle was 1,860 in killed and wounded. Our army captured 1,200 prisoners. If his account of his loss in killed and wounded is correct his total loss was 3,060. Assuming that Early's statement of his loss in killed and wounded is correct, our loss in this battle was almost double that of the enemy. This could reasonably be accounted for by the fact that our army had been surprised and taken at great disadvantage.

This battle of Cedar Creek shows, in matter of moment, how important it is that the first step, the initial movement should be sure and right. When Sheridan was put in command in the Valley, he patiently bided his time, when he could, as he did, take the enemy at a disadvantage in the battle of the Opequon, gaining a great victory thereby, and thus paved the way for the strong confidence the unbounded faith in him, on the part of his army, which enabled him to snatch victory from defeat in this latter memorable battle. Sheridan won a major general's commission in the regular army by this victory. In tendering the commission a few weeks later, President Lincoln said in part, that it was "for a brilliant victory achieved over the Rebels for the third time in pitched battle within thirty days."

The next morning after the battle our brigade left Winchester at about 2 o'clock for Cedar Creek arriving there the same morning at about 8 o'clock with the wagon train. When we arrived on the battle field some of the Rebel dead were yet unburied. The following day the 21st, the Twelfth with its brigade marched down the pike about seven miles to Newtown to guard the temporary hospital at that place. We remained at this town for over two weeks. On the 25th, the soldiers here who were citizens of West Virginia voted for President. An old diary written at the time says that there were only four or five votes for McClellan; whether in the brigade or our regiment it does not say. The next day Gen. Duffie was captured between Winchester and Martinsburg.

During the stay at Newtown, Mosby was around in the vicinity twice, one time capturing a forage train within a mile or two of town, and getting off with the mules. Both times the Twelfth went out after him, but saw nothing of him. It was useless to send infantry after mounted men. On the 13th the First Virginia left for Cumberland, Md.

Chapter Eleven

While the Twelfth remained at Newtown, there was nothing of special interest occurred other than has been mentioned. As winter and bad weather were approaching, in order that we might be closer to our base of supplies, the infantry moved back from Cedar Creek on the 9th of November to Kearnstown; the next day the cavalry followed and late in the evening of this same day, and last of all, the two remaining regiments of our brigade moved down and joined our corps with the army. The next day we put up our tents. The Sixth Corps and the Nineteenth, worked at throwing up fortifications all day.

The next day after Sheridan's army left Cedar Creek, Early thinking that perhaps our force had been withdrawn to send part of it to Grant, moved his army down from New Market to Middletown. He was thus on the day, the evening of which the Twelfth left its camp at Newtown, within five miles of us at that place Sheridan was ready to meet him; and sent out the cavalry of the 12th against the Rebel cavalry, Merritt's and Custer's divisions on the right of the pike, and Powell on the Front Royal road. They drove the Rebel cavalry back. Powell attacked McCausland's brigade at Stony Point and routed it capturing its two guns and 2,745 officers and men. The army was ordered to be prepared for battle the next day, but, though Early had, according to the reports of citizens been considerably reinforced after the battle of Cedar Creek, he had by this time acquired a wholesome regard for the fighting qualities of Sheridan's army; and finding that it was still in the Valley in force, he concluded not to risk a battle, but returned to his camp at New Market the 14th.

The Twelfth remained with the army at Kearnstown for two weeks. On the 19th - the day of the month in each instance, on which Sheridan's two great battles were fought, the battle of the Opequon and the battle of Cedar Creek - orders were read to our regiment from Gen. Sheridan naming this army, the Army of the Shenandoah, and the camp here, Camp Russell. On the 23rd the boys of the Twelfth had abundance of chicken sent them from somewhere for Thanksgiving dinner.

Here is a somewhat characteristic anecdote of an Irishman of the Nineteenth Corps: It is believed that it was while the Twelfth was at Camp Russell, that this Irishman, who had evidently been imbibing freely of the ardent, was noticed sauntering through the camp singing as he sauntered an apparently impromptu song, and staggering considerably as he sauntered and sang. His corps had suffered heavily in the battle of the Opequon. And his song related to the part it had taken in that battle. This much of the song is remembered:

"The nineteenth of September
In eighteen sixty-four,
Is long to be remembered
By the Nineteenth Army Corps."

The following is an amusing episode of soldier life that will be appreciated by the boys generally, and some of them will no doubt remember it. In order that a better understanding of it may be had by others than soldiers it may be well to say that, as is well known by all soldiers who campaigned in the Valley of Virginia, the guerrilla Mosby was a dangerous enemy, and a terror to all soldiers disposed to straggle. Sheridan once remarked that Mosby was as good to keep up his, Sheridan's, stragglers as would have been a regiment for that purpose; Mosby was also something of a bugaboo, and a subject of jest among the soldiers.

It was perhaps while we were at Camp Russell that one day a merchant tailor came into camp from Wheeling, to see the officers of the Twelfth with a view to taking orders for new uniforms. He wore a plug hat. Now when a stranger appeared in camp in citizens' dress, that fact was sufficient to excite in the minds of the soldiers a suggestion of a possible spy in the person of the stranger; and Mosby being an ever present bugbear in the minds of the soldiers, his name would naturally be associated with that of the stranger. So when the

Wheeling man appeared on the streets of the camp wearing his plug hat, the boys raised a general yell of Mosby!, Mosby! Mosby mingled with some remarks about the plug hat. Men can stand almost anything better than derision, especially when it comes from a great crowd; and quickly "catching on" to the fact that he, the Wheeling man, was the object of the noisy attention, he shot into an officer's tent and would not come out until he had exchanged his plug hat for a slouch hat, which some officer managed to get for him.

The Twelfth marched from Camp Russell on the 24th to Stevenson's Depot, five miles northeast of Winchester. The railroad track had recently been relaid to that place. We remained here over three weeks. The duty at this place was heavy, our brigade having to unload all the cars which brought supplies to the army and do picket duty besides. On the 16th of December one hundred guns were fired at Camp Russell in honor of Gen. Thomas's victory the day before at Nashville. When we heard the firing at first we thought the enemy had attacked our forces at the front. But before long a dispatch came from Sheridan telling the reason of the firing. The next day another salute was fired at the front in honor of Gen. Thomas's victory in the second day's fighting at Nashville, and the fall of Savannah and its occupancy by Sherman.

Before the middle of December, Early, having sent the bulk of his command to Lee, the last of the Sixth Corps had gone to the Army of the Potomac, and on the 19th the Third Brigade of our division took the cars at Stevenson's Depot for the Army of the James. Later the same day our brigade followed, having to ride in filthy cattle cars. Owing to a scarcity of cars some of the men had to ride on top of them, and, the weather being cold, they suffered considerably, especially those who rode on top of the cars. We got to Washington at eight o'clock a.m. the next day, the cars landing us at the wharf. The men would have been glad to see the city, but they were not permitted to do so. While we were waiting for a few hours to be marched on board a transport, some citizens standing about were, as was natural, making remarks about us. One fellow was overheard to volunteer the pleasant reminder concerning us, that "There are more of those fellows going to Grant's army than will ever get back." And this citizen's tone seemed to indicate that he exulted in the thought. May be, too, the wish was father to the thought.

About 12 o'clock our regiment went aboard of the transports. A part of us went on a small craft called the Putnam. This vessel was soon on its way down the Potomac. As we passed down we got a view of Mount Vernon. About 10 p.m. we anchored for the night. We started at daylight the next morning, the 21st. We ran into the St. Mary's River at about 4 o'clock P.M. that day, and cast anchor on account of the high wind. We were now 100 miles from Washington. All the next day we were detained here by the high wind; and owing to some mismanagement we had not rations enough, and, the men ran out of them.

At daylight the 23rd our vessel weighed anchor and a run of ten miles brought us to Point Lookout at the mouth of the Potomac. We stopped here and drew three days' rations. Twelve thousand Rebel prisoners were confined here at that time. From this point we passed down the Chesapeake Bay, and some time in the night anchored near Fortress Monroe. We started up the James River early the next morning and arrived at City Point on the south side of the river, about dark. Changing boats here we ran up 20 miles farther, 80 miles from Fortress Monroe, and landed on the north side, near the Dutch Gap canal.

Before the soldiers of the Twelfth went to Grant's army they had a somewhat exaggerated idea of the fierceness and fatality of the fighting there. They had some kind of a vague idea that, like the fly in the spider's parlor, in the story of the "Spider and the Fly" where they got into it once, there was an excellent chance of not getting out of it again alive. But in so great an army as Grant had, naturally soldiers would be going to and from it all the time; and somewhere on the Potomac or Chesapeake Bay, we met a vessel with a number of soldiers aboard, going to the rear. When the returning soldiers were noticed, Major Brown remarked in a kind of serio-comic way in an illusion to the supposed extreme unhealthiness of the service in Grant's army: "Well, I notice that some fellows at least are getting back from the army before Richmond alive!"

The next morning (Christmas) after landing we got off the vessel and the other transport with the rest of the Twelfth having arrived, the regiment marched about four miles to where the other troops of our division were camped, and took the quarters temporarily vacated by Gen. Butler's troops, who had gone to attempt the capture of Fort Fisher. We remained in these quarters several days, during which there was nothing occurred worthy of mention except that the enemy kept throwing shells at short intervals at our men working at the Dutch Gap canal; and once when there was heavy cannonading toward Petersburg we were called out in line, the general in command on our side of the James apparently fearing an attack.

On the 30th some of the troops that had been on the Fort Fisher expedition returned and we had to vacate our quarters and move some three miles farther to the right and put up winter quarters. The Fifty-fourth Pennsylvania, the Twenty-third Illinois, and the Twelfth West Virginia, January 1st, 1865, were brigaded together and designated as the Second Brigade, Col. Curtis commanding.

Our division was known as the Second or Independent Division, Twenty-fourth Corps, Col. T. M. Harris, afterward succeeded by Gen. John Turner, commanding the division; and Gen. John Gibbon commanded the corps.

When the Twelfth was transferred to the Army of the James, Gen. Butler was in command of it, but having failed in his expedition against Fort Fisher, he was relieved and Gen. Ord was put in command of it, which consisted of two corps, the Twenty-fourth and the Twenty-fifth, the latter being colored troops. The Dutch Gap canal referred to was Gen. Butler's project. The object of the undertaking was to make a channel across a narrow neck of land, made by a long horse-shoe bend in the river, so as to enable our vessels to avoid obstructions in the bend, and pass up to Richmond. Of course, the enemy tried to prevent work at the canal and to this end, as before stated, firing shells at intervals at the workers (colored men) was kept up; but the work went on. The men dug holes in the side of the canal, which they called gopher holes. There was also a high lookout nearby from which a man kept a constant watch, and when the Rebels fired a shot he would cry out "Gopher hole!" and the "darks" would bounce into the holes and remain there until the shell exploded. Then they would come out and go to work again. It used to be great fun for the boys to watch the "darks" run for cover when the lookout man gave notice of a shot by the enemy. This working and shelling was kept up for perhaps a month after we had gone to the Army of the James. But the canal when it was completed as far as it could be under the circumstances, proved to be a failure, no considerable volume of water passing through it, at that time at least.

When we got to the Army of the James we witnessed a condition of affairs different from anything we had hitherto seen. On the left of our lines in front of Fort Harrison the pickets were probably not more than 50 yards apart. They paced backward and forward on their several beats as though all was serene between the opposing pickets. If, however, either side had advanced, or perhaps, if one man had shot at the enemy, a bloody ball of battle would have opened; but the one man did not fire; and all was quiet on our side of the river, while on the opposite side there was constant firing going on night and day, between the pickets there.

Our duties in this army consisted of making "corduroy" roads over the soft and muddy ground, the cutting and hauling of firewood, drilling a little and preparing for inspections, going on picket about once a week, besides for the greater part of our time here, having to stand in line of battle, just outside of our works, for an hour or so from awhile before day each morning. However, our service this winter in the Army of the James was as easy as any we had had, and very much easier than some of our previous soldiering. The picket duty was comparatively light, and then we were here free from the exhausting, killing marching connected with much of our previous service.

On the 7th of January Lieut. Col. Northcott made us a farewell speech, his resignation some time previously tendered, having been accepted. Owing to the high regard and esteem the Twelfth had for him, both as a man and as a soldier, the command parted with him with regret. Major Brown and Capt. Burley of Company A were both promoted on the Twelfth, the former to be Lieutenant Colonel and the latter to be Major, this making the second promotion for Brown and the third for Burley.

On the 17th an order came around announcing the fact of the capture of the Rebel fort, Fort Fisher, by the combined attack of our land and naval forces, the former under Gen. Terry, and the latter under Admiral Porter. A salute was fired here at 12 o'clock this day in honor of the victory. Our brigade was inspected on the 22nd, and the Twelfth, having passed the best inspection of any regiment in it, was excused from duty for one week. On the 24th, there having been heavy cannonading not far off all the night before, an order was promulgated saying that the Rebel gunboats had come down the James that night and our batteries commanding the river had sunk one, and caused two others to run aground. An attack was expected this night and we had orders to be ready to form ranks at a moment's notice.

From this time on, while the opposing armies faced each other here, desertions from the enemy were of growing frequency. February 4th, a lieutenant colonel and captain deserted from the Rebels in front of the pickets of our division. When desertions of officers of their rank were taking place, it began to look like "the beginning of the end." A few days later Richmond papers obtained from the Rebel pickets an account of the failure of the Peace Commission, composed of President Lincoln and others on the part of the Government, and Vice President Stephens and others on the part of the Rebels, which met at Hampton Roads. It was exceedingly fortunate and well for the future of the country that the fatally blind obstinacy of the Rebels that had characterized them from the first caused them to refuse to consider any proposition of peace except on the basis of their independence.

Concerning the Peace Commission, Gen. Grant tells a story of Lincoln, which will bear reproduction. Stephens was a very small man, but it seems that he wore a large overcoat on the occasion of the meeting of the commission. Some time after this Lincoln, being on a visit to Grant, after a little previous conversation, the talk turning on the commission, asked Grant if he had seen that overcoat of Stephens. He replied that he had. "Did you see him take it off?" said Lincoln. "Yes," said Grant. "Well," inquired Lincoln, "didn't you think it was the biggest shuck and the least ear that ever you did see?"

Camp life here was anything but dull. There was always something occurring of an exciting character. Besides the operations of the armies here, the booming of cannon for instance, that was not infrequently heard, causing a lively interest as to what it signified, we had orders at various times announcing victories of our armies at other places, and salutes fired in their honor. And then a camp rumor startling in character could be heard at almost any hour, by which the soldiers were not much startled, however, being used to them. In fact, there are few if any pursuits in civil life calculated to keep up the tension of excitement like life in a camp of a great army in time of war. On the 9th a soldier who was a deserter and bounty jumper was taken outside the works and shot in the presence of a whole division. The night following three of the Tenth Connecticut Infantry substitutes deserted to the enemy, passing through our lines, where some of the Twelfth were on picket. One of them shot at the deserters, but missed them. The enemy had issued an order saying that all deserters from our army should be sent through the lines North, and that was the reason those fellows deserted.

On the 21st our division was reviewed, and this same day one hundred guns were fired from Fort Harrison on the north side of the James and near the camp of the Twelfth, in honor of the taking of Charleston and Columbia, S.C., by Sherman. The next day a salute was fired in honor of Washington's birthday. Twelve days later, March 7th, the news was received in camp of Sheridan's victory at Waynesboro, in the Valley, over Early, in which nearly all the latter's force was captured. No doubt Sheridan's cavalry, the loyal people everywhere, and especially the citizens along the Baltimore and Ohio railroad in the Valley were jubilant over this final elimination of Jubal.

On the 17th our corps was reviewed by Gen. Grant and staff, accompanied by a number of distinguished gentlemen and ladies. Among them was Admiral Porter, Secretary Stanton, Mrs. Grant and many others. An incident of this review is remembered. The troops were closely massed by brigades perhaps. The Fifty-fourth Pennsylvania, commanded by Major Davis, belonged, it will be remembered, to our brigade. Davis was a nervous, excitable man. As Grant and staff were passing rapidly in front of the troops, the various brigades greeted them with a great volume of cheers. This excited Davis, and as Grant drew near, the former, eyes shining and apparently bulging out, in an excited and vehement manner, gave the command to his men to cheer, throwing in a simile more forcible than polite, saying, "Cheer like ---- men !" causing the whole brigade to burst forth in laughter. Sad to say this officer was afterward killed at the capture of Fort Gregg.

The boys generally made up their minds on the occasion of this grand review that something was about to be done. Experience had made them shrewd in interpreting transactions relating to the army in general; in putting this and that together. And right here it may be well to speak of what was regarded as a possible undertaking before the Army of the James. In front of and along part of our lines quite near to us and in plain view were the Rebel breast works with abatis in front. Back of these were numerous forts mounted with cannon, the forts commanding each other so that if one were taken it would be under the fire of the others. Besides, as was generally known after the capture of Richmond, there were torpedoes planted in front of their forts to make them still more impregnable. Looking at the Rebel defenses from our side, it seemed that to undertake their capture it would be like rushing into a death-trap. And yet our men fronting them regarded this desperate task as far from improbable.

On the 19th eight deserters from the Palmetto Sharpshooters, all from one company, came into our division headquarters. They, it seemed, had got a sufficiency of rights, also about all the dying-in-the-last-ditch they cared for, and as to the "stars and bars" and "The Bonny Blue Flag" - well, they were willing to part from them for a time at least.

On the 22nd Gen. Turner was assigned to the command of our division, Gen. Harris thereafter to command the Third Brigade. Two days later we received orders to be ready to march at 6 o'clock the next morning, the 25th. We moved out at daylight that day, Sheridan, being on his return from the Valley to Grant's Army, and as the evening might, it was supposed, try to intercept him, our movement was in aid of him. We went as far as the Chickahominy, passing over a part of McClellan's old battlefields; but we saw nothing of Sheridan, he having crossed farther down the stream. We returned to our camp in the evening. In passing over the ground of the Seven Days' Fight, numerous bones of the fallen brave could be seen. A rather grotesque incident occurred on this march to and from the historic Chickahominy.

Asst. Surgeon Neil of the Twelfth at that time was something of a wag. Moving slowly and cautiously along over the battlefield, as we did, he had ample time to pick up a skull, which he did. There was a round hole in it, just as such a musket ball would make, and it needed no telling that that was what made it. The command coming to a temporary halt, he held up the skull, and assuming an air of solemnity, began a sort of mock lecture somewhat after the manner of a phrenologist. He said in substance about as follows:

"Gentlemen," said he, "examining the bumps upon this cranium hastily, yet as carefully as circumstances will at present permit, assisted by the light of past and passing events, I think that I may say, with a confidence amounting to conviction, and that you will be justified in accepting my statement as an assured fact, that the original possessor of this poll was evidently of a more or less combative disposition. And gentlemen, judging from the light of current history, and the apparent time that this skull has lain where it was picked up, and the patent, convincing, ocular evidence sustaining me in the assertion, I have no doubt that the wearer of this cranium died of a gun shot wound."

The boys within hearing smiled, some audibly, and as the march was resumed their arms and equipments felt less heavy on account of this display of waggishness.

Chapter Twelve

On the afternoon of the 17th, as preparatory to Grant's grand movement against the forces of Lee in Richmond and Petersburg, two divisions of the Twenty-fourth Corps, ours and the First, and one division of the Twenty-fifth Corps (colored), crossed the James and the Appomattox, and marched toward the left of our lines, southwest of Petersburg. Our division marched all night, passing in the rear of the lines of the Army of Potomac, and as we marched along, pretty heavy firing of the pickets close to our right was heard for nearly the whole distance. We halted about daylight in the morning in front of Petersburg and at 10 o'clock a.m. we resumed our march toward the left, followed by the other troops of Gen. Ord's Army of the James, camping within about two miles of Humphrey's Station. The next day, the 29th, the whole army, except enough to hold the entrenchments, moved to the left, our division going that morning to Humphrey's Station. We could hear cannonading farther to the left during this day. That night it rained all night.

At daylight, the 30th, our division moved again, the rain still falling. In the afternoon a train of ambulances passed to the rear loaded with wounded from the Fifth Corps. Also a lot of prisoners were brought in and sent off on the cars. The next morning at about 8 o'clock the rain ceased, it having rained all the night before, and our division advanced to Hatcher's Run; and the enemy resisting this advance, it had some pretty hard fighting. At this time the Second Corps and the Fifth and Sheridan's cavalry were on our left. Before daylight the following day, April 1st, the Rebels charged the skirmish line of our division, but were repulsed. In this charge a Rebel soldier, either deceived, or intending to deceive our men, came running up to Company E of the Twelfth on the skirmish line, exclaiming: "You are firing on your own men!" Lieut. Hugill of that company walked up to him, took his gun and sent him to the rear a prisoner.

Concerning operations here at this time, Lieut. Col. Holliday of the Fifteenth West Virginia, commanding a brigade at the time, told of an incident, according to a comrade, about Lieut. E. F. Pigott of Company G, which may be here given. Holliday, with his brigade, undertook to capture a Rebel fort in his front and Lieut. Pigott, being on the skirmish line then at that point, when the brigade charged, cooperated in the charge with his company. The attempt failed. Holliday and Pigott were in front of their men, and the men, giving ground almost before the officers knew of it, they were left between the lines, and, the fire of the enemy being hot, they took cover behind stumps. While they were thus under cover Holliday glanced from behind his stump, and seeing an overcoat in front said that he would like to have it; and Lieut. Pigott coolly and deliberately, said Holliday, got from behind his stump, walked forward, picked up the coat, brought it back and gave it to him. Some few years since Pigott, poor fellow, passed to the Beyond.

All night of the 1st we could hear on our right, toward Petersburg, the deep sounds and see the flashes of light caused by the firing of our siege-guns. At short intervals the whole heavens were made lurid by the discharge of the artillery. This day Sheridan, with his cavalry and the Fifth Corps, had had his victory at Five Forks, southwest of Petersburg. This firing was kept up to prevent, perhaps, the enemy from detaching troops in our front for the purpose of recapturing Five Forks, a vital point to them. As the Rebels lay behind their entrenchments that night it may be that they regarded this thundering and lightning of Uncle Sam's siege-guns as betokening his vengeful wrath, and their impending doom. Grant gave orders for the Sixth Corps on our right and opposite the Rebel center, expecting the enemy troops from there to attack the lines in its front as soon as possible in the morning, the 2nd; and for all the other troops to hold themselves in readiness to attack. The Twelfth took a position and lay close up to the enemy's lines that night, fully expecting to have to attack his entrenchments in the morning; but fortunately did not have this to do.

The Sixth Corps, having broken the lines in its front, the Rebels soon thereafter evacuated their works in our front. Our brigade then moved to the right to Petersburg, arriving near the city a little after noon. By this time all the enemy's works southwest of the city had fallen into our hands, except three forts near it, and it and several thousand prisoners besides. Our brigade participated with great credit that afternoon in the capture of Fort Gregg, and the Twelfth made for itself a proud record. An incident of a little while previous to the capture is remembered. After our brigade had got within a half mile of the fort, marching along we passed near a few soldiers not on duty. They seemed to regard us seriously, as being new troops to them and the Army of the Potomac. One of them looked at us rather dubiously and said in substance: "I wonder if those fellows will stand up to it?" implying that they thought there was fighting before us. We, however, had little idea of the serious work just at hand. If those soldiers watched the part we took in the capture of Fort Gregg, they doubtless had their minds disabused of any doubts as to whether we would stand up to it, at least as well as the average soldiers.

Our brigade was marched up and halted in line on high ground facing toward Fort Gregg to the north. All was quiet as yet, there being no firing. When we reached this ground we could see some of our troops, a part of the First Division of our corps, a little to the right of a direct line from us to the fort, and pretty close up to it. They were in a wavering condition, having failed to enter the fort. A little later an aid rode up to Col. Curtis, giving an order. The colonel looked a little pale, but unflinching, and almost before we had time to think, and without any announcement of what we had to do, the order of "Attention, Second Brigade, shoulder arms; right shoulder shift, arms; forward double quick march," was given. The boys seemed to know by a common understanding what was wanted, and, giving a yell, a sort of "Rebel yell," they started on the charge, running like mad their very best, seeming to realize that the sooner they got to the fort, the fewer of them would get killed.

The fort was in plain view from the point from which we charged, and as the ground over which we charged was mainly clean and open, and the lay of the land was such that the fort was not lost sight of at any time during the charge. The distance to be charged over was perhaps 500 yards down a slope and up a slope. In the hollow or foot of the slopes, something less than half way to the fort, there was some low swamp brush. When this was reached the enemy opened on our men, apparently with grape or canister. The balls could be heard striking in the mud and clashing through the brush, but, as seemed surprising, few if any were hit just at that place. The men rushed rapidly on their ranks, necessarily much broken by their passing through the low swamp brush, their different capabilities as runners, and their all rushing toward the one point, the fort. And they never stopped or scarcely so, until the bulk of them were in the deep ditch surrounding the fort. All the time after our men had come within close range, the enemy poured into them a hot musketry fire; but they escaped being hit remarkably, owing to the rapidity of our men's movements, and the Rebels' overshooting, aided materially, evidently, by the troops of the First Division's drawing the Rebels fire, and by their return fire, compelling the Rebels to a considerable extent to keep under cover.

When the order to charge was given Private J. W. Caldwell of Company D took off his hat and, swinging it over his head, shouted: "That's our fort, that's our fort;" but the gallant boy, falling dead upon the field, failed to witness its capture. Gen. Turner, commanding the division, after the brigade had got part of the way to the fort, and was under heavy fire, believing that the brigade was insufficient to take the fort, sent an order to Col. Curtis to halt his men and await reinforcements, but the men rushed on. Col. G. B. Caldwell, who was adjutant of the Twelfth till the winter of 1864-5, in his eulogium upon Col. Curtis at the reunion of the Society of the Army of West Virginia in 1891, says in regard to the order to Col. Curtis to halt his brigade: "But American soldiers are men of intelligence. With one mind they thought they were more certain to be shot down if they turned their backs than if they went on. They rushed forward." So far as this statement implies that the men heard that order, it appears to be a mistake. It is believed that few, if any of the rank and file heard the order. It would have taken a dozen or more men of the greyhound type to have carried that order to the men after they got on the go for that fort.

When within 50 yards of the fort, Sergt. Emanuel M. Adams of Company D, color-bearer, fell wounded. The colors were picked up and bravely carried forward by Private Joseph R. Logsden of Company C, as the brigade charged on over the dead and wounded of the First Division. After our men had got into the ditch surrounding the fort, they remained there perhaps twenty minutes before they made an entrance. In the meantime the Rebels were throwing dirt, stones and various kinds of missiles upon them. At length as a movement toward entering the fort, the gallant Logsden undertook to plant the flag of the Twelfth upon the parapet, and was killed, falling back into the ditch. The colors were then seized by Lieut. Joseph Caldwell of Company A, who leaped upon the parapet, and in attempting to plant the colors there was killed, falling also into the ditch. The flag fell inside of the fort. Then the brave boys of the Twelfth rushed to the parapet to recover their flag. They were joined by comrades of the rest of the brigade. Pouring a volley into the Rebels, the boys of the Twelfth leaped into the fort and planted their flag on the parapet - the first colors on the Rebel works. The fort and its brave defenders were soon ours, all the troops present joining in their capture. But the reduction of the fort was at fearful cost to the Union troops, the loss being in killed and wounded 715, as will be seen in Col. Caldwell's address at Huntington, herein given.

After events seem to show conclusively that this great sacrifice was unnecessary, for the fort would have been evacuated the following night without it. But it was here that the Twelfth won its eagle, and Col. Curtis his star, and Capt. Bristor won promotion for his gallant conduct. It was here, too, that Lieut. J. M. Curtis won a medal of honor, and Andrew O. Apple of Company I and Joseph McCauslin of Company D also won their medals of honor. And to add to the grace and beauty of the distinction, those medals were pinned upon the lapels of the boys' coats by the fair hands of the daughter of Gen. John Gibbon, our corps commander. There are very respectable members of Private George H. Bird's Company (I), it should be added, who believed that he should have had a medal of honor, as he was among the first few who climbed upon the parapet of the fort.

The next morning, the 3rd, after the capture of Fort Gregg, it was found that the enemy had evacuated Richmond and Petersburg, and nearly all the troops before these cities, including our division, started immediately in pursuit. And not to prolong the history too much, it will simply be said that we followed the Rebels for several days, there being more or less fighting and captures of prisoners by some part of Grant's forces every day. However, a material matter somewhat closely connected with the history of the Twelfth regarding this particular time, should not be omitted. On the 6th, the Fifty-fourth Pennsylvania and another regiment of infantry, with a squadron of cavalry were sent out in the direction of Farmville under command of Brig. Gen. Theodore Read to burn a bridge near there in advance of the retreating Rebels. But they were surrounded by a large force of the enemy, many killed and wounded, including Gen. Read killed, and the rest all captured. The Eighth, two divisions of our corps, the First Division and the Independent, marched all day and until 11 o'clock at night, making in that time, it was said at the time, a distance of 35 miles. We did not then precisely know the object of this forced march. We did not know but that we were following the Rebels, but we found afterward that we were being pushed to cut off their retreat.

An incident concerning a private of Company I, Alexander B. Allison, is perhaps well worth telling here. The boys of the Twelfth, like those of other regiments perhaps, were much given to discussing the probable outcome of any military undertaking. On this forced march the boys struck up a discussion as to the probability of overtaking Lee's army, the likelihood of a battle, and the probable result of it. Finally some of the boys said that they had seen enough of the Johnnys and that they wished that they, the Johnnys, would go on until they should run into the Gulf of Mexico. Fighting the Johnnys was no longer a picnic. The time had passed when the boys were "spoiling for a fight," and as the average man is generally willing to postpone a possibly fatal ordeal, so the most of the boys were doubtless willing to delay an engagement with the enemy. Private Allison, however, then about 19 years of age, spoke up showing the grit to perform a disagreeable duty immediately, saying: "Boys, if I have to fight the Rebels at all I am willing to do it right now. I do not desire to follow them for a week or two, and then have to fight them at last."

We camped this night in a piece of woods to the side of the road not far, as we learned afterward, from the Southside railroad. It happened that the cavalry a short time before had captured a train of cars containing subsistence for Lee's army, and the train was lying not far from our camp. One of the boys of Company I somehow found out that the train was there, and he got by some sort of management a large piece of bacon, as much as he could well carry, and brought it to camp, dividing it among a number of the company. This was a welcome supplement to the rations.

Before daylight on the morning of the ever memorable 9th of April, a day that will stand out as conspicuously in our history as that of the surrender at Yorktown, if not more so, we started to cut off and surround the Rebels in their retreat, to engage and vanquish them in their Last Ditch, and give a finishing stroke to the Lost Cause; and thus to give to the loyal people of the Nation the fruition of their indomitable struggles, through hope, through darkness, and doubt, for four long and bloody years; to illuminate the land with joy, and to fill it with a great gladness such as it had not known for generations.

We marched not very far when we were started on the double-quick along the road, just as day was breaking. We had marched thus rapidly only for a few minutes, when some cavalry were observed coming out of woods on our right at a rather rapid rate, though in good order. It appeared that the Rebels had been driving them, and that they were withdrawing to uncover the infantry. Just as a squadron emerged from the woods opposite our regiment, one of the cavalrymen exclaimed: "Here come the Doe boys," and then he gave us the further encouragement of assuring us that the Johnnys had up the black flag.

Every soldier who served any considerable time in the late war will bear out the assertion that in no kind of civil life during the same length of time could a man hear a tithe of the rumors, startling in purport, that he could hear during the war. So the boys had heard too many rumors to be frightened by this story of the black flag. In a few minutes our regiment was halted, the ranks closed up and formed into line upon the road. This road, it is believed, led north, so as to intersect the road the Rebels were on, a short distance west of Appomattox Courthouse. Our part of the line did not extend as far as the intersection of the roads, but doubtless the two divisions extended beyond it, so as to completely cut off the retreat of the enemy. We moved in line toward the enemy and at nearly right angle to the road, through some woods in such a manner as to place our regiment in the west line of the closing in lines. Our two divisions from the Army of the James and Sheridan's cavalry were now barring the Rebel retreat. We advanced rather cautiously, moving up a little then, then halting, perhaps waiting on the disposition of other troops. It was not long till shells began to crash through the tree tops above us, from the enemy's batteries. They did no harm to us, however.

We now halted and remained in line for perhaps two hours, expecting to have a battle that day. The boys of the Twelfth seemed confident. There was no disposition shown by any to flinch. They no doubt were cheered by the thought that for once, since joining Grant's army, they were about to get a whack at the Rebs without having to fight them behind breast works; when about 9 o'clock a.m., the order came very unexpectedly and to our great gratification and relief, to cease firing until further orders. We did not then know that a flag of truce had been sent by Gen. Lee; but the boys generally seemed, in the phrase of the present time, to "catch on" to the fact that this probably meant the surrender of Lee's army, the main-stay of the Rebellion; and their countenances accordingly lighted up with the thought of the pleasing prospect of this glorious consummation, which all felt was devoutly to be wished for, and which had been hoped, prayed, and fought for through four long years of blood and tears, and tears and blood.

Soldiers hardly ever have knowledge before of any great military movement in which they are to engage. Sometimes they are precipitated into a hazardous undertaking without a minute's notice. They are sometimes engaged in important movements without knowing definitely what they are doing. A soldier, who was in McClellan's army in its retreat from the Chickahominy to the James, once related that he thought that all the time they were fighting and marching they were going toward Richmond instead of retreating. But, as to the matter of the early knowledge of what was about to be done, for once, that 9th of April, the soldiers got ahead of the Commander of the United States Army, for they had at about 9 o'clock a.m. that eventful day a pretty strong intimation of what was about to take place; while Lee's dispatch to Grant agreeing to surrender on Grant's terms did not reach him until half past eleven o' clock a.m., the latter being considerably in the rear of his forces, passing from the right to the left to communicate with Sheridan. He could not be found till then, and consequently did not know sooner of Lee's acceptance of his terms.

Perhaps it was shortly after 12 m. that our line moved up toward the Rebel camp into open ground, and soon their camp some half mile distant appeared in view. Not long after this a great volume of cheers was heard rolling round the lines from right to left. This we soon learned was caused by the announcement of the surrender. The cheering was not precisely continuous, but was rather somewhat intermittent. It would break out in great roars, then subside, then in a few minutes break out again, all the time coming nearer as the news was carried from organization to organization. Pretty soon our commander, Col. Curtis, rode in front of the regiment and repeated the gladsome news of the surrender, saying that the war was virtually over; that we would soon be mustered out, and sent home; that we would get home in time for harvest. The boys, inspired by the thought of final victory, that the "cruel war" was over, and especially by the thought of home, gave three such rousing heart-felt cheers as doubtless never escaped their lips before.

Such vigorous, frantic, and deep-down-from-the-heart cheering was perhaps never before heard on this continent as was heard that day, and the boys need not ever expect to hear the like again. Men acted with the delirium of joy, climbing trees, throwing their hats in the air, jumping on them and doing all sorts of frantic things. They forgot all about the long and weary marches they had made; their suffering from sickness, hunger and cold, the dangers, battles, and scenes of carnage they had passed through. All thoughts of these things were swept away by the great flood of joy that overwhelmed them, because of the glorious victory of the hosts of Union and Liberty over the hosts of Treason.

And now a remarkable feature of this almost closing scene in the great drama of the Civil War should not fail of receiving notice, especially as it has not hitherto been alluded to, so far as has been observed, in any other published account of the surrender. About a half hour after the cheering had ceased on the part of the Union soldiers, there was almost as vigorous cheering in the Rebel camp. This conduct of the enemy had something of the appearance of rejoicing over their own defeat. However, though no explanation is remembered as ever having been given for this demonstration, the reasonable inference is that they were cheering because they had heard the news that they were to be paroled upon the field and sent home, instead of being sent to prison. Like the Union soldiers they were delighted with the prospect that they should soon "breathe the air again of our (their) own beloved home." Be this as it may, this cheering of Lee's defeated veterans was a most extraordinary occurrence. And it is doubtful if a parallel to it can be found anywhere in all previous history. This was a scene the like of which could occur nowhere else, perhaps, on the earth at this time than in this free, enlightened, and humane land of ours.

Some mention here of Lieut. H. R. McCord will perhaps be not without interest. He was mustered in as First Sergt. of Company G. During the war he received promotions up to first lieutenant, and when Col. Curtis was put in command of a brigade, McCord was appointed adjutant general on the colonel's staff. The lieutenant had relations living all during the war within the Rebel lines, and he would hear, through letters from them occasionally. He came to believe and so expressed himself during the last year of the war, that the Rebels would never be conquered. Doubtless the die-in-the-last-ditch spirit breathed in those letters was responsible for that belief. He never gave up that idea until the morning of Lee's surrender. This want of faith in final success, however, in nowise interfered with his faithfulness and efficiency as a soldier, for he was ever ready to do his whole duty bravely and well. The cloud of despair that had hung over him was all swept away that memorable morning, as a fog before the breeze. And perhaps there was not a gladder man, nor one that rejoiced more heartily that day in the entire army than he, over the glorious victory and the downfall of the Rebellion.

Two divisions of the Twenty-fourth Corps and some other troops remained on the field of surrender while the Rebels were in course of being paroled. At first for about one day our guards kept the soldiers of the two armies apart and from mingling with each other. After that there was no restraint put upon them, and the late deadly enemies met and chatted in a quite amicable and seemingly friendly way, just as if they had never been at war with each other. The Johnnys were disposed to contend that if the number of their men and their means had been equal to those of Uncle Sam, they could not have been conquered. But they said nothing at that time about one Southern man being able to whip five Yankees.

There was considerable trading going on between the soldiers of the two armies. The boys on either side were disposed to trade almost anything they had. The Johnnys would sell their Confederate money for about anything they could get for it, and they would go to our sutlers and spend any "green-back" or postal-scrip money thus obtained for tobacco, being anxious to get, as they said, some "Yankee tobacco." They quite generally expressed a willingness to give up the struggle; to have the war end immediately, and to submit to the authority of the United States.

The world has heard much of the hero of Appomattox and the famous apple tree. Gen. Grant rather spoils that story of Lee's surrendering to him under the apple tree, by saying in his memoirs that it had very small basis of fact, viz., that Gen. Lee had met Grant's staff officer, Gen. Babcock, under an apple tree which stood near a road running up through an orchard, which was near the Rebel camp. After all, though this story has a pretty good basis of fact, many a good tale has less. At all events it was quite generally believed by the Union troops, and there was accordingly a scramble among them for fragments of the tree. Many of the Twelfth managed to get pieces of it, for when it came to "confiscating" things and appropriating them to private use this regiment was never far behind.

As anything relating to that historic field and that memorable day is of interest, the following as related by a soldier of the Twelfth is given:

On the day of the surrender or perhaps the next day, I was strolling about the field and chanced to approach near to where a colonel of our army and a citizen were in conversation. This citizen, it seemed, was no other than McLean, at whose house Gen. Grant drew up terms of the surrender of Lee's army. Just as I came up McLean was saying, "I own the ground where the first battle of the war was fought, Bull Run, and I own the ground where the last battle of the war was fought, at this place." This remark arrested my attention. I knew that it was generally regarded among the Union troops that Lee's surrender was the virtual collapse of the Rebellion, but I was interested in having a confirmation of this opinion from a Rebel himself, being like the rest of the boys anxious to have the cruel war over; so I could not refrain from saying: "And so you regard the war as being over?" addressing my remark to the citizen. "Yes," said McLean. The colonel answered also, saying, "And one of the greatest generals of the world, General Lee so regards it." I felt a vaguely defined sense of displeasure at and disapproval of this remark of the colonel, but said nothing.

Perhaps if this soldier had looked into his mind for the motive of this feeling, he would have found it in the fact that it was hardly consistent with loyalty to his country, its cause and his comrades to be praising this Rebel general whose hands were red with his comrades' blood, who had been fighting against the only free government at that time worthy of the name on the face of the earth, endeavoring to set up a government founded on the barbarism of human slavery, and whose so-called government had so cruelly treated his comrades at Andersonville and other prisons.

The officers of the Army of the Potomac seem to have had a very high opinion of the military ability of Gen. Lee. Gen. Grant says in his Memoirs that it was no uncommon thing for his staff officers to hear from Eastern officers: "Well, Grant has never met Bobby Lee yet," implying that when Grant should meet him he would meet a greater military antagonist than he had previously met and perhaps an overmatch. Events - the hard tug of war for about a year, however, proved that "Old United States Grant" was too much for "Bobby Lee."

Impartial history will, no doubt, record with substantially one voice that the blacks were innocently the cause of the war. Anything therefore relating to the "contrabands" in connection with the war will not be impertinent, so an incident in regard to one of them is here given. One day during the several days we were camped at Appomattox a colored man came into the camp of the Twelfth. On being engaged in conversation and asked if he knew that his people were now all free, and told that President Lincoln had two years before the then last New Years' declared all the slaves in the land forever free, and being told that he was now, since the Rebels were whipped, as free as any man, he seemed almost struck dumb with amazement, managing, however, to utter some devout ejaculations. He appeared to be though more incredulous if possible, than amazed.

It may seem to be almost incredible that this black man living not more than 80 miles from our lines, for the then past year, should be ignorant of the proclamation of Emancipation, at a time more than two years after it had been issued, especially as news is said to have generally traveled fast among the slave population. He, however, did not know of the granting of this great and long prayed for boon to his race by "Massa Linkum," or else he was a very skillful adept in assuming ignorance. It may be remarked here that in whatever degree the slaves may have been ignorant of the existence of the Proclamation, they seemed to know by intuition or otherwise that their interests lay with the success of the Union cause.

Within three or four days after the surrender Lee's army was all paroled and sent home. April 12th the Second Division (ours) marched for Lynchburg, arriving there on the 14th, and destroyed much war material at that place. The Second Brigade entered the town in advance, and as our men marched along the streets the blacks, in great numbers, many of them sent from various places - some from North Carolina - for safe keeping, thronged the streets. They were wild with joy. They threw their arms around each other, shouting "Glory to God! the Yanks am come and we're all free."

The 16th the command started back from Lynchburg and scarcely, if at all, halting at Appomattox, pushed on toward Richmond. Our division halted a few days at Burkesville, during which time the Twelfth was paid to the first of the past January. We then marched on to Richmond, arriving there the 24th. Our brigade was camped near the city. We remained here nearly two months and during this time, the 16th of June, the Twelfth was mustered out. And it was while we were here that one pleasant June afternoon we were marched to a point nearer the city than our camp, and just as the shades of night were beginning to spread over the landscape, the boys of the Twelfth who had won medals at Fort Gregg were presented them, receiving them as before written from the hand of Gen. John Gibbon's daughter. This was a proud day for those boys.

On the 20th of June, the Twelfth took transports for home. They landed us at Baltimore. We took cars there for Wheeling, arriving there the 24th. In a few days the men were paid off and, receiving their discharges, were soon on their way to their several homes to enjoy the peace they had to fight for, and yet as long as they should live, from time to time, fight battles over again. It should be said, however, that before leaving for their homes the boys were given a grand dinner by the generous citizens of Wheeling.

Col. Curtis died August 25th, 1891. There was always a high respect and filial regard entertained on the part of the members of the regiment for their late commander, and the survivors will be gratified to have here recorded Col. Caldwell's memorial address, before referred to, upon his life and character.

COLONEL CALDWELL'S ADDRESS

Comrades and Friends: - General Curtis is gone. He was a grandson of John Curtis, a patriot soldier of 1776.

General Curtis was born April 18, 1821, on now historic ground where the great battle of Antietam was afterwards fought.

In 1832 his parents removed to the town of West Liberty, in Ohio county, where on becoming of age he engaged and continued in business as a merchant until he became a soldier in 1862. In 1861 he was a member of the State convention at Wheeling, which organized a loyal State government for Virginia.

In 1776 one of the members of the Continental Congress advocated unanimity in supporting the immortal declaration of our country's independence by reminding his fellow-congressmen that "they must all hang together, or they would all hang separately." In that Wheeling convention every man had to face the same situation. Each one who cast his lot and his vote there on the Union side risked his life, his fortune and his sacred honor on what was then a doubtful result, and against the vast majority of the people of his State, against the seductions of State sovereignty, and often against the strongest influence of family ties. General Curtis had a brother who was colonel of the Twenty-third Virginia Confederate Regiment and was killed at the battle of Slaughter Mountain.

If the South succeeded, death or exile, confiscation of property and business and social proscription were sure to each member of that convention. It was a convention of Southerners true to the old flag without an appropriation. From its results was born West Virginia, fair and patriotic, devoted and loyal, in the sisterhood of States.

It is one of the proud memories that we cherish of our comrade that he served not falteringly among those true and devoted men. In 1861 he raised and tendered to the old war governor, Francis H. Pierpont, a company of volunteers. Again in 1862 he enlisted a company which became Company D of the Twelfth West Virginia Infantry. He was elected captain.

In 1863 the nine captains of the regiment, other than himself, and the other commissioned officers, elected him major. As such he commanded the regiment until January, 1864, when his worth was again recognized by his election by his fellow-officers of the regiment as colonel, and their choice was ratified by Governor Boreman. Holding that distinguished rank, he commanded generally a brigade, sometimes his regiment, until the close of the war.

Even while thus serving he suffered from disease, but was a soldier who never lost a day's duty in those trying years, or answered a surgeon's roll call. Whoever else was absent, he was always "present for duty."

At New Market, Piedmont, Lynchburg, at Snicker's Ford, Kearnstown, Winchester, Fisher's Hill, and above all at Fort Gregg, he was the leader not only in rank of his brigade, but in fact. He served under the quick, brilliant and glorious Phil. Sheridan, the Stonewall Jackson of our side, throughout the great campaign of 1864 in Shenandoah Valley.

At Snicker's Ford on the banks of the beautiful Shenandoah, we were all ranged along the shore of the river behind a low fence of stone surmounted by rails. The Confederates had lately had a blockade runner get through, and wore light blue trousers and jackets, once gray, which time and service had rendered of no particular color. Their skirmishers approached us, walking backwards and turning to fire. Our boys, when they got near, wanted to fire on them, but Colonel Curtis forbade it, saying: "Those are our men."

Directly one of them turned and took deliberate aim at the colonel, who was standing by a rail upright by his side, and blazed away. Tung! went the oak rail as it was struck by the ball close to his head. It was the only time I ever knew the colonel to forget his tactics. "Shoot them, boys, shoot them now!" he said with energy. It was not the regulation command, but it was appropriate and efficient.

The foremost of all who served, General Grant, in his Personal Memoirs, calls the assault by Curtis's Brigade on Fort Gregg in front of Petersburg, Va., "desperate." In this assault there were 715 men and officers killed and wounded on Sunday, April 2, 1865, yet Col. Curtis captured the fort. His own regiment had three color bearers killed in planting their flag on the rampart.

After he had ordered the charge General Foster regarding it as impossible of success, ordered that it should be abandoned after the troops had got near the fort. But American soldiers are men of intelligence. With one mind they thought that they were more certain to be shot down if they turned their backs, than if they went on. They rushed forward through chevaux de fris and ditch and threw themselves on their faces against the sandy front of the ramparts. General Foster exclaimed when they refused to about face: "Well, go on. You'll all be killed anyhow." A two hours' hand to hand contest over the walls of the fort resulted in its capture.

General Gibbon called it "if not the most desperate, one of the most desperate assaults of the whole war." A few days afterward at a grand review at Richmond, one officer and two privates of the regiment were called to step four paces in front of the line of battle. A general order was then read, naming them for conspicuous personal gallantry in the assault, and soon afterwards bronze medals were presented to them by our National Congress. One of these three was that brave and fearless soldier, Lieut. Mont. Curtis, now deceased, a son of Gen. Curtis.

For the part he took the eagles upon Colonel Curtis's shoulders were replaced by the general's stars by the President of the United States. The official record in the War Department of the promotion reads: "For gallant service in the capture of Fort Gregg, Virginia." The regiment was presented with a bronze eagle for its conduct. It bears the inscription:

"Presented to the Twelfth Regiment, West Virginia Volunteer Infantry, by their corps commander, General John Gibbon, for gallant conduct in the assault upon Fort Gregg, near Petersburg, Va., April 2, 1865."

Richmond was immediately evacuated when this fort surrendered. General Curtis was afterward elected a member of the Legislature, and rendered important civil services to the State, and has continually held positions of honor and importance bestowed by his comrades in the G.A.R.

Owing to declining health he had for some years lived in retirement before his death on the 25th of last August at his home in

West Liberty, at which time he was one of our vice presidents. Our deceased comrade was a modest man, but we have no reason to be modest in speaking of him.

It was the fortune of your speaker to sleep in the same blankets with General Curtis for two years and a half during his service, being his adjutant, and he was the most indulgent, considerate and generous of men, manly and Christian in all his character. He had the rare faculty of attaching those he led to himself in unwavering confidence, and that enthusiastic, affectionate personal regard without which no military captain of any degree can be a success.

Like the Old Commander who received the sword of Lee at Appomattox, he was level-headed, and never lost his head in the hour of danger; had full possession of his faculties and capabilities in the hour of battle, as well as on dress parade.

In time of peace he was a man of peace. When war came he became a soldier. When peace returned again, he returned to the paths of peace. He was a splendid type of the citizen-soldier. At the end of his "three score years and ten" he leaves a memory which will be revered, honored and cherished by his comrades, and perpetuated in the history of a grateful country.

Conclusion

A few words in conclusion are ventured. From a military point of view it would appear that one of the lessons of the war, if not the most important one, teaches that we should not over-estimate our own valor, strength and resources, or under-estimate those of the enemy. Accordingly, when it becomes necessary to go to war, making full allowance for any possible inadequacy of estimate in these regards, we should strike with ample and overwhelming force. The force should be double or triple that which would seem to be enough, rather than of doubtful sufficiency. In fact, where there is uncertainty as to the possible magnitude of a war, it is best to be on the certain side, and to strike the first blow with utmost strength, rather than feebly - with the big end of the bludgeon of war, rather than with the little end; and not do as was done by the government in the late war, begin it with an inadequate force. The example of the Prussians in the Franco-Prussian War teaches a lesson in warfare. They struck in the beginning with overwhelming force, and made short work of the war.

Perhaps the most striking fact in connection with the conduct of our late war was the lack of appreciation of this guiding principle of precaution, or the disregard of it on each side of the contending powers. There are many examples illustrating this fact. The failure of the government to fully measure the task of the suppression of the Rebellion prolonged the war through four years, seriously jeopardized the result, and caused the sacrifice of a million of men, and the expenditure of many millions of money to finally suppress it, which otherwise might have been accomplished with one-tenth of the cost of men and money. Twenty thousand more men on the Union side at Bull Run, for instance, which additional number could easily have been had; would probably have gained the day there, and put an end to the war.

On the other hand, if the Rebels had not under-estimated the valor of their foes, thinking that one of them could whip five Yankees, and had they made their supreme effort at an earlier stage of the war instead of at the last of it, when they were "robbing the cradle and the grave" to recruit their armies - if for instance they had had at Antietam 110,000 men instead of 60,000 or 70,000, over which McClellan failed to gain a decisive victory, which larger number they could have had as easily as they could bring on the field of Gettysburg 100,000 men almost a year later, after meeting heavy losses at Chancellorsville and on other fields, it is no violent presumption to say that they might have won the day and gained their independence.

However, regarding the war from a moral and political standpoint, it sometimes seems as if the war did not last long enough. It took years of the terrible scourge of war, it would appear, to convince the people of the seceded states, and to wring from them the acknowledgment that they were better off without slavery than with it. And perhaps if the war had lasted a little longer, and the Rebels had felt still further the scourge of war, those who now have so much respectful regard for the flag of treason, and the Lost Cause and their defenders, might have finally become convinced that one flag and one cause and its defenders are enough to honor, and that there should be no place in the patriotic regard and affection of the people in this free land of ours for the Rebel flag, the Lost Cause or their defenders. Big as this country is it ought to be too little to give room for any display of honor to the Rebel flag, the Lost Cause, or their champions, dead or alive. Therefore, no soldier who would be faithful to his country and the cause for which he fought should join in any ceremony of decorating Rebel graves, of holding reunions with Rebels, or of putting up monuments to them.

A few years since Gen. Sherman, at a Soldiers' reunion, said that it was commendable to decorate Union graves, to encourage reunions and to put up soldiers monuments, as to do these things was to create and nurture a patriotic sentiment. Granting the truth of this, it follows then as the night follows the day that to take part in these or similar ceremonies, when done in honor of or with Rebels distinctively as such, in contradistinction to being Union soldiers or citizens, is to engender and to nurture disloyalty. No Union soldier should do it. The reason given by those of them who do so, is that they wish to remove the animosities of the war, and to cultivate a fraternal feeling between the sections. The motive is good, but is it not paying too dearly for kindly feeling and fraternal regard when they are obtained at the cost of the inculcation of disloyalty?

The people of the late seceded States claim to be now as loyal as those of the rest of the Union; but while there is a growing improvement in respect to the loyalty of the former, there is too much of the old disloyal spirit among them yet. Many instances might be given; but only that of the utterance of the following sentiment by Gen. Early at the unveiling of the monument erected in 1891 to the memory of "Stonewall" Jackson, and the manner in which it was received, is given: "If I am ever known to repudiate the cause for which Lee fought and Jackson died," said Early, "may the lightning of heaven blast me, and the scorn of all brave men and good women be my portion." According to the Charlottesville, (Va.) Chronicle, from which the above quotation is taken, this sentiment was cheered by twenty thousand throats. The fair inference is that Gen. Early and those cheering his sentiment are as much Rebels as they ever were.

The same newspaper above named says that there were ten thousand Union soldiers present at the unveiling of this monument. While the loyal sentiment of the land thus suffers the inculcation of treason, and itself to be insulted by demonstrations like that of the unveiling of the monument referred to, and others of similar character in honor of late Rebels or the cause for which they fought, by those who lately bore arms against the government there is no obligation of good feeling or of fraternity that demands of Union soldiers the countenancing and aiding of these traitor-breeding demonstrations, by their presence at them. It is to be hoped that the country is to be spared the humiliating spectacle of many more such disgusting manifestations of falsity on the part of the Union soldiers to the cause for which they fought, as that it had to witness at the unveiling of the monument erected to the memory of "Stonewall" Jackson at Lexington, Va.

The Story

of

ANDERSONVILLE

and

FLORENCE

By
JAMES N. MILLER,
COMPANY A, 12TH WEST VA. INF.

Past Commander Gen. Sherman Post,
Sac City ; Member Crocker Post, Des Moines.

Introduction

Those who took part in the civil war, and who wish to leave any record of its scenes and incidents, must do so soon. Another decade will muster out of life's service the soldiers, or leave them too old for historical or other work.

This little book is written without pretense to extended detail of the events described, but only to tell to those who do not care to read the larger works, in plain and simple language the story of the two famous prisons of the civil war. The reader will discover that it is without prejudice or undue feeling. Time has softened the intensity which formerly existed, and it is now seen that what was once believed to be diabolical and intentional cruelty was the result of circumstances partly beyond the control of those who were placed in charge of prisoners.

To the remaining white-haired comrades of the war, some of whom were confined with me, I trust this will prove of interest; and the general reader will also, it is hoped, find the simple narrative both interesting and instructive. A diary kept during the imprisonment is the basis of the narrative, and certainly it is a truthful one.

THE AUTHOR

Chapter One

The Twelfth West Virginia Infantry was formed during the summer of 1862, and was mustered at Wheeling Island on the 16th of August. It was composed almost entirely of Virginians, a few Pennsylvanians and Ohioans being in two or three companies. It was characteristic of most of the people of the western portion of Virginia that they were as intensely loyal to the nation as those of the eastern portion were loyal to the state. Between the two sections there had long been an antagonism, both industrial and political. In the western part there were few slaves, both because the industries there made it unprofitable to keep them, and because the proximity to the free states rendered escape comparatively easy. Beyond the Ohio river, and Mason's and Dixon's line, there lay freedom for the fugitive, who was hurried forward on the "underground railroad" to Canada. The people of western Virginia were mountaineers, earning a scanty existence from the hard soil, their houses poor, living on corn bread and hominy and salt pork, with an occasional feast of venison and b'ar meat. The vast resources of coal, and iron, and oil, which in the last two decades have brought wonderful wealth to the state, were then either unknown or undeveloped.

The people of eastern Virginia — the ruling forces especially — were the descendants of the aristocracy, the F. F. Vs. who scorned to labor themselves and despised those who did, and who therefore depended largely on slave labor to maintain them in splendid idleness, and devote their time particularly to politics. Their state had been the "home of Presidents," its nearness to the national capital giving it additional interest in politics; it possessed able statesmen and soldiers, and from the very inception of the rebellion the people espoused the cause of the south. The affair at Harper's Ferry, within the borders of the state had alarmed the people, and it is not to be wondered at that they honestly believed a separation from the northern states was absolutely necessary to the preservation of that great industrial institution on which their prosperity had largely depended. A generation after the war we may write calmly of these things, and even those who participated in the stirring scenes have forgotten the fierce strife and the tumultuous passions which arrayed the people of the north and the south against each other.

As family quarrels are always most bitter, so the feeling between the loyal and the disloyal people of Virginia, Kentucky, Tennessee and Missouri was far more intense than that between the people of the other northern and southern states. In the fratricidal conflict there were found fathers and sons, brothers, relatives and neighbors arrayed in arms against each other, and there were many occasions when these met on the field of battle, or in prison, or on the picket line.

CHARACTER OF THE REGIMENT

Hence it was that the Twelfth West Virginia was composed very largely of men who were intense in their hatred of those who had seceded from the union. They were mountaineers, used to tramping over the hills in search of game, skillful with the rifle, swift on the march, inured from the beginning to hardships and privations. Every soldier thinks his own regiment the best. But it can truly be said of the Twelfth, that while it was not engaged in as many battles as some other regiments, and its losses were not as heavy, it fulfilled faithfully every duty placed upon it, and did not falter in the hour of battle. And this is all that can be demanded of any regiment, for the extent and character of its services are dependent on the commanding officers.

LIMITED IN EDUCATION

Living in a state where there were no free schools, and few private ones, a number of the regiment could not read or write. This did not detract from their valor and efficiency as soldiers. It was the lot of the writer to be the penman for several members of his company, and to write their letters to loved ones at home, and read the answers. Sometimes this duty included writing letters to sweethearts, and in this art he became quite proficient, and after the war found it useful on his own account. There were certain poetical couplets with which these letters were generally ended, as —

> My pen is poor, my ink is pale,
> My love for you will never fail; and —
> The rose is red, the violet's blue,
> Sugar is sweet, and so are you.

In return for this writing my comrades often took my place on picket and other duty, and in many ways eased the hard life of the soldier. Being the youngest boy in the company, and frail in body and health, these strong men were always kind to me, and their services saved my life on more than one occasion.

HARD TO PLEASE

A few men in the regiment were tinctured with the virus of slavery, so that it was with difficulty they held to their loyalty when the emancipation proclamation was issued. One member of our company swore a round oath that he would not "fight to free the damned nigger," and sure enough after the first battle in which we were engaged he deserted, and it was not until near the close of the war that he was found in the fastnesses of his mountain home and returned to the regiment.

OFF FOR THE FRONT

It was in the latter part of August that the organization of the regiment was completed, and it was at once ordered into active service. An invasion of West Virginia was threatened; and we were sent to help repel it. As the regiment marched off the island, through the streets of Wheeling, it received a royal welcome from the people of the city, and as I looked at the long line of blue, it seemed to me that when we once got into battle the war would be of short duration. Our first trip was over the Baltimore & Ohio, the historic railroad of the war, which we were, destined to guard and repair and ride over many times during our three years of service. Going east to Grafton, we changed to the Parkersburg branch, and rode to Clarksburg, where we alighted and pitched our first camp. This town was on the border line of the war, and a number of its inhabitants were in the southern army. One company of our regiment was recruited in the town and surrounding country.

On this trip our first arms and ammunition were issued to us. The rifles were of the Austrian pattern, very roughly made, so that our hands were often sore from their handling. They shot fiercely, but the recoil was heavy, and the boys were glad when we exchanged them for the far better Enfield.

A MAN OF PEACE

On arriving at Clarksburg one member of our company was missing. He was an old man, John Scantling by name, somewhat eccentric. No one knew what had become of him, and it was feared he had fallen from the cars and been killed. But in two or three days he came into camp all right. To all inquiries where he had been, and what had befallen him, he would only answer, "I am a man of peace," and we concluded that the sight of arms had frightened him. He was soon afterward discharged, as being unfit for service.

Since the war, Clarksburg has been improved very much, and is now a bustling town. The Lieutenant-Colonel, of our regiment, R. S. Northcott, has made it his home, and a number of the boys have lived in and near the town.

Chapter Two

After a few days spent at Clarksburg, five companies of the regiment, including Company A, to which I belonged, were sent under command of our Lieut-Col, to Buckhannon, some twenty-five miles away. Here we saw the first effects of real war in the shape of some arms, and also grain, which had been piled up in the street and burned by a company of southern cavalry which had dashed through the town a few days previous, and captured some union soldiers who were stationed there. Resting a day or two, we resumed our march to Beverly, going on the way over Rich mountain, the scene of one of the first conflicts of the war, where Gen. McClellan and Gen. Rosecrans bore a part. The breastworks yet remained, as well as the graves of some southern soldiers. Our stay at Beverly was brief, and we returned to the remainder of the regiment at Clarksburg. On the way we passed through the town of Philippi, where nearly the first battle of the war was fought, and Gen. B. F. Kelley was wounded.

OUR FIRST BATTLE

The reader will not be wearied with details of the career of the regiment. In June, 1863, it engaged in its first battle, at Winchester. The union forces stationed there, under command of Gen. R. H. Milroy, met a disastrous defeat by a superior force of Gen. Lee's army, on their march to Gettysburg. Our loss in killed, wounded and captured was heavy, and the retreat into Pennsylvania was a long and severe one. We did not recover in time to be of much service in the campaign which ended so victoriously for the union army.

THE GREAT CAMPAIGN

In the spring of 1864, at Martinsburg, in the Shenandoah valley, an army had been gathered under command of Maj. Gen. Franz Sigel. It was intended that this force would march simultaneously with Grant's army in their advance to Richmond, and by threatening the rear of Lee's army compel him to detach a portion to resist us and thus draw off from the defensive forces of the confederate capital. On the 29th of April this army set out on its march up the valley. With our regiment was the 1st W. Va., the 34th Mass., the 18th Conn., the 54th Pa., the 28th, 116th and 123d Ohio, with cavalry and artillery in proportion. On the march we passed our old battle ground at Winchester, and on the 9th of May camped at Cedar Creek, the scene afterward of Sheridan's famous battle, in which our regiment took part.

Here we lay a few days waiting for the completion of a bridge across the stream, which was swollen by rains. After it was finished we resumed our march, and on the evening of the 14th of May camped near Woodstock. Here we heard the booming of cannon in the south, and reports soon came in of fighting near the town of New Market. The next morning, Sunday, we were on the move bright and early, and the sound of battle grew constantly plainer and nearer.

HIS WISH GRANTED

There was a member of our company named Chrisman, who had come to us as a recruit during the previous winter. He was jolly and good natured, always ready for singing and dancing. He and I were in file together, he in the rear rank and I in the front. As we were going into the battle he said to me, "Miller, I hope I will be killed today." I replied, "Chrisman, you ought not to talk that way." "Well, I don't care what becomes of me," he said. In the confusion that ensued, we changed places, he taking the front rank and I the rear. We lay down in line of battle, awaiting a charge which the enemy was making upon us. Chrisman lay in front of me, and as he was large of body I crouched behind him for shelter. Soon I heard a dull sound of something striking, and Chrisman stretched himself out at full length, dead from a bullet through the heart. Our conversation, and the fact that it was only by accident that we had changed places, thus taking his life and saving mine, made an impression on me that has never worn off.

Chapter Two

"HALT THERE, YOU YANK!"

A battery near us was firing on the advancing foe, and hearing an officer give the command, "Fire by section," I looked up and saw Gen. Sigel sitting on his horse, smoking a cigar, and seeming as calm as on parade ground, while I was so excited as to scarcely know what was going on. This was the last time I saw the General, though we have corresponded since the war. Our company was ordered to the right of the line to prevent a flank movement, and the main body of our army being soon driven back by the superior force brought against it, in the rout which ensued four members of our company, including myself, were taken prisoners. Fortunately we fell into the hands of brave captors, who treated us kindly. As we walked back over the battle field, the bodies of blue and gray were mingled, showing that both armies had suffered severely. My guard permitted me to pick up a blanket, and also a well filled haversack and both these became of good service to me in my long imprisonment. And so for the second time our regiment had suffered defeat.

DISCUSSING SLAVERY

It being late in the day, the prisoners taken, about one hundred and fifty in number, were marched a short distance beyond the town of New Market, and camped for the night in a field. Next morning a count of the prisoners was made, and the officers were very bitter against the men of our regiment, who as Virginians they said were "fighting against their state." On informing them that I was a Pennsylvanian, their wrath against me was mollified, and one of them engaged me in conversation on the war, slavery, etc. Now, I had always believed in slavery, supposing it to be right, but from sheer contrariness took the other side from the officer, and argued against slavery with a readiness that surprised myself, while a number of comrades gathered around to listen to the discussion. Finding that the southerner was getting warm in the argument, I prudently brought it to a close.

GOING DOWN TO DIXIE

At noon we were started on the march and at night reached Harrisonburg, and were quartered in the court house. Here we drew our first confederate rations, and they were about the last good ones we received. Next morning we resumed the march, under guard. It was a long tramp, hot and dusty, and we began to realize that being a prisoner was no light matter. At one time during the day a southern officer drove past us in a buggy. The guards saluted him, and told us he was John C. Breckinridge, formerly Vice President of the United States, and now a Major General in the confederate army, and commander of the forces which had defeated and captured us. A brief sight of him showed a well formed and fine looking man.

By night we reached Staunton, tired and hungry. Here we joined other prisoners, of the 1st New York cavalry, who had been captured in skirmishes. This place is on the Va. Cen. R. R., and next morning we were placed on the cars and taken to Charlottesville, the seat of the Virginia university, where Gen. Robt. E. Lee taught after the war. We lay a short time in the beautiful grounds of the institution, and saw some of the young cadets of the military school, who had taken part in the battle of New Market. As our forces were retreating down the valley, these cadets had returned to their studies. Our stay at Charlottesville was not long, and we resumed our ride to Lynchburg, where we got off the cars, and in a pouring rain marched to a camp in a deep valley, in which were already confined a large number of prisoners from the army of the Potomac. Here we were kept two days, and again boarding the cars we rode to Danville, where we stopped. The country through which we rode was very poor, and at the few little stations we saw only women and children, the men being in the army.

TASTE OF PRISON LIFE

At Danville we were quartered in a four-story brick building, and as my assignment with 97 others was to the top story, an attic, it was very hot and stifling. The guards kept us away from the windows, and the only rations we drew were corn bread and black bean soup, very thin. Fortunately we were kept here only a day, and again on board the cars we started for Georgia. Our first stopping place was Greensboro, N. C., but here we only changed cars, and stopped next, at Charlotte, in the same state, where we camped for the night, in an old corn field, in a pouring rain that continued all night. The next day, while making a stop at Winnsboro, the engine of our train, which had gone a short distance in front of us to take water, on its return crashed into us, smashing two cars and injuring some of our men. Many of us jumped from the cars, but the guards compelled us to get back again. The southern railroads were all in horrid condition, and the runs would be very fast down hill and very slow up hill.

Friday morning, May 27, we reached Augusta, Ga., and it seemed that I was nearer starved here than at any other time during my term of imprisonment. Having been accustomed to the liberal rations of our own army, my stomach had not sufficiently contracted to the different allowances of the confederacy. We drew a reasonable ration of corn bread and raw salt pork, and were allowed some liberty to wander around the outskirts of the town. It was often my regret that I did not attempt to escape here, though doubtless it would have ended only in recapture.

Saturday afternoon we resumed our journey, passing through Macon, where there was a prison for the officers of our army, and at noon on Sunday, May 29, just two weeks from the day of our capture, we reached a little station in the pine woods, and were ordered off the cars. After a march of nearly half a mile we came upon some tents, and then looking over and beyond them we saw a great moving mass of humanity, and instinctively knew that we were about to enter—

ANDERSONVILLE.

Chapter Three

Being drawn up in line, a little, dried up, weazened faced man, with coarse hair and beard, wearing an officer's uniform, a sword at his side and a revolver in his belt, made his appearance, and in a piping voice commanded, "Prisoners, Attention!" This was the famous and infamous Captain Wirz, commander of the prison, who after the war was tried, convicted and hanged for cruelty to those under his charge (a small man executed where larger ones should have been). For myself, neither from Wirz nor from any other officer or guard did I ever receive any personal abuse or punishment, perhaps because I studiously avoided giving them cause for offense, realizing that they had their duties as soldiers, and that their place was a hard and unpleasant one, with many annoyances. It is always best for a prisoner to obey orders, and to avoid giving his guards annoyance and trouble.

DISCOUNTING OUR INTELLIGENCE

Having secured our attention, Wirz again announced, 'If there is any sergeant here who can read and write, let him step out." The idea of there being a sergeant who could not both read and write was so strange to us that we were nonplussed, but we learned that this was not uncommon in the southern army, and Wirz supposed the same condition existed among our soldiers. One of my comrades whispered to me to step out, and although only a private I did so, but was a moment late, and a real sergeant was placed in charge of the squad of prisoners, and this charge he retained in the prison, receiving an extra ration for his services. Was not this ill luck for me?

SHOWING HIS TEMPER

Some delay was occasioned in going into the prison, and a few of the boys straggled down to the brook which ran near us to get a drink. Whereupon Wirz gave us an exhibition of his uncontrollable temper, swearing he would put as into the stocks if we didn't stay in ranks. I afterward saw a prisoner who had attempted to escape, confined in the stocks, sitting in the hot sun, his back uncovered and blistering with the heat, and his tongue lolling out with thirst.

Finally the order to march was given, and we entered the prison at the north gate, the guards standing with cocked muskets ready to repel any attempted outbreak by the prisoners.

"FRESH FISH!"

This was the cry that greeted us from our fellow prisoners, which we afterward used in welcoming new sufferers who came in. Despite all the misery and torture and death, there was always plenty of humor which helped us to endure the life there. One day a storm that blew upon the prison carried up into the air some hats and other articles of clothing, and deposited them outside the stockade, while the boys made the prison ring with shouts and laughter.

A NARROW ESCAPE

Being very thirsty, my first act was to go down to the brook to get a drink. Inside the stockade, about twelve feet therefrom, ran a line of posts three feet high, on top of which was nailed a two by four, and this was the celebrated dead line, beyond which it was death to pass. Ignorant of its purpose, and of the penalty for crossing it, and seeing that the water running in the brook was clearer inside this line, I was about to step over the railing, when a comrade caught me and pulled me back, and pointing to the sentry in his box at the top of the stockade, told me of my danger. There the guard was standing with musket cocked and leveled, ready to fire had I gone over. Several men were shot here during the summer, and it was believed among the prisoners that a guard who shot a "yank" was given a furlough therefor. But about this I have no knowledge, and believe there is no evidence to substantiate the charge.

PITCHING OUR TENT

After finding the boys of my company—Freeman Younkin, Wm. Stine and Clark Gamble—we proceeded to locate our home, near the southeast corner of the prison, and to pitch our tent, made from the blankets of which we each fortunately possessed one. Two blankets made the tent, of the A. or dog, pattern; one was spread on the ground and the fourth was used as a covering. We drew our rations, and worn and weary lay down to sleep on the sands of Andersonville. Awaking early next morning we saw a few feet from our tent the body of a prisoner who had died during the night, entirely stripped of clothing, taken off no doubt by other prisoners. He was a young lad, and it was a pleasant (?) thought that came to me that perhaps I, too, should lie down there and die like a dog, and loved ones at home would never know my fate. But this was for a moment only, and after that I never lost heart, and of course grew indifferent to suffering and death.

THE PRISON

Andersonville, at the time of our entrance, contained about sixteen acres, enclosed by a stockade of pine logs of one to two feet in diameter, twenty-five feet long, set on end in a trench dug five feet deep, as close together as possible, forming thus a wall twenty feet high that could neither be seen through nor surmounted without the aid of a ladder or a rope. Through the center of this enclosure ran a small stream, about as large as what would be called a "run" in Pennsylvania or a brook in other places. It was rather swift flowing, the water tinged with black, and having a decaying vegetable taste. There was often a scum of grease on the water, which came from the cook house located over the stream a short distance outside the stockade. About half the length of the stream was used for washing clothes and bathing, and the other half, next the outlet, served as a sink. On each side of the stream was a morass or swamp, varying in width from fifty to a hundred feet, through which one could not walk, and which was of course uninhabitable, taking off, therefore, that much from the available space of the prison. At times this swamp would be so alive with wriggling maggots that it seemed to rise and fall in undulating billows. From the edges of the swamp the ground rose, especially on the north side, which was quite steep. Aside from the swamp the location was a very good one.

PLENTY OF SAND

The soil, if it could be called such, was sandy, and this was of great benefit to those confined, in point of health. Every rain, and it is a land of copious rainfall, washed off the sand, and carried with it the accumulated filth, down to the brook, and thence away from the prison.

When the site for the prison was selected, it was a forest of Georgia pitch pine trees. These were cut down and used to form the stockade, leaving only the stumps and limbs, which were soon used by the prisoners for fuel. If a few trees had been left for shade, it would have been of great benefit, but those who planned the prison did not think of this, or perhaps did not care. Beneath the blazing sun of June, July and August the sand was so hot that one could not walk on it in his bare feet, and a number of the prisoners were without shoes, their captors having appropriated them for their own use.

SHOOTING BOXES

At proper distances around the prison, at the top of the stockade, were covered platforms, for the use of the sentries or guards. These stood always with muskets ready, and generally they evinced an unnecessary readiness to shoot at any provocation, though some of them were not of that character. Very often they were ready to trade with the prisoners, giving food and tobacco in exchange for trinkets. The articles were either thrown back and forth or pulled with a string. One day I saw a prisoner who had become insane, rush inside the dead line, and baring his breast call on the guard to shoot him. Ordinarily this would not have needed a second invitation, but this guard happened to be humane, and called to the comrades of the man to take him back to his tent. Another day a prisoner who was sleeping in his tent alongside the dead line, and whose foot in his sleep protruded within the limit was fired at and wounded. So in the southern army, as in our own, there were various grades of soldiers. Generally speaking, the guards who had seen real service were kind in their treatment of prisoners, while the men who had never smelt powder on the battle field were anxious for the opportunity to "kill their man."

At night the guards would call the hours, beginning with the one at the south gate, who would announce, "Post numbah one, two o'clock, and all's well," and this would be repeated by each one in turn, changing only the number of his post. If a guard wanted anything he would call out, "Co'pal of the gua'd, post numbah foah." It was very often hard to distinguish between the language of the negro slaves and that of some of the southern soldiers.

THE DEAD LINE

Concerning the dead line much has been written about it as a measure of cruelty. But in fact it would not have been possible to have maintained the prison without it. If the prisoners had been permitted to put their tents up to the stockade, it would have been undermined the first night. The only other cruelty or barbarity connected with the line lay in the over readiness of some of the guards to shoot those who unknowingly walked over its boundaries. We believe every northern prison of open character maintained such a line.

THE WATER SUPPLY

This came partly from the brook, and partly from wells dug throughout the prison. The soil being sandy, it was comparatively easy to dig wells, even with only a tin plate or half a canteen, and in ten to twenty feet there would be found a moderate supply of water, of fair character. This would be raised to the top in a tin cup tied to a string, more primitive even than the wells dug by the patriarchs in ancient Palestine. Some time during August this water supply was augmented by a spring which broke out near the north gate, between the stockade and the dead line. The commanding officer kindly allowed a spout to be put in to run the water to the prison, and thereafter it furnished a large part of the prisoners with pure water. It is no wonder we called it "providence spring," though it was only the uncovering of a former spring which had been covered over by the washing of sand and soil. Such ebbs and flows are not uncommon in hilly countries.

Chapter Four

The rations furnished to the prisoners in Andersonville were partly raw, and partly cooked. Those who drew cooked rations received corn bread, corn mush, cooked beef or pork, cooked beans or cow peas, and cooked rice. (not all of these at one issue, but from time to time). The quantity varied, but the quality was always the same, rather poor. The bread and mush were made of unsifted corn meal, ground cob and all we always believed, and it was very often only half cooked. Then the mush was dumped into pine boxes, giving it a taste of resin and turpentine, which none but starving men could have eaten. The beans, or peas, were a southern product, used for stock, but they were nutritious and healthful, despite the bugs which made their habitation in them.

Those who drew uncooked rations received the same articles as above, in their raw state, and the same in quantity. It was always my fortune to receive my rations raw, and it was much better, for I could vary the style of cooking. The coarsest parts of the meal could be taken out and these in the cooked rations were a prolific cause of diarrhea. Sometimes I made corn cakes, and at other times corn dumplings. My cooking utensils were a quart cup and half a canteen. The bugs in the peas bothered me by trying to crawl out of the cup when the boiling process commenced, but by careful watching, and pushing them into the soup, it made the food more nutritious and palatable.

The fuel used was pitch pine, the smoke from which entered into the pores of the skin and blackened us until we lost the semblance of white people. I often think this smoke has never gotten out of the faces of the prisoners, and that they can be readily recognized. Sometimes I drew more rations than I could eat, the stomach revolting. In this case the surplus corn meal would be made into a beer or vinegar, used for the scurvy, or it would be traded with other prisoners for vegetables.

DRAWING RATIONS

This was the important event of each and every day, and likewise a neverending topic of speculation and conversation. When the gates were opened, and the wagons were driven in with the food, a crowd gathered around, and any crumbs that dropped on the ground were eagerly seized by the hungry wretches. The sergeants in charge of the detachments received the portions allotted to them, and taking them to the assigned places, distributed them to each individual member, and the sub-divisions were pretty small on some of the articles. Perfect fairness was enforced, or a fight ensued. It was not required for the members of a detachment to have their tents together, but generally this was done for convenience. As soon as the prisoners received their rations, they hurried to their tents, to eat the cooked food, or to cook that which was raw. Very often the whole ration was eaten at one meal, so intense was the hunger, but this was a bad thing to do.

SOME EXCUSE

In extenuation of the rations furnished, it can be said that the confederacy was in hard straits to secure sufficient food to feed its own soldiers. Indeed, at this writing I am inclined to think the officers in command were more incompetent than they were deliberately cruel. Much of the suffering, and the heavy death rate, were unavoidable from the large number confined in so small a space, in a debilitating climate, with unsanitary conditions, and the lack of sufficient shelter. A part was also due to the homesickness of the prisoners, especially of those who had left families at home. When once the disease of longing for home seized a prisoner, he began to decline, and it was seldom he recovered. A case in point was one of the members of my company, Clark Gamble. As soon as he entered the prison he grew home sick, and began to go down. Seeing he was in this condition, the rest of us began to abuse and torment him, and by getting his spunk up, and leading him to forget his troubles, he commenced to improve, and lived to get out all right. Of the four of our company who were captured at New Market, all lived to return home, and I believe that very few of our regiment died in prison.

ABOUT THE VERMIN

Here is a subject concerning which it is distasteful to write, yet the description of prison life would be incomplete without it, for it formed a considerable part of our daily life to exterminate the pests. We had encountered these in some degree in our own army, but they were as nothing compared to those which infested the sands of Andersonville and Florence. If the plague of lice sent upon Egypt was like that which infested us, I cannot conceive why Pharaoh did not get rid of the children of Israel at once. Travelers in Egypt say that remnants of the plague are numerous there to this day. When we entered the prison our curiosity prompted us to count the number we killed on our clothing each day, but after running up to nearly two hundred it grew too tedious. Two or three times a day we were compelled to go through the searching process, and woe betide the poor fellow who was too weak, or too indolent, to rid himself of the parasites. He soon succumbed to the diseases which their attacks produced. The fear of my veracity being questioned leads me to forbear giving accurate statistics, but in Andersonville, as in other places, eternal cleanliness was the price of life.

BATHING AND WASHING CLOTHES

It may well be supposed that these duties were attended with some difficulty. Bathing, indeed, could be carried on with reasonable regularity at the brook, but when one had no change of clothing, and the process of washing was known to wear out garments rapidly, it may well be surmised that as little was done in this direction as possible. I am therefore not ashamed to say that during my last three months of imprisonment I did not wash the one suit of underclothing which I possessed. Winter was approaching; release seemed uncertain; there was no opportunity to replace clothing were out; and so I decided to be on the safe side, and save as long as possible the scanty covering which might be necessary to protect me from the cold and wet. Many others were compelled to do the same.

TRYING TO ESCAPE

It is one of the rules of war, at least among civilized nations (who ought never to go to war with each other), that prisoners have a right to escape, and should not be punished for attempting it. They may make use of any means to escape, even to taking the lives of the guards. The captors, on the other hand, are at liberty to use every means to prevent escape, and may shoot down those who attempt it. But after the attempted escape had been foiled, or the escaped prisoner had been retaken, there should be no punishment further than additional necessary precautions and safeguards against future attempts. It is therefore a just cause of complaint against the keepers of Andersonville prison that they inflicted undue and barbarous punishment on those who attempted to escape. The most common method of escape was by means of tunnels, dug from a point, near the dead line, at a depth sufficient to pass under the stockade, and after a short distance beyond to dig up to the surface and thus escape. The work was done at night, with the same rude tools used in digging wells, and the dirt taken out would be thrown into an abandoned well, or carried to the brook to be swept away with the current. One prisoner would crawl into the tunnel and dig, putting the dirt into a sack, which his companion would pull out with a string, empty the sack and the digger would pull it in again. It was very hard work, and great care had to be used to keep it from being known, and also to prevent accidents in the tunnel which might result fatally.

If the tunnel was carried to completion, a dark night would be selected and as many as were in the secret would creep into the narrow opening, and crawl and squeeze through the passage until the end was reached, when they would work their way up to the opening. If they succeeded in eluding the ever watchful guards, they would steal silently out into the forest, generally one by one, to meet again on a signal of whistling, or perhaps to try their fortune alone.

Various other means were adopted, but were seldom if ever successful. I do not believe that one prisoner ever got entirely away from Andersonville, between April 1 and October 1, 1864.

PREVENTING ESCAPE

The methods used by the prison keepers to prevent escape, or to recapture those who escaped, were various. Workmen would make the rounds of the prison, next the dead line, with sharp pointed poles, to discover any tunnels by pounding on the ground or running the sharp point down. Some times the location of a tunnel would be revealed by an unfaithful prisoner, who would receive some reward from the keepers. But if he became known to his fellow prisoners he would be punished by having half his head shaved, the word "traitor' written upon his forehead or breast, in which condition he would be marched through the prison, execrated by every one who saw him, and sometimes set upon and beaten.

THE BLOODHOUNDS

But the most effectual means used were the bloodhounds, of which several were kept ready for use. Every morning they made the circuit of the prison, at a short distance outside the stockade. If a tunnel had been used during the night it would be discovered by the hole through which the escaping prisoners had crawled, and the hounds soon found the trail. And then woe betide the poor prisoner, for it was only a question of a short time until he would hear the ominous bay upon his track, and his life could only be saved by taking to a tree. As to the justification of this method of capturing escaping prisoners I pass no judgment. As Gen. Sherman said, "war is hell," if not in one way then in another. These hounds are now used in many counties for tracking criminals.

UNJUST PUNISHMENT

The punishment inflicted on these men, who had a perfect right to escape, was to give them lashes on the bare back, or confine them in the stocks, or bind a heavy iron ball about their leg, or deprive them of food for a time. For this there can be no justification whatever, and it is the greatest stain upon Wirz and his fellow officers that it was done. It is with no small gratification that we are led to believe that hereafter in civilized war the treatment of prisoners will be far more humane than it has been in the past. The horrors of Andersonville were probably no greater than those of the British prison ships in the revolutionary war. During the late American-Spanish war prisoners were treated very humanely by both nations.

Chapter Five

The most important and exciting incident in all the history of Andersonville was the capture, trial conviction and execution of THE RAIDERS.

These were a band of thieves, robbers and murderers, mostly from New York City, who had probably enlisted as bounty jumpers or substitutes had been captured, and now in prison banded themselves together to continue their old occupation. It was never possible to tell how many of them there were, and doubtless their forces were exaggerated. They made up by organization and discipline what they lacked in numbers. Their mode of operation was to note the new prisoners who came in, and who appeared to have money, or who wore good clothes, or had plenty of blankets or other comforts. Locating the place where one or more of these prisoners would put up their tent, the raiders would go there at night, and if possible steal anything on which they could lay their hands. If the owners discovered them, and resistance was made, a fight followed, in which the raiders by standing compactly together generally won out, unless the cries of the victims drew too large a crowd, in which case the raiders would scatter to their tents. Whistle calls regulated their movements. Some of them were well known, but so great was the terror inspired by them that no one dare molest them. During the month of June they became especially bold and active, and scarcely a night passed that their whistle calls were not heard, followed by cries from their victims, with a rush of hurrying feet throughout the camp. Prisoners mysteriously disappeared, and no one could trace them. Our tent was never molested, doubtless because it presented an aspect of poverty which did not in any way belie the actual condition of its occupants, for there was not one of us possessed a penny.

ARRESTING THE RAIDERS

At last the robberies grew so numerous and unbearable that some of the prisoners who had been victims banded themselves together to exterminate the raiders. An appeal for help was made to Capt. Wirz, and to his credit be it said he responded to the call. Guards were furnished who arrested the raiders as they were pointed out, and took them outside the prison. This occurred on the 29th of June, and one or two succeeding days. The raiders fought desperately, and in my diary it is recorded that two of them were killed. This is not mentioned by Sergeant McElroy in his book, and it may have been only a rumor. I had no part in the affair, but my feelings were strong against the raiders. The regulators, as those who fought the raiders were called, were deserving of great credit for their brave work, done at peril of their lives, for had they not taken matters in hand the condition of the prison would soon have become unbearable. It is a hard thing to say that the worst treatment the prisoners received came from some of their own number; but it should be borne in mind that these brutes were not real soldiers, who had enlisted to fight the battles of their country, but were thieves and murderers who had joined the army to ply their trade, and perhaps to escape the penitentiary for crimes committed.

TRIED AND CONVICTED

Over a hundred of the raiders were arrested and taken outside, where they were kept under guard by the regulators. A jury was empaneled, made up of new prisoners who were unprejudiced. A fair and impartial trial was held, the accused being allowed counsel. The evidence showed innumerable robberies, and several murders, the bodies of the victims having been buried under the tents of the raiders, thus accounting for the mysterious disappearances. After a full hearing the jury found six of the accused guilty of murder, and sentenced them to be hanged. Several others were found guilty of robbery and theft, and were sentenced, some of them to wear a ball and chain, and others to run the gauntlet. These latter were turned into the prison one at a time, and compelled to run through a line of men who set upon them and beat them, three being killed in the process.

As usual where a community takes the law into its own hands (though this was absolutely necessary here) excesses were committed.

THE EXECUTION

Monday, July 11, was fixed as the day for the execution of the six murderers, though this was kept secret except to a few. On the morning of that day timbers were brought in, and the erection of the gallows was begun near the south gate. The raiders who were left in the prison mustered their forces for a last rally, and trouble was looked for. At this time there were over twenty thousand men in the prison, and all who were able to do so gathered about the gallows, or on the opposite hillside, to witness the sight. A little after noon the south gate was opened, and Capt. Wirz entered on his old white horse, with guards conducting the six condemned men. Wirz made a short speech in his usual broken tongue (he was of Swiss birth), and turning the men over to the regulators he rode outside, taking the guards with him.

A WEIRD SCENE

And now occurred a scene, which in its settings and dramatic effects has seldom been equaled, and certainly never surpassed. Around the scaffolding in every direction ten thousand men were gathered as tightly as they could be wedged. On the opposite hill side another ten thousand were standing, tier above tier, like those in the old Roman Coliseum, straining their eyes to see the strange proceedings. Outside, the stockade the guards were gathered in the forts which commanded the prison, ready for any emergency which might occur, the infantry in ranks, the artillerymen at their guns, which were loaded and ready to be fired at a signal. Many spectators were also standing on the walls of the forts, watching the unwonted scene. Alongside the scaffold were ranged the six doomed men, their faces pallid, but lips firmly set, and eyes sending forth defiance. Around them were the regulators, with clubs in hand, keeping back the ever surging crowd from the cleared space, and closely watching for any attempt at rescue by the partners of the murderers. A priest in his robes stood with prayer book in hand, and on being given leave to speak he began an appeal for mercy. But a mighty shout of protest went up from the entire vast multitude, until his words were drowned. Again it was like the scene in the Coliseum, when the fallen gladiator saw no hands uplifted in all the great throngs bidding his conqueror to spare.

SELLING HIS LIFE DEARLY

The priest, seeing his appeal was useless, read the last rites, and the condemned were ordered to ascend the scaffold. With an oath one of them broke from his captors, and fighting his way through the crowds ran towards the brook. Outside the keepers, seeing the commotion, thought an outbreak was at hand, and officers called to their men to be ready, while the spectators (many of them women) screamed with terror and scattered in every direction. It was reported that Wirz commanded the officers to fire, but they, seeing there was no movement of the prisoners toward the stockade, refrained from repeating the order to the artillerymen. The crowd around the scaffold, very few of them knowing what had happened, was panic stricken, and in the mad rush some were pushed into wells, and suffered broken limbs. If the regulators had not been men of cool heads and determined nerve, every doomed raider would have broken loose, and all the efforts would have come to naught.

But they stood by the captives with uplifted clubs, while the two who were in pursuit of the fleeing criminal overtook him in the swamp and dragged him back to the scaffold. They passed close to me, and I can never forget the look of hopeless terror in his face, mingled with a tiger-like ferocity, as with foaming mouth he cursed his captors.

THE FINAL SCENE

Once again the order was given to ascend the scaffold, and with trembling limbs the helpless murderers obeyed. Walking up the steps, and out on the narrow plank, they stood ranged in line, with the ropes dangling at their heads. Leave was given them to speak, and they employed their last moments in calling to friends among the crowd, giving them directions, and sending messages to their homes. Again the priest commended their souls to heaven, the heads were covered with sacks, the ropes adjusted, the signal to drop given, and the six souls swung off into eternity.

NO MERCY SHOWN

But no, not all. Mosby, the leader of the gang, whose station was at one end of the plank, broke his rope, and fell to the ground in an unconscious condition. The regulators lifted him to his feet, and dragged him up the steps again. He revived and begged piteously for his life. But he who had never given mercy was denied it now when he most needed it, and for the second time he was swung off, this time effectively. An awful hush fell on the vast multitude as the bodies swayed to and fro.

The work was done, justice had performed its vengeance, and law and order had triumphed.

After a sufficient time the bodies were taken down, and turned over to their friends, who gathered around and tended them carefully, muttering curses and threats against the regulators. Both outside and inside the prison the spectators returned to their various places. So fearful had been the punishment that it was never necessary to repeat it, and thereafter both life and property were reasonably safe within the prison, except from sneak thieves.

The six men who were hung were as follows:

William Collins, called Mosby, 88th Pa. Inf.

A. Muir, U. S. Navy.

Terence Sullivan, 77th N. Y. Inf.

Charles Curtis, 5th R. I. Art.

John Sarsfield. 144th N. Y. Inf.

Patrick Delaney, 83d Pa. Inf.

Yes, "war is hell," but an equal hell can be found any night in the slums of our great city.

Chapter Six

The most common diseases to which the prisoners were subject were scurvy, diarrhea and dysentery. The first was the result of an inactive life, the salt meat used, and the lack of vegetables. Its symptoms were swelling and discoloration of the limbs, ulceration of the gums, and followed by lassitude and depression. I have seen prisoners take out their teeth and replace them, so badly was the mouth affected. The disease was believed to be communicable through the common use of drinking cups, but this was probably an error. The only certain cure was to procure a supply of vegetables, especially Irish potatoes eaten raw, and a change from one prison to another was beneficial. It was not in itself a fatal disease, but it induced through weakness other diseases, the combination of which ended in death. Very few prisoners were free from it, and the effects of it have continued to this day upon some who survived the war.

The kindred diseases of diarrhea and dysentery were the most fatal in their results. They principally arose from the coarse food, especially the unsifted corn meal, and the half-cooked condition in which most of it was eaten, while bad water contributed its share. Those who drew cooked rations were more subject to them than those who did their own cooking. Each disease was rapid in its effects, and unless it was speedily checked there was but one end, and that was death. Very little medicine was issued by the authorities, partly because they had little to give. On several occasions I went out at sick call to the physicians in charge, both for myself and for others, and received only some sumach berries for scurvy, and white oak bark for diarrhea. For the latter disease I added charcoal made from the pine fuel, and cured myself of a severe attack. The scurvy clung to me until I was sent to Florence, and its effects still remain with me.

CASES OF GANGRENE

At one time a number of prisoners were afflicted with gangrene, resulting in part from vaccination, which had been performed by the southern surgeons, their arms being in terrible condition. It was charged that the vaccine matter was intentionally poisoned, but it is practically certain that the resulting gangrene was caused by the physical condition of the patients. Any wound or cut made on the body was hard to heal, and there were numerous eases where fingers and toes were cut off to stop the spread of gangrene.

HOMESICKNESS

This was undoubtedly a prolific source of sickness and death. The prisoner affected would sit down and grieve, instead of exercising; he would refuse to eat; if genuine sickness came upon him he gave up hope, and after that it was not long until his comrades were called on to carry him outside, either to the hospital or to the dead house, and the former was generally only a half-way house to the latter.

CARRYING OUT THE DEAD

When a prisoner died, his friend, if he had any, took immediate possession of the body, to prevent other claimants doing so. At the proper time two or more would carry the remains outside and lay them in the dead house. On their way back the carriers were permitted to gather up loose wood for fuel, and this was the incentive which made every one so eager to perform the gruesome service. Once the members of my tent fought with those of the adjoining tent over the body of a soldier who had crawled into the little street in front of us, and died during the night. Our force won, and I was one of the two detailed to carry out the body, and returned with an armful of wood.

THE CEMETERY

From the dead house the bodies were hauled in wagons to the cemetery, being thrown into the wagon promiscuously. I saw a load of these bodies once, with an entirely naked corpse stretched out on the top, and the sight nearly made me sick. At the cemetery the bodies were placed side by side in a trench, covered with earth, and at the head of each body a little board was put up, on which was painted the name and regiment where known, but on three thousand of them there was the one word, "unknown.'"

Since the war this cemetery has been cared for by the government, and is said to be well kept. Miss Clara Barton devoted much time to identifying the graves, and marking them wherever possible.

MORTALITY AND DEATH RATE

The official records of Andersonville show that 45,613 prisoners were admitted, and that the average term of imprisonment, from first to last, was about four months. Of this number, 12,920 died in the prison and in the hospital, or over 28 per cent. Very few regiments during their three years service lost that per cent of their members killed in battle or dying of disease. To this number should be added probably 20 per cent, who died after removal to other prisons, or soon after being released, from disease or injuries contracted in the prison, making a total mortality of nearly fifty per cent, or one-half. Nothing else so fully shows the terrible suffering endured here, and its significance can hardly be realized. Suppose that one per cent of the people of a town or city should die on a given day, what an awful visitation of providence that would be considered, and the weeping and lamentation would be like that which followed the edict of Herod nineteen hundred years ago. But on the 10th of August, 1864, there were three hundred dead union soldiers carried out of Andersonville, or about one and one-fourth per cent, of the number then in the prison. Yet so hardened had we become, and so hopeless were many, that it occasioned no particular comment.

MIGHT HAVE BEEN LESS

The death rate in Andersonville could have been largely reduced by leaving some trees for shade when the ground was cleared; by permitting the prisoners to erect houses for shelter out of the wood which stood in abundance all around the camp; by sifting the meal used for bread and mush; by cooking the food more thoroughly, and by giving the prisoners more exercise. But all this was above and beyond the mental capacity of Wirz, no matter what his disposition might have been.

WRITING LETTERS HOME

One privilege granted to the prisoners was to write letters home, and also to receive them from friends at home, though I never saw any of them that thus came. Early in June I wrote to a sister at home this letter:

In Prison at Anderson's Station, Ga.

Dear Sister: I was taken prisoner on 15th May and brought here. Am well, in good spirits. Don't tell Mother where I am, if you think best not to. Write and direct to Commander Co. A, 12th Va., tell him Gamble, Younkin and W. Stine are here and well. I hope soon to be exchanged. We are treated pretty well. Get enough to eat. Write to me. Direct to J. N. Miller, Co. A, 12th Va., prisoner at Andersonville, Ga., via flag of truce boat. Good bye. Don't be alarmed about me. From your Brother.

This letter, in an unsealed envelope, was placed in the box at the south gate, where such letters were ordered to be deposited. On the 17th of Jan., 1865, seven months after writing, it was received and postmarked at Old Point Comfort, Va., and it reached its destination in Pa. about the first of February, a month after I had arrived at home. During all the seven months of my imprisonment my fate was unknown, for I was reported "missing" on the field of battle, and the anxiety of my aged mother, and of brothers and sisters, cannot be conceived by those who have not passed through similar experiences. What was the cause of the long delay in forwarding the letter I of course never learned.

HOPES OF RELEASE

Every succeeding day brought an innumerable batch of rumors and stories about exchange and release. These were the universal topic of conversation. No one could ever tell the origin of the stories, but as they passed from lip to lip they grew in detail and certainty. The constant failure of our hopes never brought discouragement, for a new crop sprung up in place of those which failed. Like Jonah's gourd, they grew to full vigor in the night, and perished in the heat of the day. The keepers of the prison seemed to encourage the rumors, probably to keep us quiet and prevent an outbreak.

Then there were ever recurring hopes of release by our invading armies. Stoneman's raid, when he reached Augusta, gave us high hopes, and the alarm felt by Wirz was manifested when he caused a shell to he fired over the camp by way of warning, and notices were posted forbidding us to assemble in crowds for any purpose. Alas, we were so thick in the prison that it might be said we were a perpetual crowd.

DEPENDING ON SHERMAN

But it was when Uncle Billy Sherman started on his march to the sea that our hearts beat fast. The capture of Atlanta was announced to us by one of the sentinels, who called out one night,

Ten o'clock, and all's well,
But Atlanta's gone to hell.

A wild cheer went up from those who heard him, and soon the whole camp knew it. Every fresh lot of prisoners brought in were quickly interrogated, and in this way we kept track of the movements of our armies, it was seen that the confederacy was doomed, and that our release was only a matter of time—but, could we hold out? That was the serious question. Yet had it not been for this constant hope within us, renewed from day to day, very few would ever have survived the horrors of our prison life.

MADE ME KIND

My confinement in prison had one effect upon me; it has made me sympathetic in feeling for those confined in states' prisons. Not that I condone their crimes, or would release them until they have been punished, but I often think of their lonely hours, their separation from home and loved ones, the cold reception which awaits them when they go out into the world again, and I think of Him who came to open the doors of the prison and give release to the captives.

NO GLORY FOR US

One cause of perpetual regret to us was that while Sherman was marching through Georgia, and Sheridan was whirling up the valley, and Grant was pounding his way to Richmond, we could bear no part in these glorious campaigns, but must make up our daily little life of monotonous routine, in which the most exciting incident was the hunting for vermin. Is it any wonder that the minds of some of the prisoners gave way, and they become raving maniacs?

Chapter Seven

> Each heart recalled a different name,
> But all sang Annie Laurie.

Some might think that a prison would be barren of music. It was not so in Andersonville. There were few instruments, as I remember. But singers were there in plenty, and every evening the strains of the Star Spangled Banner, America, and other patriotic songs were heard throughout the camp. Mingled with these would be the hymns and sacred songs sung at the prayer meetings. And now and then a cultured voice would sing a song of love, or of home. I often recall a night in July, a clear, manly voice near me sang the Sword of Bunker Hill. When he ended the guard near him called out, like Oliver Twist, for "more." I seldom heard any of the southern soldiers singing, and believe they were not as given to music as our boys. Their favorite and almost only tune for the little drum corps was the Bonnie Blue Flag, and they played it over and over again, until everybody grew heartily sick of it. Whenever any of the negro slaves were working near the prison we would hear their weird, sad and monotonous songs.

RELIGIOUS MEETINGS

A Catholic priest was the only minister who was ever known to come into the prison. He did not hold any public service, but would talk privately with the soldiers, and give sacrament to the dying. One day some ladies made us a visit, but the scenes witnessed were so sad they did not stay long. Almost every evening there would be several meetings for prayer held, and one may feel assured the petitions to the throne of grace were very fervent. I possessed a copy of the New Testament and read it through several times, to my profit. The last moments of many of the dying were cheered by words of hope and comfort from those who had made their peace with God, while others, sad to say, died cursing the government, and even reviling their Creator.

PROFANITY

It was a terrible place for swearing. This is common in war. Away from home, and the restraints which society imposes, the prisoners grew peevish and cross, and vented their feelings in senseless oaths that were shocking. They cursed each other on little provocation; cursed the government for not procuring their release; cursed the confederacy for not bettering their condition, and cursed God in sheer wantonness.

DISCUSSIONS

There were men of all shades of opinion—political, social and religious in the prison, and naturally these men very often came together in discussions, which sometimes grew heated and personal, ending occasionally in blows. Strolling one day near the north gate, I saw an elderly man who was defending the course of our government in respect to exchange of prisoners (requiring negro soldiers to be exchanged the same as white soldiers), and urging our duty to stand by Abraham Lincoln. Looking closely at him I saw it was a townsman of mine, Jos. Cook—Col. Cook, he was called—of the 18th Pa. Cav., one of the best of men. Right glad we were to see each other, and through him I found other acquaintances who helped me much. Among them was Sergeant, afterward Captain, John Rogers, also of the 18th Pa. Cav., a brave soldier, who had escaped from prison in Lynchburg by breaking past the guards, was recaptured in sight of our lines, and sent to Andersonville. He afterward escaped from Florence, and reached home after numerous adventures.

Once I had an unpleasant discussion with a couple of Englishmen, who were berating our country, and claiming that the British were much superior to the "bloody" Yankees. I casually mentioned Bunker Hill, and for this was set upon and had to scurry back to my tent.

FIGHTING

In spite of the weakened condition of the men, and the miserable circumstances which ought to have made them patient and forbearing with each other, quarrels and fights were all too frequent. Ordinarily the fistic encounter was of short duration, but a prize fight (generally between New York City bruisers) now and then created a passing spectacle. In one of these, death resulted to one of the combatants.

ODD FELLOWS

Near the southwest corner of the prison was a good sized house made of logs, whose occupants seemed to be better dressed and fed than the balance of the prisoners. Inquiring the cause of this, I was told that they were Odd Fellows and that through their connection with the order they were enabled to secure supplies from the outside. It occurred to me that it would be a good thing to join them at once, but the ballot could not be "spread" at that time, and it was not until after the war that I learned by actual experience the benefits of the order of the three links.

GAMBLING

Perhaps the reader will think that this subject should be treated like the famous chapter on snakes in Ireland. But in fact there was a continuous run of games among the prisoners, there being plenty of professional gamblers. The main street leading from the north gate was lined with men manipulating cards and dice, while gathered around would be others watching the game. New prisoners staked their money, and generally it quickly changed hands. Old prisoners, whose funds had long been exhausted, wagered rations of food, or tobacco, or cooking utensils—anything and everything to gratify the insatiable passion for gambling. It was a source of great evil, but there was no way of stopping it. Throughout all the prison there was a great deal of harmless card playing, the packs from long usage being so well marked that each particular card was known nearly as well by its back as by the face. Home made checkers, chess and dominoes were also used to while away the tedious hours.

TRADING

Yankees are never happy except when trading, and this propensity was carried to its fullest extent in Andersonville. Walking back and forth through the prison, men would cry their wares, "fresh corn cakes," "tobacco for meal," "molasses," "buttons," and on through the gamut of every possible article. It seemed that one could not offer any article but that he would find some one ready to "swap" with him. Very often the guards were ready to exchange with us, giving us tobacco, and vegetables, in return for trinkets, which had great attraction for them. I remember the surprise of a guard who one day came into possession of a little pocket mirror, in which he surveyed his lank face and uncombed hair with childish satisfaction.

MORE ROOM

On the first of July an addition to the north end of the prison was opened, and all the detachments above forty-eight in number were moved into it. This comprised about eleven acres, making the total area twenty-seven acres. It was my fortune to be assigned to this new part, and I secured a place next the dead line, on the north side, midway east and west. The ground was higher, was fresh and there were numerous stumps of trees, limbs and chips left, which we quickly stored up for fuel. This also gave us much more room, although it was not long until the influx of new men made the prison almost as crowded as before. The great battles of the summer campaign of 1864 were being fought, and while our armies were steadily forcing their way to Richmond and Savannah, yet their losses in captured were necessarily heavy, and Andersonville being the main prison received most of them. When the prison was fullest the available space for each man was not over thirty square feet—five by six feet.

BARBER SHOPS

Several tonsorial artists set up shops in the prison, where shaving and hair cutting were done. If the customer had no money, he gave a ration, or made a trade of some kind, and these barbers were enabled to live well by their labor. Perhaps all trades and professions were represented among the prisoners, but there was no opportunity for them to ply their calling. Wirz sought to enlist some machinists to go out and work in shops, making arms and ammunition, but they refused to go.

THE PLYMOUTH PILGRIMS

Among the noticeable prisoners were those who had been captured at Plymouth, N.C., in April. Their chief distinction was they were so much finer dressed than the others, and in better flesh. They had seen but little service, having always been in barracks, and when captured they were permitted to retain everything they had about them. But they did not endure prison life well, and the mortality among them was great, while they were an easy mark for the older prisoners.

BLACKS AND REDS

There were several negro prisoners, who had been captured in Florida. Naturally they did not receive any consideration at the hands of Wirz and the other officers, who were enraged at the idea of former slaves fighting to destroy slavery. One poor fellow was said to have sixteen wounds on his body, and could only crawl on his hips, being denied even the privilege of going to the hospital.

There were also a few Indians, who had been used as scouts in the armies beyond the Mississippi. They were well formed, vigorous looking men, but how long or well they endured prison life I never knew.

> Soldier, rest! thy warfare o'er,
>   Sleep the sleep that knows not breaking;
> Dream of battled fields no more,
>   Days of danger, nights of waking.
> In our isle's enchanted hall,
>   Hands unseen thy couch are strewing,
> Fairy strains of music fall,
>   Every sense in slumber dewing.
> Soldier, rest! thy warfare o'er,
> Dream of fighting fields no more;
> Sleep the sleep that knows not breaking,
> Morn of toil, nor night of waking.

Chapter Eight

Tuesday evening, Sept. 6, eighteen detachments of prisoners received orders to be ready to move at any moment. Immediately all was excitement throughout the camp, every possible surmise being made as to the meaning of the order. All hoped it meant exchange, but some, the older prisoners, especially, feared it would end in only removal to another prison. But even this would he better than to remain. A feverish night was spent, and in the morning six of the detachments, and a number of inmates of the hospital, were taken to the railroad, placed on the cars, and the train started toward Macon. For the next five days this movement continued, until all the old prisoners, who had come from Libby, Belle Isle and other prisons, had gone away, and the new prisoners were commenced on.

"FLANKING OUT"

As the lower numbered detachments, beginning with number one were being taken, and my number was 87, I began to fear that before this number would be reached there would be a stop put to the taking away, and I would be left. So on the evening of the 11th, Col. Cook, Capt. Rogers and I went over near the south gate, and lay down to sleep with a detachment which had received orders to go out the next morning. Soon after daylight we were called up, and began to move toward the gate. Several other fellows were attempting to flank out the same as we were doing, and a fight ensued between them, and the police who were endeavoring to prevent it, some of them getting their heads clubbed. In the melee the Captain and I got close to the gate, when we were stopped, and my heart went down to my old shoes. But it was only for a moment, and again we were ordered to march, and we passed out forever from the walls of Andersonville. Rogers kept close by me, but Cook was nowhere to be seen, and we feared he had been captured by the police, but when we reached Augusta we found he was on the train with us. On the way to the station we passed the tent of Capt. Wirz, who was sitting there, looking very feeble from an attack of sickness. He reminded me of the giants in the Pilgrim's Progress, sitting in their cave and biting their nails at the pilgrims passing by.

As we crossed the brook on our way, I stooped down to get a cup of water, and was seized with a peculiar cramp and pain in my left leg, which doubled up so I could hardly walk, and this did not leave me for nearly a month. It arose from the scurvy.

GOING HOME?

At the train we were given what was announced to be two days' rations, and boarding the freight cars we started toward "God's country," as we fondly supposed. Next morning we reached Augusta, the broad streets of which, with rows of trees through the center, looked very inviting. The second morning, before daylight, our train stopped in what seemed to be a city. Presently we heard a low boom, and then a shell shrieked through the air and burst near us, and we knew we were in Charleston. How good it was to hear our own guns once more, and how near we seemed to freedom. Surely we would now be sent into our lines. But then the thought flashed on us, had we been brought here to be placed under the fire of our own besieging army? We had heard that this was being done, and we were ready to believe almost any story. However, our fears were soon relieved, and likewise our hopes of exchange blasted, for after an hour's stop the train pulled out, and we found ourselves going northward.

By this time the rations we had received at Andersonville were exhausted and we began to be very hungry, with no prospect in sight for any addition to our haversack. At noon we reached

FLORENCE, S. C.

and lay that night in the cars, the station being some distance from the town. Next morning we were taken off the cars, and at noon were marched a mile or more to a camp. On the way we passed through a thick wood and as the guards were not very plenty a number of our boys darted off through the brush. Whether any of them got through to our lines is doubtful, as the country around was closely watched by patrols, and recapture was almost certain. I would have made the attempt, but my leg was so sore that it was with difficulty I could walk. I urged Rogers to go, but he refused to leave me. At night, when it seemed as if our powers of endurance had reached its last point, we drew a pint of meal, and managed to cook and eat it.

BLASTED HOPES

Learning the location of Florence we soon realized that we had been brought there, not for exchange, but to be placed in another prison, and we learned that this was being prepared for us near by. The spirits of everyone sank and we became desperate. A bold leader only was needed to head an outbreak, which would undoubtedly have succeeded, as the guards were few, and there was no stockade to restrain us. But while there was no organization, there were numerous escapes, both by day and by night, and the number of these must have been several hundred. Nearly all of them, however, were soon captured and returned to the camp.

Next day the sick of the camp were permitted to go outside of the lines, and wander at will. I was among them, and in my wanderings went into a farm house—a typical southern one—where the women treated me kindly and gave me something from their scant hoard to eat. At night I slept under a tree, feeling very faint and sick from the scurvy, and my leg sore and lame. It began to look as if my days were numbered. But the fresh air, with some vegetables which I procured and ate raw, revived me somewhat. The following day we were all sent back into the camp, and then I learned that Rogers had run past the guards the previous night, and so far had not been brought back. My prayers went up for his success.

ENLISTING IN THE SOUTHERN ARMY

While we lay in this camp awaiting the completion of the prison, offers were made to the prisoners to enlist in the southern army. They were told that they would be used to guard forts, and thus relieve their own soldiers who could be sent to the front, where it was evident they were badly needed. A large number of prisoners accepted the offer, and after taking the oath of allegiance to the confederacy, were sent away. I always looked upon this leniently, for it was commonly talked that they would seize the first opportunity to desert to our lines, and this proved to be the case. Yet I could not make up my mind to desert my government, even though it seemed to have deserted us and left us to our fate. But one day, when we had drawn no rations, and it seemed as if we would surely be starved, I went up to the headquarters, intending to enlist, with the idea that the first night I was placed on picket, the officer of the guard would find a deserted post when he made his rounds. When I reached the place, and saw the hated stars and bars flying from the staff, and a vision of our own beautiful and loved flag flashed upon me, I turned and hurried back to my tent, and in answer to the questions of my comrades replied that I would lie there and rot before I would swear allegiance to the southern confederacy. If there was nothing else in my career as a soldier to be proud of, this one action was sufficient, for at this time I was only eighteen years old, naturally feeble, at the point of starvation, with indescribable misery all around, a new prison being prepared to receive me, and no apparent prospect of release.

THE NEW PRISON

At last, on the 2nd day of October, our camp was broken up, and we were marched into the new stockade which was to be known as Florence prison. It was an enclosure of some fifteen acres, very similar to Andersonville, with a stream through the center, the wall of logs, the dead line (here only a furrow in the ground), the stumps of trees, etc. It was enough to take all the heart out of us, but we set bravely to work, and with the other boys with whom I had joined forces, began to build us a house.

THE NEW MANSION

Selecting a spot near the brook, where the ground sloped, we dug out a space sufficient for five of us to lie down in. Setting up tent poles we stretched our blankets over them, chinking in at the bottom with dirt, making it as tight as possible. Spreading one blanket on the ground, we had one left for covering the five, and it will be seen we had to sleep spoon fashion in order to make the blanket cover all. My place was at one end of the row, and I would grip the blanket in my hand and try to hold on to it in my sleep. In this little hut I spent over two months, waiting, waiting, for the release which it seemed would never come.

LIEUTENANT BARRETT

Here we made the acquaintance of a new type of prison commander. Wirz was old, sickly, peevish, small brained, incompetent, but at times kindly. Barrett, in charge of Florence prison, was a young man, well built, erect, active, fairly intelligent, with red hair, a typical southern blood. He realized to the fullest extent the great importance of his office. He was always fully armed, his pants stuck into his boots, a jaunty uniform, and an air of bravado that only partly concealed a really cowardly heart. Woe betide the luckless wretch who got into his pathway. A curse and a kick were the lightest he could expect to receive. One day he had ordered all the prisoners to one side of the camp for the purpose of counting them. Barrett was standing on the other side of the brook, and ordered a company of prisoners to move on. They did not hear, or did not obey, and he drew his revolver and fired at them. The shot fell short, and the boys yelled in derision. Seizing a gun from a guard, he again fired, but without effect, and another yell greeted him. In his rage he gave the gun back to the guard, and started toward his quarters, swearing, and evidently intending to return with a force and take summary vengeance, but for some reason he did not come back. Wirz was mad most of the time, but Barrett was always mad.

> How sleep the brave, who sink to rest
> By all their country's wishes blessed!
> When Spring, with dewy fingers cold,
> Returns to deck their hallowed mould,
> She there shall dress a sweeter sod
> Than Fancy's feet have ever trod.

Chapter Nine

It may well be supposed that Barrett was brutal in his punishment of prisoners who had either purposely or unwittingly given him offense. One day—Nov. 12—piercing cries were heard from the direction of the gate. Hurrying there I saw a prisoner hanging by the thumbs, his feet clear of the ground, while he screamed with pain. The sight was so sickening that I had to go back to my tent. His only offense was attempting to escape, a privilege which every prisoner should have by the rules of war. It seemed to be impossible to please Barrett, or to escape his punishment if you came in his way.

TUNNELS AND STARVATION

Again, on Monday, Nov. 21, no rations were issued to the prison. It was a cold, rainy day, and the men suffered much. Next day, Tuesday, no rations were given out, and we were informed that Barrett had declared that a tunnel had been dug, and that he would issue no rations until it was discovered. This day was also cold and wet, and some of the prisoners, having no tents, had to sit on the ground, or walk about as long as their feeble strength permitted. Wednesday morning came, and the dead carried out were the largest number on any day of the history of the prison. What was to be done? We could not endure much longer. In the afternoon the usual rations were issued, either because Barrett relented, or because the location of the tunnel was revealed. Some said that a short tunnel was dug, purposely, and shown to Barrett. This act was the most barbarous in all my prison experience, and far exceeded anything Wirz ever did. Fortunately this inhuman wretch died near the close of the war. Had he lived he would undoubtedly have shared the fate of Wirz, unless some of his victims had taken just punishment into their own hands, as many declared they would if given opportunity.

ELECTING A PRESIDENT

Tuesday, Nov. 8, 1864, was the day for the election of President in the loyal states. Interest in this contest ran high in the prison, as well as throughout other parts of the country, even though we could have no part in it. Barrett (or perhaps some superior officer) conceived the idea of obtaining an expression of the feeling of the prisoners, and to this end made arrangements to hold a mock election. Bags of beans were provided, both black and white. A black bean, the symbol of war, was to be used to vote for Lincoln, while a white bean, betokening peace, indicated a vote for McClellan. The prisoners who chose to do so marched up to the gate, selected a bean of the color of their choice, and deposited it in a bag. It was evidently expected by Barrett that a large proportion of the beans used would be white ones, and this result would be used to influence opinion in the north. But notwithstanding there were many democrats among the prisoners, they stood by Lincoln and the government and not more than one in ten of the beans voted were white. Finding this to be so, Barrett discontinued the ballot, and the result was never announced. I myself cast a black bean, though I was not 21 years old, and had always considered that I was a Democrat. And this was the nearest I came to voting for the greatest American, Abraham Lincoln.

"GALVANIZED YANKS"

About this time the prisoners who had enlisted in the southern army began to be returned to the prison. They proved to be of no use whatever as guards, and were constantly deserting. A partial uniform, of gray color, had been given them, and this caused them to be nicknamed Galvanized Yanks. They had improved in flesh and health, but were coldly received by the prisoners who had remained true to their government and their oath. As soon as possible they got rid of their gray clothing, and concealed as far as they could the evidence of their unfaithfulness. During one of President Cleveland's terms he vetoed a bill granting a pension on the ground that the soldier was one of those who had thus taken the oath of allegiance to the southern confederacy. While his decision was technically right, yet there were extenuating circumstances.

NO TURKEY, THANK YOU

Thanksgiving Day, Nov. 24, was known in the prison, but there were no family reunions, no football, no turkey, no cranberries, and no pumpkin pie. In their stead we had a pint and a half of corn meal, with no meat, or beans, or rice, or molasses, or sweet potatoes, as we sometimes drew on other days. Barrett was determined we would remember the day in some way. But we thought of the loved ones at home, and knew that they remembered us as they sat down to the well filled tables.

And this reminds me that often at night, when we had lain down to sleep hungry and weak, I would dream of sitting down to a table loaded with good things, which in some way disappeared before they could be tasted. Especially did the form of a neighbor, Mrs. Ruth Craft, who was a very good cook, and at whose table I had often eaten when a boy, appear to me in my dreams.

ISSUING CLOTHING

Reports of our condition had reached the north, and the Sanitary Commission, which had done so much good work for our soldiers, obtained permission from the confederate authorities to send clothing through the lines to us. This reached us during November, and while it was gratefully received there was not enough to supply very many of the needy ones. My one suit of clothing was in fair condition, but I was of course anxious to secure a new supply, not knowing how much longer my imprisonment would continue. So taking my shirt, I tore several rents in it, and giving it to a comrade whose detachment was called before mine, told him to wear it when he went before the distributing officer. He did so, and came back with a new shirt. When my detachment was called I put on my torn shirt, and appeared before the officer who was giving out the clothing. When he saw me, he asked me if that was my shirt. I promptly replied that it was. "Is it the only one you have?" "Yes, Sir." "Well, I am sorry for you, my boy, but I have given out one new shirt on that today, and cannot give another." Can you imagine how I felt? I went back to my tent chagrined and crestfallen, to bear the badinage of my comrades, and procuring a needle and thread sewed up my torn shirt as best I could.

INCREASING MY RATIONS

During part of my stay in Florence I had the good luck to be associated with a member of my regiment, John Crow, of Company C. Being a stout fellow, he got on the working squad which was used to clean up about the prison. For this work he received an extra ration, and this he divided with me, I doing the cooking for us both. In this way I fared much better, and no words of mine can express my gratitude to him. Since the war we have never met, and I do not know if he is living or dead.

LIFE IN FLORENCE

Our condition in Florence was not very different from that in Andersonville, except that the number of prisoners was less. The highest number at one time was about ten thousand, and this gave us much more room. The rations issued were smaller than at Andersonville, a result due partly to Barrett's vicious disposition, and partly to the straitened resources of the confederacy, which was now drawing to its close. The guards at the prison were living on short rations.

The weather grew quite cold, and ice was formed a quarter of an inch thick. This added to the discomfort of the prisoners, but did not probably increase the mortality. It was not as fatal as the burning heat at Andersonville.

The hospital was in one corner, and was but little better in its attendants and supplies than the rest of the prison. Fully a third of all who were confined in Florence died there, a result partly due to the fact that the prisoners were mostly those who had been long in prison, and were therefore weaker.

There were the same vermin, gambling, cursing, fighting, stealing, an equal disregard for suffering and death, as at Andersonville. Life was held dear, and every one sought first his own welfare. Yet there were not wanting cases of kindness and self-denial.

Police regulations were kept up here, and detected violators were punished, mostly by sound "spanking" on that portion of the body best, fitted by nature, administered with a shingle. Some times an unusual offender was tied up to a stake and whipped on the bare back, and I have always thought that this punishment, ought to be inflicted on every man who beats his wife. Altogether, it was harder at Florence than at Andersonville.

GENERAL WINDER

Here I first saw this confederate officer, who had general command of all southern prisons. He has been severely denounced as cruel and unfeeling in his office, and this charge was made by southern as well as northern papers. I never came into personal contact with him, and therefore express no opinion. He, like Barrett, died near the close of the war. In the death struggles of the confederacy the feelings were very bitter, and it is but fair to believe that most of the officers in command of the prisons did not trouble themselves much about the comfort of the prisoners, nor care particularly for an increase in the death rate.

HOPES OF RELEASE

The few new prisoners brought in kept us informed of the progress of the war and our hearts were cheered by the constant victories our armies were winning, making sure our early release. Especially did we pin our faith and hope to Uncle Billy, who was known to he cavorting around through Georgia and South Carolina pretty much as he pleased. We felt certain he would come to deliver us, and much of our time was spent in discussing how we would assist his forces when he came. Included in these plans was the death of Barrett by the most slow and miserable processes our imagination could devise. Why our armies never reached Andersonville or Florence is to this day an unsolved problem.

Chapter Ten

"All things come to him who waits," and at last the day of our deliverance dawned. On Sunday, Nov. 27, orders came to Barrett to parole one thousand of the sick. This meant one in ten of the prison population. Immediately there was an alarming increase of sickness among the prisoners, as every one was anxious to go, whether it meant home or another bull pen—anywhere to get out of here. In Florence the division of the prisoners was by thousands, subdivided into hundreds. The first thousand was therefore called up, and the examining surgeon selected one hundred of the weakest ones, and they were sent outside. The same process was repeated next day with the second thousand. On the third day none were taken out, but instead a fresh batch of prisoners were brought in, who reported that they had been taken from Andersonville to Savannah (now in possession of our troops), had been paroled, but for some reason were not sent within our lines, but were brought here instead.

SINKING HOPES

This was a dampener to our prospects, and we knew not what to expect. The next two days no more of the sick were taken out, and on the third day, December 2, the sick of the second thousand who had been taken away were brought back, reporting that they were not able to reach Savannah, and that they were to be exchanged. Nothing more was done until the 5th, when the sick of the second thousand were again taken out, and our spirits were cheered. On the 7th, the third, fourth, fifth, sixth and seventh thousands were examined, the selections made, and they went outside. My thousand, number eight, received orders to be ready next morning. It may well be imagined that the intervening night was one of feverish anxiety for me.

TELLING THE TRUTH

Next morning, after a hearty (?) breakfast, our detachment was called up to the gate, and formed in rank inside the dead line. The examining surgeon passed along the line, questioning the boys, and making his selections for parole. I noticed that he took the second man from me, and also the one next to me, both being fellow townsmen, though not of my regiment. My chances looked decidedly slim, and perhaps this thought increased my haggard and woe-begone appearance. When the surgeon asked me what was the matter with me, I assured him that I was afflicted with the scurvy, the diarrhea, the dysentery, and several other diseases the names of which I do not now recall. Now, I had been afflicted with all of these in turn, but had partly recovered, and was at this time in fair condition. But who can blame me, and who would have done different? The surgeon hesitated, and seemed about to pass on, when by sudden inspiration I asked him to feel my arm. Naturally very slender, and still more so then, when he took hold of my puny arm he said, "you may go." It took just half an instant for me to get outside the gate, and I have wondered that he did not call me back, as being too active to be very sick.

COL. COOK'S QUICK WIT

When Cook's detachment was examined, he was not selected for parole. As the next detachment was being examined, he was standing near, looking very disconsolate. Now, the examining surgeon had been passing out the sergeant in charge of each thousand, whether sick or not. It happened that the sergeant of the thousand which was being examined had gone back to his tent to say good bye, or to get something. When the surgeon had finished the examination, he called out, "where is the sergeant of this squad?" No answer. Again he called in louder tones, "where in ---- is the sergeant of this squad?" "Here I am," came a voice from the crowd, and Col. Cook pushed his way up to the officer, seemingly in great haste, and puffing as if he had been on the run. "Well, get out of here mighty quick." roared the officer, and the Col. needed no second command, but went out at the gate as fast as his legs would carry him, was paroled and taken home, which he reached very weak and sick, but recovered and lived several years. It was the sharpest trick I ever saw played, and I always felt that he was justified, even if I did sometimes think of the poor sergeant who came back to find his place taken, and he doomed to remain.

OFF FOR CHARLESTON

Once outside we were marched into a field, where the oath of parole was administered to us, and our descriptive lists taken. This took considerable time, and it was not until the next evening that we were put on board the cars, and started for the famous city where the first gun of the war was fired. It was the 9th of December, the air was cold, and we shivered, but what of that? We were going home. A few of our number died on the cars.

At daylight the next morning we reached Charleston, and again we heard the booming of the "swamp angel," and the whistling of the shell. The siege was still going on. Alighting from the cars, we were marched to the shore of the bay, where we were put on board a boat that carried at the bow a white flag. It looked more like release. Out we steamed, past Fort Sumter, until our boat met and signaled another boat bearing also a white flag, and better still, the glorious STARS AND STRIPES.

The boats pulled up alongside each other, a plank was run across the intervening space, and with feeble but joyous steps we walked from bondage to freedom, from death to life. No one can tell how we felt, as we cheered, and laughed, and wept, and danced, and hugged each other. The southern boat soon left us, and then we steamed outside the harbor, and were transferred to the steamship United States. A bath followed, and provided with a new suit of clothes we threw our old rags into the sea, when strange to say they at once made a bee line for the shore, and the boys declared it was the graybacks going back to Florence. A cup of coffee, some hard tack, and a piece of well cooked pork were given us.

LIFE ON THE OCEAN WAVE

The exchange was made on Saturday, December 10. We lay here over Sunday, receiving other prisoners. On Monday we weighed anchor, raised steam, and began our voyage north. Passing Wilmington we saw the blockading fleet commanded by Commodore Porter. Wednesday morning we reached Fortress Monroe, and here we saw another portion of Porter's fleet. At two o'clock on Thursday we reached Annapolis, and were put on shore, feeling pretty well, for I had not gotten sea sick. And here, just as we felt ourselves to be once more safe and at home, some of our comrades died, the saddest sight in all my seven months of prison life.

After a few days in the parole camp, we drew pay, and were given a furlough to go home. Christmas was spent in Baltimore, and in spite of the tragedy in that city at the opening of the war, I was everywhere treated and feasted until almost glad to get away. Reaching home, I remained until the end of my furlough, returned to Annapolis, was transferred to Camp Chase, at Columbus, Ohio, where I was kept until muster out in June, never having been exchanged, but only paroled, so that I could not return to my regiment, which had the honor to be at the famous apple tree at Appomattox. During my imprisonment it bore a prominent part in the campaigns of the valley and the Potomac, being engaged in twelve general battles in all its term of service.

Chapter Eleven

Mention has been made of the diary kept during my imprisonment. It was given to me soon after capture by Younkin. In it are recorded briefly the prominent events of each day, and from it my memory has been refreshed in preparing the foregoing narrative. A few extracts from it may serve to deepen on the mind of the reader the impression made at the time and present more vividly the character of the life and sufferings endured.

May 31 (two days after entering Andersonville): Last day of spring. A few more prisoners came in. All seem to think the war will soon be over, and we will be released. I hope it may soon be. Drew better rations today.

June 1: First day of summer. God grant that ere it ends we may all be within our own lines. The Col. (probably Wirz is meant) says we will soon be exchanged or paroled. 1,500 more prisoners came in.

June 4: A great lot of ladies came to the stockade to see the prisoners. Some seem to be union at heart.

(For 21 consecutive days I record that it rained — some times only a little, but mostly hard.)

June 17: Fourteen prisoners ran away from wood squad in evening, taking nine guns along.

June 21: Two men were shot by guard for going over the dead line.

June 22: Made a good meal of beans, meat and corn dumplings. It is said an exchange or parole will take place July 7.

June 24: All prisoners who had money taken from them can get it tomorrow morning. It does not affect me.

June 30: Our rations were stopped until the raiders were taken out. Men organized and took them out by force. Found great deal of stolen property.

July 3: No rations issued on account of some prisoners being missed. Bridge built across the branch.

July 4: The anniversary of our National Independence. No celebration by the rebels. Would that I were home. A very poor place for us to celebrate it. All the detachments were changed in number. Very loud thunder.

July 7: This is the day parole was to take place, but nary parole.

July 11: (Records the hanging of the Raiders).

July 13: A prisoner was shot by a guard while getting water at the brook. Belonged to the 20th Pa. Cav. Was not over the dead line. 'Twas nothing but a cold blooded murder.

July 14: The sergeants of detachments wore taken out and informed if the men did not keep away from the gate they would be fired on. Two blank cannon shot were fired in evening, and a lot of musketry. Don't know what it was for.

July 16: Petitions are being gotten up to the loyal Governors to have us released.

July 20: The rebels commenced throwing up fortifications outside, I suppose to resist an anticipated attack.

July 27: Went out to Doctors today on account of having scurvy in my mouth.

July 29: Four white flags were put up in camp as a mark not to collect in crowds between them and the gate while prisoners were being brought in.

July 31: Reported that our cavalry are in the direction of Macon, making a raid. Rebels worked all last night and today fortifying.

Aug. 2: A lot of prisoners came in. Say Gen. Stoneman and a large lot of his men were captured near Macon.

Aug. 5: All the sick out of eleven detachments were taken out. Begins to look like paroling.

Aug. 6: Quite a lot of slaves are here working on fortifications. Seem to be happy, sing as they work.

Aug. 9: Rained very hard. A lot of the stockade fell down at the brook. Rebs fell out into line double quick. None of the prisoners got away.

Aug. 10: The men are dying off at a fearful rate. About time hundred within twenty-four hours.

Aug. 11: It is sad to see the sufferings the men endure in this prison. Some one will have an unpardonable sin to answer for in keeping them in here.

Aug. 20: Felt pretty bad today. Mouth very sore with scurvy.

Aug. 25: Am a good deal better today. This is my birthday (18). A poor place to celebrate it.

Aug. 26: A man was tried today for murder. Was taken outside. (Have no further record of this.)

Aug. 31: The last day of summer — a summer spent in prison. What can our government mean by allowing its soldiers to be confined in this manner? There is surely some way of releasing us.

Sept. 5: A lot of prisoners came in from Sherman's army. Say Sherman has whipped Hood badly, and drove him from Atlanta. Think he will come down here.

Sept. 23: (at Florence): A petition to the rebel government was got up in camp, asking them to parole us. Don't think it will do much good.

Sept. 26: Drew very small rations, barely enough to support life. Last night was cold. Some of the men have no clothes, and no shelter.

Sept.28: Drew nothing but half a pint of very coarse meal, and a few spoonfuls of beans. At this rate men will die of starvation. Threats are being made of a "break."

Sept 29: An opportunity was offered for those wishing to take the oath of allegiance to the C. S. A. Don't feel like it myself.

Oct. 1: Drew one and a half of hard tack, four spoonfuls of meal, and a little molasses, for a day's ration. Begins to look like starvation.

Oct. 14: A larger number took the oath of allegiance than at any other time before. What the end of this will be God only knows. May He grant to have us released.

Oct. 16: Prayer meetings were held in prison in the evening.

Oct. 20: Some of the men were allowed to go outside to get brush to fix up their tents with.

Oct. 25: The rebels moved their artillery away from around the camp, for some purpose. It is said our forces are making a raid from Georgetown S. C.

Oct. 31: Another month gone, and still in prison. I think our government is rather too stubborn about an exchange.

Nov. 5: 270 prisoners took the oath of allegiance, and went to join the rebel army.

Nov. 8: Election day at home. A vote was taken in prison, resulting in a large majority for "Old Abe." May like success attend him elsewhere.

Nov. 17: A great lot of prisoners who had taken the oath of allegiance were sent inside. Had been at Charleston doing duty.

Nov. 30: The last of autumn. Is it possible that we are never to get out of prison? I fear but few will live to see home if not released soon.

The record from this time has been set forth in the body of the book.

Congressional Medal of Honor Recipients

12th West Virginia Infantry

Apple, Andrew O.
Rank and organization: Corporal, Company I, 12th West Virginia Infantry. Place and date: At Petersburg, Va., 2 April 1865. Entered service at: ------. Birth: Northampton, Pa. Date of issue: 12 May 1865. Citation: Conspicuous gallantry as color bearer in the assault on Fort Gregg.

Curtis, Josiah M.
Rank and organization: Second Lieutenant, Company I, 12th West Virginia Infantry. Place and date: At Petersburg, Va., 2 April 1865. Entered service at: Ohio County, W. Va. Birth: Ohio County, W. Va. Date of issue: 12 May 1865. Citation: Seized the colors of his regiment after 2 color bearers had fallen, bore them gallantly, and was among the first to gain a foothold, with his flag, inside the enemy's works.

Durham, James R.
Rank and organization: Second Lieutenant, Company E, 12th West Virginia Infantry. Place and date: At Winchester, Va., 14 June 1863. Entered service at: Clarksburg, W. Va. Born: 7 February 1833, Richmond, W. Va. Date of issue: 6 March 1890. Citation: Led his command over the stone wall, where he was wounded.

McCauslin, Joseph
Rank and organization: Private, Company D, 12th West Virginia Infantry. Place and date: At Petersburg, Va., 2 April 1865. Entered service at: Ohio County, W. Va. Birth: Ohio County, W. Va. Date of issue: 12 May 1865. Citation: Conspicuous gallantry as color bearer in the assault on Fort Gregg.

Reeder, Charles A.
Rank and organization: Private, Company G, 12th West Virginia Infantry. Place and date: At Battery Gregg, near Petersburg, Va.,

2 April 1865. Entered service at:------. Birth: Harrison, W. Va. Date of issue: 3 April 1867. Citation: Capture of flag. [Note: According to Col. William B. Curtis, Private Reeder found a Confederate flag lying on the ground at the Confederate position on Hatcher's Run several hours before the assault on Fort Gregg. For more on this, please see *The Confederate Alamo: Bloodbath at Petersburg's Fort Gregg on April 2, 1865*, by John J. Fox III, Angle Valley Press, pg. 290]

Roster

FIELD AND STAFF OFFICERS

Colonels

John B. Klunk

Date of commission: August 20, 1862

Commissioned as colonel, August 20, 1862 to rank from same date. Resigned September 1, 1863, to take effect September 5, 1863.

William B. Curtis

Date of commission: January 26, 1864

Muster out: June 16, 1865

Was 41 years of age at date of muster in. Elected captain of Company D, August 20, 1862. Promoted to major and commissioned, order of July 27, 1863, to rank from June 17, 1863, vice F.P. Pierpont resigned. Promoted to colonel, January 28, 1864, vice Klunk resigned. Muster out at Richmond, Va.

Lieutenant-Colonels

Robert S. Northcott

Date of commission: August 23, 1862

Commissioned as Lieutenant-Colonel, August 23, 1862. Was captured June 16, 1863. Prisoner in Libby Prison, Richmond, Va. Resigned January 5, 1865. Resignation accepted per Special Order #5, Headquarters W.Va., N.C.

Richard Hooker Brown

Date of commission: January 25, 1865

Muster out: June 16, 1865

Was 25 years old at age of muster in as Captain of Company I. Promoted to Major, February 6, 1864

COMPANY A

Captains

Tomlinson, Hagar [Commissioned April 16, 1862. Resigned November 1, 1864.]

Burley, William [Commissioned November 16, 1864. Promoted to Major.]

Roberts, William L. [Commissioned January 25, 1865.]

First Lieutenants

Magruder, Thomas S. [Commissioned August 16, 1862. Resigned January 17, 1863.]

Burley, William [Commissioned February 3, 1863. Promoted to Captain.]

Riggs, William H. [Commissioned December 16, 1864.]

Second Lieutenants

Burley, William [Commissioned August 16, 1862. Promoted to 1st Lieutenant.]

Bier, Philip G. [Commissioned February 3, 1863. Promoted to Captain and A.A.G. U.S. Vol.]

Manning, Thomas W. [Commissioned April 6, 1864. Resigned November 16, 1864.]

Caldwell, Joseph [Commissioned December 16, 1864. Transferred to Company C.]

Enlisted Men

Allison, Oscar L.
Anton, William
Argo, William
Baird, Joseph H.
Baker, John C.
Baker, S. B.
Baker, Timothy B.
Barnhart, Benjamin F.
Birch, John
Boyd, Reuben G.
Brockaway, Thomas
Brown, Samuel
Bryson, John A.
Byrnes, William F.
Cain, Jeremiah
Carr, Edward
Cecil, Andrew
Chambers, Morrison
Chrismond, John A.
Coe, Isaac R.

Coe, James W.
Conaway, George W.
Conner, Alexander
Criswell, Oliver W.
Crow, Absalom
Crow, John C.
Darrah, James
Devor, John N.
Dornan, Norman E.
Dorsey, Basil
Dorsey, William H.
Dunlap, James
Echels, William H.
Edwards, John W.
Flannagan, John H.
Freeman, Samuel
Gamble, William C.
Geurin, Alexander
Geurin, Mahlon
Gillett, William
Gossett, George
Gregg, Gans
Gregg, Isaac
Hammond, George W.
Holmes, Henry
Holmes, Peter
James, Isaac
Jones, Abraham
Jones, George A.
Jones, George L.
Jones, John G.
Kane, Jeremiah
King, Francis W.
Kupfer, August
Leach, Joseph W.
Leach, William H. H.
Logston, James
Logsdon, John E.
Magers, David

Magers, James A.
Magers, William F.
Manning, Lewis
Massena, Samuel
Mathews, Andrew J.
Mathews, Christopher C.
McGarey, Thomas
McKnight, John
Miller, James M.
Morgan, Thomas R.
Morris, Daniel
Moslander, William
Nice, William
Orum, George
Pelley, Philip Mc.
Porter, John
Pratt, Jonathan D.
Riggle, George
Riggs, Alexander B.
Riggs, Alfred R.
Scantlin, John
Schofield, Edward
Shillings, Alexander
Shook, Israel
Simms, John
Sims, Martin
Stine, Jacob
Stine, William
Tolbert, John R.
Tomlinson, Joseph
Trenton, John A.
Turner, Thomas M.
Williams, Charles W.
Wilson, James L.
Wyrick, Joseph W.
Younkin, Samuel F.

COMPANY B

Captains

Bonar, Martin P. [Commissioned August 22, 1862. Resigned January 25, 1863.]

Roberts, John C. [Commissioned February 11, 1863. Resigned on account of wounds.]

Fleming, Thomas A. [Commissioned February 13, 1865.]

First Lieutenants

Fish, Nathan S. [Commissioned August 22, 1862. Resigned February 3, 1863.]

Dunnington, James W. [Commissioned February 11, 1863. Dismissed May 28, 1864.]

Wallace, Henry C. [Commissioned August 6, 1864.]

Second Lieutenants

Roberts, John C. [Commissioned August 22, 1862. Promoted to Captain.]

Anshutz, Henry T. [Commissioned February 11, 1863.]

Enlisted Men

Allen, Leander
Allen, William M.
Allman, Joshua
Anderson, Joseph H.
Biles, John
Blair, James M.
Blake, Joseph
Blake, Thomas
Blinquo, Thomas
Bonar, William N.
Booth, John J.
Bryson, Abram
Burch, James
Burch, Talbott
Burris, John W.
Bush, William
Cecil, George W.
Clayton, John W.
Coffield, William M.
Coffman, Adam
Collins, William H.
Conley, William M.
Coulter, Andrew
Craig, Samuel
Criswell, Charles
Criswell, John C.
Criswell, William H.
Crow, Henry
Crow, James M.
Davis, Wilson
Enix, Brice
Evans, William

Fletcher, David A.
Francis, Emanuel
Francis, Joseph T.
Fuller, George W.
Games, Alfred
Giles, Hamilton
Goodrich, Franklin
Goodrich, Nathan D.
Goodrich, Nelson
Goodrich, Timothy M.
Greathouse, Amos
Greathouse, Hiram
Greathouse, John
Greathouse, Thomas
Griffith, Amos
Griffith, Benjamin
Griffith, John
Griffith, Zachariah
Hall, Daniel C.
Harbinson, John W.
Hartsell, John
Henry, Robert A.
Hollingshead, Venus
Johnson, John W.
Kidder, Ira
Kimmins, William R.
Knapp, Andrew
Manning, James B.
Manning, William M.
Marple, George
McDonald, James A.
McHenry, James N.
Miller, Joseph
Miner, Alexander
Moore, John L.
Morgan, David L.
Morgan, James J.
Morgan, Oliver H. P.
Muldrew, Andrew W.

Myres, Joseph
Parsons, Thomas
Peters, Samuel W. M.
Pyles, Joshua
Reece, George W.
Reed, Dolphus
Reed, Ezra M.
Reed, Josephus
Riggs, Thomas G.
Rine, David
Ritchie, Andrew K.
Ritchie, Crozier
Roberts, Jacob J.
Robinson, George
Robinson, James
Robinson, Philip
Rulong, Morris
Rulong, William H.
Scears, John
Siberts, Barney
Snider, Wilson
Standiford, William S.
Stillwell, Joseph
Stillwell, Timothy C.
Sutter, Jacob
Taylor, Francis
Taylor, John
Truman, Elias
Truman, James M.
Truman, Robert T.
Vanscoy, Josiah
Wallace, Joseph
Wallace, William T.
Wetzel, Martin
White, Alexander
Wilson, James
Wilson, Joseph G.
Wilson, Samuel
Wilson, Samuel H.

COMPANY C

Commissioned Officers

Captain
Bartlett, Erastus G. [Commissioned August 23, 1862]

First Lieutenants
Roberts, William L. [Commissioned August 23, 1862. Promoted to Captain, Company A.]

Gardner, Michael [Commissioned February 1, 1865.]

Second Lieutenants
Lydick, John B. [Commissioned August 23, 1862. Resigned December 25, 1862.]

Whittingham, James [Commissioned January 8, 1863. Promoted to Captain and A.Q.M., U.S. Vols.]

McCord, Henry R. [Commissioned October 24, 1864. Promoted to 1st Lieutenant and Adjutant.]

Caldwell, Joseph [Commissioned December 16, 1864. Killed in assault and capture of Ft. Gregg while planting the regimental colors on the fort.]

Enlisted Men

Abercrombie, William H.
Aston, Thomas J.
Bane, George
Bane, Jesse
Bane, Henry
Bassett, Jacob W.
Billeter, Munger
Briggs, James M.
Carothers, Jackson P.
Caulfield, Joseph H.
Chaddock, J. J.
Chambers, Benjamin
Chambers, John
Chambers, Wilson
Clark, Thomas B.
Clegg, John
Clegg, John E.
Clegg, Thomas
Conner, Joseph H.
Cross, William
Crouch, James C.
Crow, Harmon
Crow, John W.
Daken, John
Dardinger, Stephen
DeGarmo, James
Deitz, Andrew
Earlewine, Reuben

Fish, Isaac N.
Founds, John W.
French, Samuel
Gorby, Josephus
Gosney, James
Gray, Francis M.
Grimes, James
Gunn, William R.
Hadsall, John E.
Hagerman, Joseph C.
Harris, George W.
Harris, Samuel
Hicks, John A.
Hicks, William H.
Hobbs, Isaac N.
Hummel, Jonas
Kirkendall, John A.
Knapp, Alva
Knapp, Robert
Knapp, Stewart
Koch, Joseph H.
Logsden, Anthony
Logsden, John T.
Logsden, Joseph R.
Low, Alexander
Lowry, Benjamin C.
Marple, Thomas W.
McCon, James W.
McKnight, Gordon S.
McRichmond, William
Miller, Michael W.
Miller, Marquis D. L.
Moore, William
Nice, Thomas
Nixon, James
Ormsby, Thomas J.
Powell, Melvin
Pritchett, Wesley W.
Redd, John S.

Redd, Parker S.
Richmond, James F.
Roberts, Jacob D.
Roberts, John A.
Ruckman, Isaac D.
Shepherd, Joseph W.
Shipley, Robert
Sisson, Andrew M.
Sockman, Francis M.
Sphar, John
Standiford, Benjamin
Standiford, Jacob
Stewart, Levi C.
Stump, Albert
Wait, Allen N.
Whetzel, James
White, Milton B.
Williams, Samuel H.
Williams, Samuel K.
Williams, Wesley
Williams, William H.
Williamson, Marion
Workman, Benjamin M.
Wright, William S.

COMPANY D

Commissioned Officers

Captains

Curtis, William B. [Commissioned August 20, 1862. Promoted to Major.]

Smiley, William A. [Commissioned October 12, 1863. Promoted to Paymaster, U.S.A.]

Blayney, David M. [Commissioned May 9, 1865.]

First Lieutenants

Smiley, William A. [Commissioned August 20, 1862. Promoted to Captain.]

Blayney, David M. [Commissioned October 12, 1863. Promoted to Captain.]

Peirson, James C. [Commissioned May 9, 1865.]

Second Lieutenants

Blayney, David M. [Commissioned August 20, 1862. Promoted to 1st Lieutenant.]

Peirson, James C. [Commissioned November 23, 1863. Promoted to 1st Lieutenant.]

Enlisted Men

Adams, Emanuel M.
Anderson, Robert J.
Armstrong, Thomas B.
Atkinson, William
Barnes, Joseph M.
Bier, Philip G.
Blayney, Henry G.
Buckhannon, John A.
Buckhannon, Robert E.
Burke, Thomas
Bushfield, John M.
Caldwell, James W.
Carroll, Orvill
Carson, William
Clark, James W.
Clendenen, Samuel E.
Clendenen, William W.
Craig, David M.
Cramp, William N.
Cunningham, John
Curtis, Josiah M.
Degarmo, William J.
Denniston, Robert M.
Dunlap, Eugene M.
Dunlap, William M.
Ferrill, Thomas M.

Fleming, David B.
Fleming, Samuel
Foreman, William W.
Frays, Jacob
Frazier, Daniel A.
Giffin, Daniel A.
Giffin, William
Gilbreath, William L.
Gilmore, Alexander K.
Gilmore, John
Gilmore, Joseph
Greer, Henry C.
Halstead, Joseph S.
Hamilton, Charles W.
Hanna, William R.
Hemphill, Josiah Q.
Harvey, Henry C.
Hosic, Morrison L.
Hutchison, Thomas B
Jackson, David M.
Kennedy, James B.
Kiger, George
Kiger, James B.
Kiger, William
King, George W.
Long, James
Mack, John
Munnell, Charles W.
Maxwell, Daniel
Maxwell, William D.
McCammon, Robert
McCauslin, Joseph
McCoy, James R.
McKeller, James
McNear, Jesse
McQuown, Robert L.
Milligan, Hugh W.
Montgomery, Joseph
Morrison, Giffin
Morrison, James

Murray, John W.
Murray, William M.
Nickerson, David
Nickerson, Nehemiah
Orr, Thomas J.
Padgett, James
Parry, Henry H.
Parry, William M.
Patterson, John K.
Pemberton, William D.
Pierson, James W.
Pinkerton, Thomas B.
Ray, James
Reynolds, Joshua
Reynolds, Samuel
Rodgers, Ezekiel H.
Rodgers, William
Rose, John B.
Ross, William
Smith, William C.
Speare, Henry
Stamm, John L.
Stewart, David
Tanner, Charles W.
Tanner, James M.
Teagarden, George H.
Terrell, Thomas M.
Thornburg, William
Vanaman, Nathaniel
Vermillion, Richard J.
Waddle, John W.
Wallace, David C.
Wallace, Theodore A.
Whitham, Joseph D.
Whitham, William F.
Wiles, Barnabas
Wiles, George W.
Yarnall, Peter
Yates, Andrew F.

COMPANY E

Commissioned Officers

Captains
Mercer, Cornelius [Commissioned August 22, 1862.]

First Lieutenants
Tate, Oscar H. [Commissioned August 22, 1862. Dismissed March 6, 1863.]

Durham, James R. [Commissioned July 9, 1863.]

Second Lieutenants
Durham, James R. [Commissioned August 22, 1862. Promoted to 1st Lieutenant.]

Hugill, Asa S. [Commissioned July 9, 1863. Promoted to Captain and transferred to 10th W. Va. Infantry.]

Enlisted Men

Anderson, James R.
Baccus, James
Baccus, Jesse
Bennett, John H.
Bennett, William O.
Blackwell, Enoch
Bowser, Jacob
Brison, James E.
Brown, Henry W.
Carder, John W.
Carson, Robert
Coffman, John M.
Cork, Harrison
Cottrill, Robert H.
Cottrill, Thomas J.
Criss, David J.
Davis, James U.
Dillon, Daniel
Dillon, James
Drain, Isaac
Drummond, Jasper
Ebert, Charles W.
Farance, Granville
Fittro, Alstropheus W.
Fittro, James J.
Flanigan, Elisha
Flanigan, Martin V.
Flanigan, Philbert
Flowers, Seldon E.
Fox, George F.
Gaines, John J.
Gaines, Peter
Gleason, Joseph
Hall, Fabius E.
Hardman, Abner
Hardman, Josiah D.
Hardman, Nicholas
Harrison, Benjamin J.

Hartzell, Benson R.
Haymond, Rufus
Howard, John H.
Hughes, Peter
Hursey, Thomas S.
Israel, Isaac
Jasper, Andrew F.
Johnson, Frederick F.
Jones, Montello
Klaiser, Joseph
Leeper, William
Loughry, John
Loughry, William E.
Lyman, Daniel
Martin, Jesse J.
Martin, Luther J.
Matthey, Frederick G.
Maxwell, Isaac N.
Maxwell, James T.
McAtee, George W.
McQuain, Joseph W.
Merriman, George S.
Metz, Henry
Miller, Jesse
Moran, Alpheus
Munday, John J.
Peck, John C.
Perine, Isaac W. M.
Perine, Jacob
Primm, Charles E.
Reed, Alexander
Reed, James D.
Rider, John G.
Riley, John W.
Robinson, Edmund S.
Root, Stephen M.
Shackelford, John H.
Shinn, Leonidas
Shutter, Gottleib

Simms, Peyton H.
Smith, John D.
Smith, Martin B.
Stiers, Cleatus L.
Strother, Wesley
Sutton, John
Swiger, Francis M.
Swiger, William H.
Towles, Jason L.
Walker, Samuel C.
Washburn, Lloyd
Welsh, John
White, James J.
Wildman, John H.
Williams, Jeremiah
Williams, Waldo
Young, Francis R.
Young, John C.

COMPANY F

Commissioned Officers

Captains
Pritchard, Amos N. [Commissioned August 25, 1862. Resigned March 24, 1865.]

Pierpoint, Jr., Francis H. [Commissioned May 9, 1865.]

First Lieutenants
Fleming, Thomas A. [Commissioned August 22, 1862. Promoted to Captain, Company B, February 13, 1865.]

Pierpont, Jr., Francis H. [Commissioned February 13, 1865. Promoted to Captain.]

Cunningham, Duncan [Commissioned May 9, 1865. Transferred to 10th West Virginia Infantry.]

Second Lieutenants
Haymond, Thomas H. [Commissioned August 25, 1862. Resigned February 7, 1863.]

Ben Gough, John T. [Commissioned March 4, 1863. Killed in action at Winchester.]

Pierpoint, Jr., Francis H. [Commissioned December 1, 1863. Promoted to 1st Lieutenant.]

Cunningham, Duncan [Commissioned February 13, 1865. Promoted to 1st Lieutenant.]

Smith, Craven [Commissioned May 9, 1865.]

Enlisted Men
Amos, William M.
Anderson, Henry
Anderson, Newton B.
Anderson, Robert R.
Arnett, Jonathan
Barnes, Silas
Berry, Isaac C.
Billingsley, John E.
Birmingham, William B.
Bowers, Joseph D.
Bowman, William H.
Brown, Francis M.
Brummage, Daniel D.
Burgoyne, Louis E.
Conaway, Henry
Cook, Thomas

Davis, Daniel H.
Davis, Henry S.
Davis, Jonathan B.
Dragoo, William B.
Dudley, William
Dunnington, James W.
Evans, Alfred C.
Evans, William L.
Faucet, James
Fisher, Adam
Fesler, Frederick
Fleming, Calvin L.
Fleming, Thomas M.
Fleming, William A.
Fletcher, David F.
Floyd, James P.
Floyd, Levi C.
Fortney, Henry
Goodwin, John L.
Grubb, Benjamin
Hall, George
Hall, John C.
Hall, William S.
Harr, Rufus E.
Hawkins, Alexander
Hawkins, John
Hawkins, Samuel
Hawkins, William
Hayhurst, Eli
Heiskill, Robert L.
Hibbs, Thomas W.
Hibbs, William W.
Hill, Winchel
Hite, Reason D.
Hobbs, Enoch N.
Houston, John C.
Hunt, Lebbins C.
Jemison, John F.
Johnson, William

Jones, Hiram E.
Keller, James C.
King, James W.
Layman, John J.
Little, Thomas A.
Lough, Calvin J.
Lough, Hezekiah T.
Lough, Newton
Martin, Thomas
Mason, Charles E. W.
McCray, Raymond R.
McDonald, John I.
Mercer, John W.
Monroe, Josiah
Monroe, Riley
Morgan, Archie
Morgan, Eber D.
Morgan, Samuel
Morris, Josephus
Morrow, Bernard F. L.
Musgrave, John C.
Nuzum, Zadoc K.
Parker, Eli L.
Pitzer, John F.
Poling, Richard
Redd, John S.
Rex, Francis M.
Rice, Isaac H.
Ritchie, John S.
Robinson, Edwin S.
Satterfield, Eli
Shafer, James T.
Shaw, Joshua
Sheets, John
Shore, Martin L.
Shore, Simon F.
Shroyer, Andrew M.
Snodgrass, Eugenius
Stephens, Samuel S.

Stewart, James M.
Sturm, Enos E.
Thorn, John M.
Toothman, Urias W.
Upton, Abraham S.
Vandegrift, Marshall
Walker, John T.
Wallace, Ezra

Wamsley, Abia
Wells, Francis M.
Wells, Richard D.
Wells, Richard J.
West, Jonathan J.
Williams, Eli
Wilson, James L.
Zinn, James I.

COMPANY G

Commissioned Officers

Captain
Moffatt, James W. [Commissioned August 25, 1862.]

First Lieutenants
Hall, Van B. [Commissioned August 25, 1862. Resigned February 13, 1865.]
Fortney, George W. [Commissioned February 13, 1865.]

Second Lieutenant
Pigott, Elam F. [Commissioned August 25, 1862.]

Enlisted Men

Ashcraft, Armstead
Ashcraft, Ezekiel
Barnes, Josephus
Barton, James
Belch, Lewis
Bennett, Theron D.
Boggess, Alonzo H.
Brown, Stephen F.
Burns, Frederick J.
Carder, George F.
Coffman, Isaac M.
Coffman, Lemuel D.
Coffman, Theodore
Crim, Fielding
Crim, James E.
Crowl, Griffin
Cunningham, Robert W.
Cunningham, William D.
Davis, Samuel B.
Dawson, John N.
Denham, Andrew J.
Drain, Azariah

Drain, George W.
Drain, Presley
Drain, Richard
Ebert, David
Elder, Loyd H.
Elder, Nathaniel
Exline, Joseph
Fincham, Lafayette
Fortney, John M.
Fortney, John C.
Fortney, Joshua D.
Fortney, Joshua N.
Fortney, Seth F.
Furns, John H.
Gabbert, John M.
Garrettson, William E.
Gifford, Waldo W.
Green, Isaac N.
Griffin, Luther C.
Harbert, William E. L.
Harbert, Eli
Harbert, Luther C.

Harbert, William E.
Hardin, James C.
Harrison, Joseph B.
Harvey, Bazil T.
Heflin, James A.
Heldreth, Benjamin H.
Heldreth, Joseph G.
Holder, Jesse F.
Jackson, Irving
Jackson, Rolley
Jarvis, Noah W.
Jones, Joshua
Kelly, Levi
Koon, Robert W.
Lindsey, Arville W.
Lucas, George
Lynch, Simon P.
Madden, Jesse H.
Martin, David
Martin, Elihu
Martin, John O.
Martin, Presley
McCarty, Greenberry T.
McClung, George W.
McClung, James A.
McClung, William H.
McCord, Henry R.
McIntyre, Elias
Mennear, Samuel W.
Metz, Francis B.
Nay, Fielding
Nay, Marsena J. D.
Ogden, William R.
Pierce, Isaac N.
Pitcher, Martin V.
Potts, Thomas C.
Reeder, Charles A.
Robinson, Dennis M.
Roby, Andrew J.

Roby, James A.
Sevier, David
Shaw, David N.
Shaw, Lemuel R.
Shinn, Quillen H.
Shinn, George
Shrader, Bazil T.
Shrader, George W.
Shrader, William L.
Slaughter, Francis M.
Smith, Edmund J.
Smith, William D.
Spencer, Otha H.
Sprout, David
Sprout, Jesse
Stark, Silas
Tichenal, Daniel
Tucker, Jeremiah M.
Vincent, Jacob L.
Willis, Henry L.
Winemiller, Adam
Wiseman, Job
Wiseman, Lemuel H.
Wright, Benjamin
Wright, William
Wright, Zebedee
Wyer, Alpheus

COMPANY H

Commissioned Officers

Captain

Bristor, Jacob H. [Commissioned August 20, 1862.]

First Lieutenants

Powell, David [Commissioned August 20, 1862. Mustered out by order War Dept.]

Means, Thomas H. [Commissioned February 13, 1865.]

Second Lieutenants

Means, Thomas H. [Commissioned August 20, 1862. Promoted to 1st Lieutenant.]

Martin, William D. [Commissioned May 9, 1865.]

Enlisted Men

Arnold, Richard H.
Bailey, Cornelius H.
Bailey, John F.
Bailey, Thornberry
Bircher, Henry
Bircher, Thomas C.
Blake, George B.
Bolyard, Henry
Brake, David C. J.
Bunner, Hiram
Campbell, Howard
Carpenter, Lewis C.
Cassell, John
Cassell, Peter
Conley, Patrick
Day, Benjamin F.
Day, John
Demoss, Eugenius W.
Demoss, Francis M.
Demoss, James H.
Demoss, William M.
Eichelberger, James D.
Elkins, James P.
Fanley, Jacob
Finley, William
Funk, Isaac B.
Funk, William M.
Goldsbury, Townsel
Grimes, William M.
Haddox, Harvey
Hammond, Jr., George
Harritt, Joseph
Harvey, William F. L.
Haymond, Daniel S.
Haymond, Edward O.
Henderson, Hiram H.
Henderson, William
Henline, John W.
Houston, John H.
Howard, William
Hull, Abraham S.
Hull, Albert G.

Hull, Octavius H.
Hunt, Philip
Jones, John M.
Jones, Martin
Kerns, Thomas J.
Leach, Albert G.
Leonard, Bowen E.
Ludwick, Jacob M.
Ludwick, Nathan
Luzadder, Abraham
Luzadder, Edward
Luzadder, Jr., James
Luzadder, Sr., James
Luzadder, Obadiah J.
Malone, James H.
Marquess, James
Marquess, Laquilla
Marsteller, Squire B.
Mayes, Lewis S.
McDaniel, Alpheus
McDaniel, Anson
McDaniel, John
McDaniel, Samuel
McIntosh, Elijah B.
McIntosh, William F.
McVickers, Franklin
McWilliams, Robert W.
Means, James K.
Menear, James P.
Mentzer, William G.
Michael, Isaac
Murphy, David G.
Murphy, James P.
Murphy, Joshua M.
Newlon, John
Nichol, James H.
Nose, Eli
Nose, Jacob
Nose, John
Nose, Samuel
Osborn, Micajah W.

Osborn, William L.
Palmer, Edward
Park, Levi
Pierce, Adam W.
Pool, James W.
Randall, Malsias
Reese, James W.
Robinson, James M.
Rogers, James
Rosier, Edgar
Rosier, Lemuel L.
Shingleton, John
Shroyer, Tyler M.
Smallwood, Charles
Smell, Daniel
Smell, George W.
Snider, Amos
Snider, Joseph
Spring, James W.
Spring, Joseph J.
Stewart, Oscar T.
Thomas, Doctor A.
Thomas, James W.
Thomas, William A.
Trader, John W.
Wallace, Richard M.
Waller, Benjamin F.
Watkins, William
Watson, Robert
Whitehair, Henry J.
Williams, Isaac W.
Williams, William H.
Wolf, John W.
Wood, Archer
Wood, John
Woodyard, Jerome
Woodyard, John M.
Woolard, John R.
Wotring, William J.

COMPANY I

Commissioned Officers

Captains
Brown, Richard H. [Commissioned August 28, 1862. Promoted to Major.]

Melvin, John Henry [Commissioned February 10, 1864.]

First Lieutenants
Melvin, John Henry [Commissioned August 15, 1862. Promoted to Captain.]

Campbell, Milton B. [Commissioned February 10, 1864. Dismissed September 13, 1864.]

Hewitt, William [Commissioned November 11, 1864.]

Second Lieutenants
Bradley, Thomas W. [Commissioned August 27, 1862. Killed in action at Winchester.]

Campbell, Milton B. [Commissioned January 19, 1864. Promoted to 1st Lieutenant.]

Hewitt, William [Commissioned April 6, 1864. Promoted to 1st Lieutenant.]

Curtis, Josiah M. [Commissioned November 11, 1864.]

Enlisted Men

Abrams, James M.
Allison, Alexander B.
Allison, James
Allison, John G.
Allison, John W.
Allison, Peter B.
Allison, Richard O.
Allison, William G.
Allison, William H.
Allison, William W.
Apple, Andrew O.
Applegate, Benton
Aten, James
Atkinson, William A.
Bailey, Jesse
Bailey, John S.
Bailey, Joseph
Baxter, John R.
Baxter, William H.
Beal, Samuel
Beal, William
Bernard, Thomas B.

Bernard, Van B.
Bird, George H. H.
Brobeck, John H.
Caldwell, Cyrus
Campbell, James Y.
Campbell, William B.
Carson, Martin L.
Cochran, David W.
Cullen, Isaac N.
Cullen, Marion M.
Cullen, Samuel H.
Debee, Sylvanus H.
Dornan, John M.
Dougherty, Andrew
Durbin, Joseph B.
Fernsworth, Robert H.
Fernsworth, William
Finney, William
Flowers, John W.
Geer, Charles A.
Geer, Jacob
Geer, John W.
Goddard, George W.
Goddard, William E.
Graham, Charles
Halleck, Homer B.
Halstead, Samuel
Haney, William W.
Harper, John L.
Harper, John U. S.
Henderson, Franklin
Herbert, Peter
Hewitt, Joseph A.
Hineman, Alexander
Hobbs, Wheeler
Howard, Harvey
Hukill, William M.
Hunter, John G.
Jackson, Andrew

Jenkins, Sylvester B.
Jewell, William
Jones, William H. H.
Kerr, Andrew J. L.
Lyons, Joseph R.
Mackey, George B.
Mahan, William C.
Minor, Samuel H.
McRalston, Harper
Miller, Morgan H.
Miller, Isaac H.
Moore, Thomas M.
Moore, William H.
Moorehead, George W.
Morrow, John C.
Owens, James W.
Patterson, David M.
Pees, George W.
Porter, James
Pugh, Daniel
Pugh, Robert W.
Quear, Henry
Quear, Jacob
Ramsey, Robert
Ridinger, John
Robb, William B.
Ross, Cornelius H.
Russell, David H.
Scott, John A.
Scott, Joseph
Scott, William A.
Simpson, George S.
Snowden, David H.
Snowden, James R.
Snowden, Robert
Stewart, Samuel B.
Stewart, William W.
Swearingen, Alexander
Swearingen, James

Swearingen, William W.
Thayer, Milton H.
Thompson, William
Thorn, John M.
Troup, Samuel
Wasson, Thomas
Wilkinson, Silas
Wilson, James
Young, Intrepid M.

COMPANY K

Commissioned Officers

Captains
White, Thomas [Commissioned August 29, 1862. Resigned August 1, 1863.]

Jester, John B. [Commissioned October 28, 1863.]

First Lieutenants
Jester, John B. [Commissioned August 29, 1862. Promoted to Captain.]

Brenneman, John R. [Commissioned October 28, 1863.]

Second Lieutenants
Brenneman, John R. [Commissioned April 29, 1863. Promoted to 1st Lieutenant.]

Briggs, John A. [Commissioned October 28, 1863.]

Enlisted Men

Adams, Eli
Arbaugh, Robert
Arney, Joseph F.
Baxter, Daniel
Baxter, George A.
Billingsley, William A.
Britt, Elias L.
Brownlee, Martin V.
Burgoyne, Rufus J.
Carens, John R.
Colwell, Albert
Cornelius, David
Cox, Jonathan
Craig, Roland
Crooks, Isaac
Cupples, James
Davis, David S.
Davis, Joseph A.
Degarmo, Thomas
Everett, John B.
Fenwick, John W.
Fleming, James E.
Fleming, Joseph R.
Freshwater, John
Gilchrist, John B.
Glass, George
Glass, John J.
Green, John W.
Hall, Augustus C.
Hall, Henry M.
Hall, Leonard C.
Hall, Lewis C.
Hallbritter, William H.
Haney, John H.

Harding, Joseph E.
Harvey, Benjamin
Hays, Marshall
Hendricks, Harrison
Hendricks, John H.
Hindman, Samuel
Homer, Robert H.
Hunt, Eugenius
Houston, William C. A.
Keith, John
Kelly, McKendree
Kelly, William T.
Kimmins, John
Knipple, Jacob
Kimberland, Henry C.
Lee, Bazil B.
Lucas, Philip
Mahan, Richard
Marks, Thomas Hartley
Marsh, Joseph
Mason, Charles E. W.
Maxwell, George W.
McConneha, Alexander
McCormick, Jacob
McHugh, William
McNally, Arthur F.
Montgomery, Joseph E.
Nelson, Nathaniel
Odburt, Charles H.
Paden, William
Perkins, James A.
Pepper, James M.
Phillips, William
Platenburg, Henry C.
Plummer, Joseph
Roberts, John M. M.
Roberts, Martin J.
Robinson, Armor W.
Robinson, Gabriel

Robinson, Jesse
Rush, William
Scott, Hugh
Sears, Stephen S.
Sims, Robert D.
Smith, Clarence A.
Smith, Edward J.
Smith, James S.
Smith, William H. H.
Spears, Henry
Speidel, Clemens
Stock, Benjamin
Strong, George
Swan, Mathew
Teter, George W.
Thompson, John
Wells, William B.
White, Albert H.
White, James
Williams, George W.
Williams, Joseph H.
Wise, Pleasant William
Wright, Derias
Young, Harvey H.
Younkin, Samuel F.

Index

1st New York Cavalry 35, 37, 43, 46, 66, 68, 70, 96, 182
1st West Virginia Infantry 78, 80, 81, 129, 130, 131, 133, 139, 140, 180
2nd Maryland Infantry 95, 120
4th Pennsylvania Cavalry 117
4th West Virginia Infantry 11, 95, 118, 131
5th Maine Cavalry 66
5th New York Heavy Artillery 95
5th Rhode Island Artillery 201
6th Maryland Infantry 24
9th Maryland Infantry 63
9th West Virginia Infantry 12
10th Connecticut Infantry 147
10th West Virginia Infantry 4, 21, 76
11th West Virginia Infantry 4, 76, 117
12th Pennsylvania Cavalry 24, 37, 38
13th Pennsylvania Cavalry 24
15th West Virginia Infantry 4, 117, 152
18th Connecticut Infantry 80, 81, 119, 180
18th Pennsylvania Cavalry 88, 210
20th Pennsylvania Cavalry 232
21st Pennsylvania Cavalry 66
23rd Illinois Infantry 18, 144
23rd Virginia Infantry 163
28th Ohio Infantry 76, 82, 85, 106, 180
34th Massachusetts Infantry 64, 65, 66, 70, 78, 80, 81, 84, 85, 86, 87, 89, 95, 96, 97, 136, 180
44th Virginia Cavalry 122
45th Virginia Infantry 103
54th Pennsylvania Infantry 78, 144, 147, 155, 180
67th Pennsylvania Infantry 24
77th New York Infantry 201
83d Pennsylvania Infantry 201
87th Pennsylvania Infantry 12, 13, 17, 32, 46
88th Pennsylvania Infantry 201
110th Ohio Infantry 34
116th Ohio Infantry 35, 37, 82, 85, 117, 180
122nd Ohio Infantry 46
123rd Ohio Infantry 46, 80, 81, 180
144th New York Infantry 201
160th Ohio Infantry 95

A

Adams, Emanuel M. 101, 154
Adams, Samuel 106
Alexander, Captain 84
Alexander, Major 58, 59, 60, 61
Allen, Charles G. 85
Allison, Alexander B. 155
Ambercrombie, William H. 101
Anderson, Captain (rebel spy) 44, 45
Anderson, General Richard H. 44, 45, 128, 129, 130, 131, 132, 134, 206, 240, 244, 246, 248

Anderson, Robert J. 101
Anshutz, Henry T. 35
Apple, Andrew O. 155, 235
Ashby, Turner 96
Averell, General William Woods 105, 119

B

Babcock, General Orville E. 160
Bachus, James 102
Banks, General Nathaniel P. 95
Barnes, George 101
Barrett, Lieutenant Thomas G. 218, 219, 221, 222, 223, 224, 225, 227
Bartlett, Captain 80
Bartlett, Erastus G. 5
Barton, Clara 205
Baxter, John R. 102
Beal, William 102
Bell, Lieut. 54, 55, 56
Bengough, Celia 49, 51, 53, 54, 56, 58, 60
Bengough, Harry 49
Bengough, John T. 34, 35, 48, 49
Bengough M'Caffrey, Mrs. Lottie 48, 62
Benjamin, Judah P. 59
Bennett, John H. 102
Bernard, Thomas B. 44
Bernard, Van 44
Bier, Philip G. 36, 139
Billings, Lieut. 46
Bircher, Henry 102
Bird, George H. 155
Blaney, David M. 6, 47
Bonaparte, Napoleon 1
Bonar, Martin P. 5
Boreman, Arthur I. 163
Boyd, Belle 60
Boyd, Reuben G. 101

Bradley, Thomas W. 7, 16, 33, 35
Breckinridge, General John C. 81, 82, 83, 86, 89, 117, 122, 182
Brenneman, J. R. 7
Bridgeford, Major 56
Briggs, John A. 122
Bristor, Jacob H. 6, 44, 155, 253
Brown, John (of Allegheny) 59
Brown, Lt. Col. Richard H. 6, 10, 71, 76, 78, 121, 122, 123, 130, 146
Brown, William H. 103
Bryan, Samuel 5, 19, 21, 77
Buell, General Don Carlos 65
Burke, Thomas 33
Burley, William 5, 32, 146
Butler, General Benjamin F. 144, 145

C

Caldwell, George B. 5, 32, 47, 95, 97, 103, 132, 154, 162
Caldwell, James W. 154
Caldwell, Joseph 154
Campbell, William B. 102
Carlin's Battery 81, 98
Chambers, Benjamin 101
Chambers, Wilson 101
Chrismond, John A. 88, 180
Cleveland, President Grover 222
Cluseret, General Gustave P. 19, 20, 21
Cole's Maryland Battalion 66
Collins, William 201
Cook, Joseph 88, 210, 215, 228
Craft, Ruth 223
Crook, General George 74, 76, 83, 85, 105, 107, 108, 117, 119, 120, 121, 122, 125, 127, 128, 129, 130, 133, 137, 138, 139

Crow, Harmon 101
Crow, John W. 80, 224
Cullen, Isaac N. 100
Curtis, Charles 201
Curtis, Col. William B. 6, 33, 36, 40, 43, 65, 66, 69, 70, 71, 74, 76, 81, 82, 83, 86, 95, 97, 100, 103, 104, 105, 106, 115, 118, 120, 121, 122, 135, 137, 139, 144, 153, 154, 155, 158, 159, 162, 163, 164, 165
Curtis, Josiah M. 155, 235
Custer, General George 128, 141

D

Dacon, John 101
Darnell, Captain Morgan A. 21
Daugherty, Andrew 102
Davis, Jefferson 59, 112
Davis, Major Nathan 147
DeBee, Sylvanus H. 87
Delaney, Patrick 201
Devin, General Thomas C. 128
Duffie, General Alfred N. 116, 140
Dunham, Colonel 60
Dunnington, James W. 5
Dupont's Battery 84
Durbin, Joseph B. 102
Durham, James R. 6, 35, 235
Duval, General Isaac H. 119, 129

E

Early, General Jubal 51, 68, 69, 70, 71, 89, 96, 108, 110, 115, 116, 119, 120, 121, 124, 125, 128, 129, 130, 131, 132, 133, 134, 135, 136, 138, 139, 141, 143, 147, 169, 206
Eighth Corps 11, 128, 129, 132, 137

Eleventh Corps 43
Ellsworth, Col. Elmer 57
Ely, Col. William G. 119, 120, 129
Ewing's Battery 84

F

Faulkner, Boyd 104
Faulkner, Charles James 41
Fifth Corps 151, 152
First Corps 40
Fisher, Isaac N. 101
Fish, Nathan S. 5
Fleming, David B. 5
Fleming, James E. 102
Fleming, Thomas A. 6
Flemming, Calvin L. 102
Foreman, William W. 107
Fortney, Henry 102
Foster, General Robert Sanford 164
Fremont, General John C. 96
Frizzell, John 5
Frost, Col. Daniel 117

G

Gamble, William C. 186, 192, 206
Garrittson, William H. 102
Gibbon, General John 145, 155, 162, 164
Gilmore, Alexander 101
Gilmore, Lotta 60
Gilmore, Major Harry 45, 46
Grant, General Ulysses S. 17, 43, 48, 65, 73, 86, 106, 107, 108, 116, 119, 125, 127, 128, 130, 131, 132, 134, 135, 136, 141, 143, 144, 146, 147, 148, 151, 152, 155, 157, 160, 161, 164, 180, 207
Grant, Mrs. Ulysses S. 147

Gray, Francis M. 101
Greeley, Horace 2, 34, 36, 124, 132

H
Haddox, Harvey 25, 26
Hallbritter, William H. 102
Halleck, General Henry 36, 86, 118, 136
Hall, Van B. 6
Halpine, Charles G. 104
Halstead, Joseph S. 99, 101, 104
Hamilton, Charles W. 101
Hammond, George 5
Haney, John Henry 72, 73
Harris, General Thomas Maley 4, 145, 148
Hay, Col. George 12
Haymond, Edward O. 102
Haymond, Thomas H. 6
Heiskill, Robert 102
Herbert, William E. L. 101
Hewitt, William 83, 127
Holliday, John W. 152
Hood, General John B. 233
Howard, General Oliver O. 43
Hugill, Asa S. 152
Hull, A. H. 45
Hunter, General David 82, 85, 95, 96, 97, 105, 106, 107, 108, 110, 112, 115, 116, 118, 124, 125, 127, 139

I
Imboden, General John D. 63, 82, 96
Imboden, George W. 98

J
Jackson, General Thomas J. 96, 107, 169
Jenkins, Betty 52
Jenkins, General Albert Gallatin 9
Jester, John B. 7
Johnston, Col. J. Stoddard 82
Jones, General Sam 20, 21, 27, 29
Jones, General William E. 97, 99, 100, 104
Jones, George L. 101
Jones, John G. 101

K
Kelley, General Benjamin F. 71, 179
King, George W. 13, 14
Klunk, Col. John B. 5, 9, 11, 14, 38, 43, 71

L
Lapole, Captain 24, 25, 26, 27
Leach, Sergeant Wm. H. 101
Lee, Fitzhugh 58
Lee, General Robert E. 50, 55, 56, 107, 130, 157, 159, 160, 165, 169, 179, 180, 182
Letcher, Governor John 107
Lincoln, Abraham 2, 3, 133, 139, 146, 147, 161, 210, 222, 234
Lincoln, William S. 85, 86
Logsden, Joseph R. 154
Lomax, General Lunsford L. 134
Longstreet, General James 34, 130, 136
Lowell, General Charles R. 129
Lydick, John B. 5
Lyons, Joseph R. 102

M

Macks, Joseph 102
Magers, William F. 101
Magruder, T. S. 5
Mahan, Richard W. 122
Mahan, W. C. 89
Manning, James B. 101
Manning, Lewis 101
Marks, Thomas H. 100, 102
Maxwell, Daniel 101
McAdams, Lieut. 50
McCandless, Mrs. Surgeon 58
McCausland, General John 110
McCauslin, Joseph 155, 235
McClellan, General George B. 3, 131, 140, 148, 157, 168, 179, 222
McConneha, Alexander 102
McCord, Henry R. 159
McCormick, Jake 13
McDaniel, Samuel 25, 26
McDonald, Captain 17
McElroy, John 198
McEstee, Captain 84
McEwen, James M. 62
McIntosh, Elijah 25
McIntosh, General John B. 25, 130, 254
McLean, Wilmer 160
McNeil, Jesse 74
McReynolds, Col. 27, 43, 45, 46
McVicker, Frank 102
Means, Thomas H. 6, 25, 26, 27
Meigs, John Rodgers 97
Meigs, Quarter Master General Montgomery C. 43
Melvin, John H. 6, 15, 33
Melvin, Thayer 74
Mercer, Cornelius 6
Merritt, General Wesley 129, 136, 141

Metz, Francis 101
Miller, James N. 87
Milroy, General Robert H. 16, 17, 25, 27, 31, 34, 35, 38, 49, 73, 79, 179
Minor, Captain 66
Minor, Samuel H. 102
Moffatt, James W. 6, 21, 46
Moore, William H. 102
Moor, General Augustus 81, 83, 84, 97
Morgan, General Daniel E. 22
Morris, Lt. Col. Thomas 117
Mosby, Col. John Singleton 24, 26, 77, 135, 140, 142, 143, 200
Muir, A. 201
Mulligan, General James A. 18, 49, 53, 54, 121
Murphy, James P. 44
Murray, John W. 101

N

Neil, Alexander 148
Nineteenth Corps 119, 124, 127, 128, 141, 142
Northcott, Lt. Col. Robert S. 5, 9, 11, 18, 32, 35, 43, 71, 75, 131, 135, 146, 178, 237
Nose, Jacob 102

O

Odbert, Charles H. 5
Ord, General Edward 145, 151
Ormsby, Thomas J. 109
Orr, Thomas J. 13, 15, 16
Orum, George 101

P

Palmetto Sharpshooters 148
Patton, Frederick H. 4, 35, 67
Pendergast, R. G. 84
Pierce, Col. Francis 38, 63
Pierpont, F. P. 49
Pierpont, Francis H. 163
Pierpont, Francis P. 76
Pierpont, Major F. P. 14, 15, 32
Pigott, Elam F. 6, 152
Porter, Admiral David Dixon 146, 147
Porter, Commodore 229
Porter, James 27
Powell, David 6, 24, 25, 26, 27
Powell, General William H. 25, 26, 141, 243, 253
Price, Adam 102
Prichard, Amos A. 6, 15, 127
Putnam, T. G. 84

R

Read, General Theodore 155
Reeder, Charles A. 235
Ringgold Cavalry 14, 92
Roberts, John C. 5
Roberts, William L. 5
Rodes, General Robert E. 117
Rogers, John 88, 210, 215, 217
Rosecrans, Gen. William S. 179
Rosser, General Thomas L. 134, 135
Rowand, Captain 58
Ruggles, Dwight 5

S

Sarsfield, John 201
Scantling, John 178
Schenck, General Robert 27, 36, 38

Scott, William A. 5
Second Corps 151
Severe, David 101
Seward, William H. 2
Sheridan, General Philip 11, 65, 89, 106, 109, 110, 127, 128, 129, 130, 131, 132, 133, 134, 135, 136, 137, 138, 139, 141, 142, 143, 147, 148, 151, 152, 157, 158, 163, 180, 207
Sherman, General William Tecumseh 106, 133, 147, 168, 195, 207, 225, 233
Shinn, Private 103
Shroyer, Andrew M. 102
Sigel, General Franz 75, 76, 78, 79, 81, 83, 86, 87, 88, 95, 96, 115, 116, 180, 181
Sixth Corps 11, 70, 116, 117, 118, 124, 127, 128, 129, 134, 135, 136, 138, 141, 143, 152
Smiley, William A. 6, 95
Spear, Henry 36
Stahl, General Julius 83, 97, 104
Stanton, Edwin 147
Stephens, Alexander H. 146
Stine, William 186, 206
Stoneman, General George 66, 70, 232
Strother, David Hunter 112
Sullivan, General Jeremiah C. 64, 65, 84, 97, 104, 139
Sullivan, Terence 201

T

Tate, Oscar H. 6
Teagarden, George H. 13
Terry, General Alfred 146
Thoburn, Col. Joseph 78, 79, 81, 84, 97, 98, 103, 104, 117, 118, 120, 121, 132, 135, 136, 139

Thomas, General George H. 143
Thomas, James W. 102
Thompson, William 89
Thurber, N. U. 5
Tomlinson, Hagar 5, 101
Torbet, General Alfred T. A. 134
Trainer, Thomas H. 5
Turner, General John W. 145, 148, 154
Turner, Major Thomas Pratt 58, 59
Turner, Thomas M. 101
Twelfth Corps 43
Twenty-fifth Corps 145, 151
Twenty-fourth Corps 145, 151, 159

V

Vallandigham, Clement 46
Vaughn, General John C. 66, 96
Von Kleiser's Battery 84

W

Wallace, Ezra 102
Wallace, General Lew 116
Wamsley, Abia 102
Ward, Artemus 20
Washburn, Col. James 37, 117
Washington, Col. John A. 16
Washington, George 147
Watkins, William 44
Wells, Col. George D. 65, 66, 67, 70, 84, 85, 87, 117, 136
Wells, Nathaniel 29
White, Albert W. 102
White, Thomas 7
Wildman, John H. 102
Wiles, Barnabas 19, 100
Winder, General John H. 60, 225

Wirz, Henry 92, 185, 186, 195, 198, 199, 200, 205, 206, 212, 213, 216, 218, 219, 222, 231
Wise, Gov. Henry 59
Wolfe, John R. 102
Wood, Archer 102
Wright, General Horatio G. 116, 117, 118, 119
Wyckoff, Jesse F. 25, 26
Wyer, Alpheus 102

Y

Young, Samuel B. M. 117
Younkin, Samuel F. 89, 186, 206, 231

www.ingramcontent.com/pod-product-compliance
Lightning Source LLC
Chambersburg PA
CBHW071701160426
43195CB00012B/1542